THE
GREEN
AMENDMENT

Securing Our Right
to a Healthy Environment

MAYA K. VAN ROSSUM
the Delaware Riverkeeper

DISRUPTION BOOKS

AUSTIN NEW YORK

Published by Disruption Books
Austin, TX, and New York, NY
www.disruptionbooks.com

For ordering information or special discounts for bulk purchases, please
contact Disruption Books at info@disruptionbooks.com.

Cover and text design by Sheila Parr
Cover photo by Tracy Carluccio

Print ISBN: 978-1-63331-021-6
eBook ISBN: 978-1-63331-022-3

First Edition

To the rivers, plants, and animals . . .
We must be their voice in our human world.

And to the future generations . . .
We must secure their future by fighting
to protect our environment today.

CONTENTS

ACKNOWLEDGMENTS

I wish to express my immense gratitude to my beautiful Delaware River, and to all of the streams, plants, soils, critters, and watershed communities that inspire me every day to rise up and advocate on their behalf. These precious beings have made this book possible.

Thank you as well to my family: my amazing husband, David Wood, for bringing unending love, joy, and support to my life; my daughter, Anneke, and son, Wim, for being the budding advocates and special people that they are; and my four step kids—Steven, Jessica, Scott, and Tommy—for becoming such a wonderful part of my family and my world.

Thank you to my mother, Marijke, and my father, George. I have no words to describe what spectacular people they were, and how much I miss them. Each and every day, they inspire me to be a better person and to advocate more passionately for our river and the earth.

The Delaware Riverkeeper Network's staff support this work in a myriad of ways, from the facts and figures they provided for this book to the efforts they contribute every day to advance our organization's mission. Tracy Carluccio, Mary Ellen Noble, Chari Towne, Fred Stine, Faith Zerbe, Claire Biehl, Tim White,

Bridget Brady, Aaron Stemplewicz, Clifton Biehl, Ed Rodgers, Nick Patton, Andrew Edkins, Kelly Gallagher, Corinne Bell, Deanna Tanner, Molly Atz, Amanda Vendetti, Matthew McCann, Erik Silldorff, Jill Kauffman, and Peter Tran—you are a truly amazing team. Thank you for championing the rights of communities to a Delaware River and tributary streams that are free-flowing, clean, healthy, and abundant with a diversity of life.

Special thanks go out as well to the Delaware Riverkeeper Network's board of directors. Christina Perrone, Tish Long, Judy Sherry, Janine Bauer, Harriet Anderson, and Bob Meek all energetically advance our organization's work, and their enthusiasm for this book in particular has been wonderfully uplifting. I also wish to acknowledge all other members of the Delaware Riverkeeper Network family, including funders, members, and supporters. With your visionary activism on behalf of the environment, you help to make our world a better place each and every day.

I would like to thank all of the foundations that have supported the work of the Delaware Riverkeeper Network, helping us to protect our river, watershed, and environment for the benefit of all. Thank you to the William Penn Foundation, the Woodtiger Fund, the 11th Hour Project of the Schmidt Family Foundation, the Cedar Tree Foundation, the Civil Society Institute, the George and Miriam Martin Foundation, the Geraldine R. Dodge Foundation, the Environmental Endowment for New Jersey, the Moses Feldman Family Foundation, the Park Foundation, the Claneil Foundation, the Heinz Endowments, the Foundation for a Better Tomorrow, the Wallace Research Foundation, the GreenWatch Institute, The Philadelphia Foundation, the Norman Raab Foundation, the Austelle Foundation, the Fund For New Jersey, the Johnson Ohana Charitable Foundation, Patagonia, the National Fish and

Wildlife Foundation, the New World Foundation, the Norcross Wildlife Foundation, the WaterWheel Foundation, and the 1675 Foundation. Your steady support over the years has allowed us to accomplish so much good for so many, including communities described in this book.

I am immensely grateful to Rachel Gostenhofer and Seth Schulman for their amazing writing talent and for working with me to write this book. Together, I hope we have delivered a message that will help inspire communities and change the world. Thank you as well to Disruption Books for believing in me, and to members of the BerlinRosen team for helping us spread the good word.

To Mark Ruffalo, my gratitude and thanks for lending your support to this book and for being a leader in the fight for clean water and clean, renewable energy through The Solutions Project and Water Defense, two organizations critical to empowering citizens to stand up for their right to a healthy environment.

Finally, thank you to Franklin L. Kury who, as a Pennsylvania state legislator in the 1970s, had the courage and vision to propose an environmental rights amendment in Pennsylvania's constitution and ensured its ultimate passage. It is from Franklin Kury's original leadership those decades ago that this book is inspired.

FOREWORD

By Mark Ruffalo

In 1962, conservationist Rachel Carson published *Silent Spring*, a clarion warning to the world about the consequences of environmental degradation. Her book and her later efforts are often credited with sparking the birth of the modern environmental movement. It was a call to action to political leaders and regular citizens alike: to defend our natural resources with extraordinary urgency, on behalf of the planet and all of its species, and in the name of future generations. When Carson testified before Congress the following year, one Senator described her work this way: "Every once in a while in the history of mankind, a book has appeared which has substantially altered the course of history." And indeed, in the more than fifty years since *Silent Spring's* publication, we have won critically important battles, from the passage of the Clean Air and Clean Water Acts to the establishment of the Environmental Protection Agency. Yet any honest accounting of where we are as a country must acknowledge that what has been won is woefully insufficient, that in the broader war to prevent the poisoning of the world, we are losing badly.

The basic things we have come to expect can no longer be taken for granted. We cannot assume that it is safe to swim in our lakes and rivers. We cannot assume that the soil beneath our feet is safe for growing food. We can't even assume that the water coming out of our faucets is safe to drink.

We see this tragedy playing out across the country, in places like Flint, Michigan, where more than 100,000 people spent years drinking, cooking with, and bathing in lead-contaminated water. Residents had long reported brown, foul-smelling water and unexplained sickness, but state and local officials chose to do nothing—even after they were confronted with the reality of the danger. This incident is, perhaps, the most notorious, but it is far from unique. According to a 2016 analysis by Reuters, there are nearly 3,000 areas in the country—with a population of more than ten million people—that have lead poisoning rates even higher than those in Flint.

Then there is hydrofracking and its deadly consequences— the poisoning of well water, of streams and rivers and lakes—as companies pump toxic chemicals into shale rock to release natural gas (none of which they are required to disclose). I live in the Catskills atop the Marcellus Shale, one of the country's largest fracking fields. I have seen firsthand the destruction this new technology has wrought—both the cost to human health and the cost to the pristine natural landscape. To corporations, and their political backers, these are simply the costs of doing business.

And this just scratches the surface. We see corporations build shoddy oil pipelines across critical water tables, downplaying inevitable oil spills. And yet it is the protestors who are demonized. I joined those at Standing Rock who were protesting the Dakota Access Pipeline, for example, and watched in disbelief as the air filled with tear gas. We see coal companies dumping ash and other poisons into waterways, poisoning wildlife, and endangering communities downstream. We allow companies to build dangerous chemical plants in populated areas with lax regulations and insufficient safety protocols. In the aftermath of Hurricane Harvey, for example, one such plant exploded multiple times in the city of Houston, sending toxic benzene plumes over the city, along with other chemicals that the company still refuses to disclose. It seems that rarely a day goes by without another man-made environmental tragedy to mourn.

What is clear is that our leaders have let us down. At nearly every turn, the profits of big business are prioritized, consequences be damned. It amounts to a moral failing of the highest degree, one with horrifying and lasting consequences. It is stunning just how often, in the courts, in state legislatures, in Congress, the interests of corporations are deemed more important than the basic things we demand for survival. We are not the sum of dollars and cents; we are people of flesh and blood. And yet it is the dollars that do all the talking.

Existing laws have clearly failed us. They are neither strong enough nor serious enough to protect what matters most. This insufficiency has exacted a heavy price, one we expect to worsen over time. After all, the effects of climate change will surely exacerbate political and corporate negligence.

What we desperately need today is a new strategy, one that recognizes two things: that our efforts to protect the environment to date, however well meaning, are insufficient; and one that mobilizes the American people in common cause and common purpose. It is time to see a safe and clean environment not just as a preference or a privilege, but as a fundamental right, to treat it with the same sanctity as the right of free speech.

I believe the book you are holding in your hand has the power to spark a new movement, just as Rachel Carson's did so many years ago. It is written with sharpness and clarity as it puts forward a road map for a new environmental compact. The ideas within these pages are the very ones we must embrace if we are to shift the paradigm of environmental protection. As the Delaware Riverkeeper, Maya van Rossum has gotten her hands dirty—literally—in the work to battle pollution and its defenders. Her work here will move you—and empower you—to do the same. van Rossum has spoken fiercely and eloquently for the kind of change we all must seek, and has put admirable action behind her powerful words. I cannot imagine a timelier or more critically important piece of writing. It offers a fast and fascinating analysis of where we are as a country, and a bold and convincing strategy for where we must go. My sincere hope is that the words written here are read and repeated far and wide, and that its message becomes the basis of a new environmental era. In an age of environmental pessimism, van Rossum gives me hope.

Mark Ruffalo
Actor, clean water activist, founder of Water Defense,
and cofounder of The Solutions Project

INTRODUCTION

WE NEED A
GREEN AMENDMENT

Early in 2008, my family drove up to my mother's beautiful sixty-eight-acre patch of forest in Columbia County, central Pennsylvania. For over twenty-five years, this rustic valley had served as my family's oasis, and when my mother had passed a few years earlier, she had entrusted the property to my daughter and me to protect for future generations. Once her estate was settled, I set about securing the loans necessary to build the dream cabin my mother had designed but hadn't had the chance to build. The cabin was now complete, and my husband Dave and I, along with our kids, were taking our first trip up to enjoy it.

We decided to drop in on our neighbor Mason, the gentleman who had sold the property to my mum and who in her later years had helped her to maintain it. As we sat in Mason's office, he filled us in on some recent happenings in the local area. He mentioned that representatives of gas drilling companies had approached several of our neighbors, describing a new technology that could extract gas from deep inside the earth without harming the surrounding environment. "They're offering us lots of money for access to our land," Mason said. "They say there's absolutely no adverse environmental impacts, and that the drilling will help revitalize our economy and community."

Absolutely no adverse environmental impacts. That's what they said back then about the process of extracting natural gas from shale rock formations using horizontal directional drilling and hydraulic fracturing (commonly known as fracking).

"Did you sign on?" I asked.

He shook his head. "A lot of the neighbors are just signing leases with the drilling companies, but I'm taking the time to look into it first. There's a lot of pressure from the drilling reps for folks to sign. A few of the neighbors asked to meet with me to talk about why I wouldn't sign. When I showed up, there was a room full of, like, seventy people asking me why I wouldn't sign and pressuring me to change my mind. But it sounds too good to be true. I'm going to wait awhile."

I'm the Delaware Riverkeeper and my job is to protect the Delaware River and its watershed, 13,539 squares miles of land spanning the states of Pennsylvania, New Jersey, Delaware, and New York. Much of the watershed in New York and Pennsylvania rests atop the Marcellus shale, a massive stretch of gas-rich shale running from New York State down to West Virginia. Around the same time we spoke with Mason, we learned that the drilling companies were also aggressively targeting properties and landholdings for development in portions of the Delaware River watershed. As 2008 wore on, my organization, the Delaware Riverkeeper Network, received more and more calls from residents in our watershed with similar stories of industry representatives knocking on doors and soliciting easements to drill for gas. My conversation with Mason had alerted me to the impact these sudden offers were having on landowners and communities. The excitement, confusion, and fear were palpable. For the good of my watershed, we would need to determine the truth about fracking, carefully comparing the industry's claims with the experiences of communities and the findings of scientific experts.

My colleague, Delaware Riverkeeper Network's deputy director Tracy Carluccio, and I acted quickly, learning about fracking and its potential impacts. The more we investigated, the more apparent it became that drilling and fracking are hardly innocuous. Although scientific evidence linking fracking with water pollution, the contamination of drinking water, methane gas emissions, increased seismic activity, extreme weather events, and human health hazards was still emerging for our region and the Marcellus shale, we discovered that the extraction process had already devastated lands and communities in Texas, Michigan, and other states early to the shale gas boom. We were also hearing horrific stories from communities in central and western Pennsylvania where fracking had already taken place.

We had to see for ourselves what was happening in these Pennsylvania communities outside of our watershed, so we paid them a visit. As we discovered, fracking operations were emitting noxious gases into residential communities and towns. They were disturbing humans and animals with 24/7 light and noise pollution. They were destroying vast swaths of forest, as shale gas extraction requires massive land clearing to accommodate drilling pads, roads, wastewater impoundments, compressor stations, and natural gas processing facilities. And they were sucking up vast quantities of water while simultaneously polluting groundwater supplies and streams.

4 THE GREEN AMENDMENT

Despite this environmental devastation, the shale gas industry had continued to consolidate its operations throughout
Pennsylvania, West Virginia, Ohio, and New York, the primary
states sitting atop the coveted Marcellus shale deposits. Within
our watershed and across the shale region, companies were
approaching more property owners to secure drilling leases.
Everywhere the gas companies went, they touted the same line:
"We have a way to extract natural gas from the ground. Natural
gas is an environmentally friendly, largely nonpolluting energy
source, and we have a way to extract it from the ground without
posing harm to the environment, your property, or your family.
We will pay you a bonus up front when you sign a lease that
allows us to drill on your property. Once we start getting gas, you
will get royalties. You will make a good, healthy income for years
to come. You can pay off your debts and start to enjoy your life.
You can even start to think about retirement." Eager to do the
right thing and also beginning to feel the impact of the Great
Recession, people began signing leases.

Unfortunately, many who signed soon came to regret their
choices. As early as 2009, residents of Clearville and Avella,
Pennsylvania, reported sick and dying livestock and dangerous levels of contamination in the soil around drill sites.[1] In
Dimock, Pennsylvania, water began turning brown and making people sick; animals began mysteriously shedding their hair;
and a water well spontaneously combusted. Dimock residents
watched in horror when in September of that year a series of
spills from a Cabot Oil and Gas shale gas well sent acid- and
detergent-laced fracking water surging into surrounding wetlands and nearby Stevens Creek. Other communities reeled as
their homes and schools, long ensconced in beautiful forests and
gently flowing streams, now gazed out onto noisy, smelly, and

hazardous industrial operations. As the months ticked along, we regularly met families whose members were suffering all sorts of harms: nosebleeds, headaches, loss of memory, dizziness, agitation, and the sickening of farm animals or domestic pets. These families were terrified and no longer able to enjoy their properties. They wanted action.

Alarmed, we voiced our concerns before the Delaware River Basin Commission (DRBC), a regulatory agency with authority over the Delaware River watershed. After collaborating with other community leaders, mobilizing residents, lobbying politicians, submitting written comments, testifying at hearings, and representing the concerns of the seventeen million people who rely upon the Delaware for drinking water, we managed in May 2010 to convince the DRBC to enact a moratorium on shale gas extraction, drilling, and fracking within our watershed. This moratorium would remain in force until the DRBC passed regulations that would allow drilling and fracking while at the same time protecting the river's water quality—a hurdle that by this time we knew they could never overcome.

The drilling industry assured the DRBC that fracking benefitted communities, the environment, and business, and that the industry could frack in a way that would not harm the river. Industry officials, lawyers, and landowners also threatened legal action if the DRBC did not open the watershed to shale gas extraction. By 2020, the industry raved, America would achieve energy independence, relying on its own natural resources instead of foreign sources of fossil fuels, and put Americans to work in the process. At most, they said, fracking was a temporary nuisance. It posed less of a threat than coal, its dirty, carbon-dioxide-emitting energy competitor. Many local people, seeking to avoid harsh local battles around fracking and wishing to believe they really *could* have it all, found the industry's arguments convincing and urged the DRBC to lift the moratorium. But a growing number of individuals and organizations joined us in opposing the industry after learning about fracking's horrors from the media and organizations like my own Delaware Riverkeeper Network.

As more and more anecdotal accounts of fracking's destructiveness accumulated, and as scientific studies documenting fracking's near- and long-term ecological impacts mounted, it became obvious that we needed to do more to stop the industry. Our moratorium on shale gas extraction in the Delaware River watershed represented the cutting edge of protection, but it was fragile—it could be lifted with a vote of five people and just a few weeks' notice. In fact, for a few weeks during the fall of 2011, the lifting of the moratorium seemed imminent. It failed to materialize at the last minute only because we lobbied hard behind the scenes and advocated heavily with the public, triggering a massive uprising. After this close call, we at the Delaware Riverkeeper Network and our partner organizations resolved to work for a comprehensive and permanent ban on fracking in the watershed. At the same time, we wanted to put in place layers of protection so that we'd be safe if the DRBC ever tried to lift its moratorium. The more layers that existed, the more communities we would help, bringing us closer to the day when we would stop *all* shale gas extraction everywhere, for everyone.

In New York, communities had invoked their municipal authority to ban fracking town by town, and the courts had upheld their right to institute these local protections. Could fracking opponents accomplish similar town-by-town bans in Pennsylvania? That was unclear. Pennsylvania communities could certainly make various legal arguments in support of a ban, but to date no court decision had actually upheld such a ban.[2] Some communities did attempt to ban shale gas extraction, testing the boundaries of existing law, but most resorted to using zoning laws to place constraints on drilling and fracking, ensuring that these operations could only take place in industrial zones and not in agricultural districts, residential areas, or critical environmental or historic preservation zones. In response, the industry got busy in the halls of the state capitol in Harrisburg. Pitching drilling and fracking as a job-creating engine for the state, they covered up the environmental, public safety, and community devastation that already was resulting.

Enticed by the industry's promise of quick wealth, or perhaps just by the big contributions they would receive in their election campaign coffers, Pennsylvania's politicians reaffirmed their support of drilling, fracking, and shale gas, passing in 2012 a sinister piece of legislation that came to be known as Act 13. Act 13 granted the shale gas industry a bag of goodies from its regulatory wish list. It required that every municipality, and every zoning district within every municipality, permit access to the drilling and fracking industry. Schools, residences, protected waterways, wildlife sanctuaries, public parks, state-owned lands—all were now open to intrusion by the shale gas industry. Not only was every community obliged to allow drilling and fracking operations in every part of their community, but the drilling industry was also given the power to seize land through eminent domain for purposes of storing its gas underground. While the law mandated that the industry notify public water authorities in the case of accidental spills threatening water supplies, the industry didn't have to notify people who obtained their water from private wells.

To make the bill more palatable, the industry had included

several carrots, such as an "impact fee" that would channel industry money into the state's general budget and also disseminate it to local communities to remediate fracking-related damages, fund schools, or support other local priorities. The industry knew, however, that the environmental impact would be far more devastating than any impact fee could cover. That may in part be why, we suspect, Act 13 included a medical gag rule, stipulating that doctors treating patients exposed to drilling chemicals or other emissions couldn't speak publicly about these medical cases. Doctors who treated patients suffering from exposure to the industry's chemicals could only obtain information needed to help their patients if they signed nondisclosure agreements. They couldn't share information about these chemicals with anyone, including other doctors who might help them properly diagnose and treat their patients. By any measure, Act 13 was a travesty—a bald-faced capitulation to the industry. In fact, we later learned that the industry itself had written the law and delivered it to legislators, many of whom didn't even bother to read it. An enormous grassroots effort to stop the bill emerged, waged by the Delaware Riverkeeper Network, municipalities, and environmental organizations from across Pennsylvania. In February 2012, however, the legislature approved the bill, and shortly thereafter, Governor Tom Corbett signed Act 13 into law.

Alarmed and outraged, the Delaware Riverkeeper Network brought legal action, joining forces with seven vulnerable towns and a concerned physician. Three attorneys would lead our legal team—Jordan Yeager, John Smith, and Jonathan Kamin. While plotting our strategy for the litigation, Jordan, Tracy, and I agreed that although the Delaware Riverkeeper Network would present a number of rationales for striking down the law from the environmental perspective, chief among them would be a long-ignored provision of Pennsylvania's constitution, the Environmental Rights Amendment. In 1971, Pennsylvania had passed an amendment to its Constitution's Declaration of Rights—article 1, section 27—that explicitly protected the right of people to a healthy environment, and that established the government's obligation to protect the state's natural resources. The provision stated: "The people have a right to clean air, pure water, and to the preservation of the natural, scenic, historic and aesthetic values of the environment. Pennsylvania's public natural resources are the common property of all the people, including generations yet to come. As trustee of these resources, the Commonwealth shall conserve and maintain them for the benefit of all the people."

With the inclusion of article 1, section 27, Pennsylvania's constitution elevated environmental rights to the status of other fundamental rights and freedoms, such as free speech, freedom of religion, due process, and the right to bear arms. The constitution's power trumped that of any piece of legislation. It proclaimed the supreme law of the state, enshrining our most deeply held values. And yet, for a variety of reasons, Pennsylvania's courts had treated article 1, section 27 as a statement of policy rather than as a binding statement of law. Still, we believed that Act 13 violated both the spirit and letter of this environmental provision, and that it was not a mere policy statement. We were determined to test this conviction in court. By including this constitutional argument as a centerpiece of our legal efforts, we hoped to obtain a decision that would set a precedent for environmental litigation of all kinds. It was a risky bet, but the stakes couldn't have been higher: pure water, clean air, and a healthy environment.

In a protracted series of actions and appeals, our legal team presented the case for why Pennsylvania courts should find Act 13 unconstitutional. Attorney Jordan Yeager took the lead in crafting our part of the case and in arguing that Act 13 violated our environmental rights as guaranteed in article 1, section 27. In December 2013, in a landmark decision, the Pennsylvania Supreme Court declared fundamental provisions of Act 13 unconstitutional, reinstating property and municipal zoning rights. Article 1, section 27 was a linchpin of the plurality opinion authored by Chief Justice Ronald D. Castille. In rendering its decision, the court vindicated the environmental rights amendment's importance and power, promising all generations of Pennsylvanians that they would benefit from pure water, clean air, and a healthy environment, and giving them the ability to defend that right in court if it were violated. The court also made clear that our environmental rights are not granted by the Pennsylvania Constitution or any legal document created by people. Rather, they are inherent and indefeasible rights given to us by nature, by virtue of our birth, and thus inalienable. The plurality of the court also emphasized that these environmental rights belonged not just to present generations living on the earth today, but extended to the future generations yet to come, thus ensuring a higher obligation of protection.

Three years later, in September 2016, the Pennsylvania Supreme Court found additional provisions of Act 13 unconstitutional, including the medical gag rule. As the Delaware Riverkeeper, I felt deeply moved and inspired by our victory. For the time being, we had thwarted the gas companies' arrogant efforts to take over the state and ruin its environment. But the victory was bigger than that. We had established that environmental activists could once again use constitutional provisions to affect transformational change.

Across the country, concerned individuals fighting a range of environmental battles are at the mercy of powerful business interests and the lawmakers they influence. In recent decades, environmentalists have sought protections via *legislative* remedies—laws like the Clean Water Act; the Clean Air Act; the Safe Drinking Water Act; the Endangered Species Act; the Toxic Substances Control Act; the Comprehensive Environmental Response, Compensation, and Liability Act (also known as Superfund); the National Environmental Policy Act; the Coastal Zone Management Act; the Marine Protection, Research, and Sanctuaries Act; the Oil Pollution Act; the Federal Insecticide, Fungicide, and Rodenticide Act; the Resource Conservation and Recovery Act; the Wild and Scenic Rivers Act; and others, as well as their affiliated regulations and state counterparts. Yet this legislative approach has largely failed us, and our precious natural resources have continued to degrade. Business interests enjoy a powerful advantage in how the laws are written, whether they pass or fail, how they are implemented, and how rigorously they are enforced. They enjoy access to politicians that regular people simply do not have. They have bought the science needed to make their case, and they've leveraged economic arguments to cloud the facts both in the courtroom and in public debate.

But more than that, when legislators have dared to oppose their plans, companies and industry groups have gone to courts of law and mobilized property rights and other widely recognized constitutional liberties to justify environmental degradation. Lacking recourse to the constitution, environmentalists have been at the mercy of elected officials and powerful business interests. When legislators haven't done the right thing and passed environmentally friendly laws, or when officials haven't properly enforced existing environmental protections, environmentalists and community groups have often lost their battles for lack of a sufficiently strong legal rationale. In Pennsylvania, thanks to our case, this situation is starting to change. We faced down a powerful, well-funded industry group with a stranglehold over legislators and regulators and we triumphed—because we had the state constitution on our side.

As of this writing, Pennsylvania's environmental rights amendment remains unique among the fifty states. Only Montana's constitution contains an analogous provision. Thirty-three other states have constitutional provisions that mention aspects of the environment, but they don't recognize environmental rights as on par with other political rights deserving of the highest recognition and protection. Many of these provisions merely refer to environmental protection as good public policy or depend upon additional state action to realize such protection. As a result, these provisions are largely ineffectual. Fifteen states have no provisions whatsoever protecting environmental rights. And of course, clear recognition and protection of environmental rights is also glaringly absent at the federal level.

Imagine what would happen if strong constitutional provisions similar to Pennsylvania's existed across our nation. Imagine if each state passed a constitutional environmental rights amendment that equaled or exceeded Pennsylvania's. Imagine if we passed a federal constitutional provision to our bill of rights—a Green Amendment to the Constitution—guaranteeing that the government has no more ability to harm your environment than it does to deny you due process or overturn your right to free speech. In courts of law, constitutional protection would change wishful thinking about the environment into a clear and well-deserved entitlement. Instead of hoping and pleading with law-makers to do the right thing, constitutional amendments would elevate environmental rights to the status of our most cherished liberties. Life, liberty, the pursuit of happiness, *and* a clean environment would now be recognized by all as being inherent and indefeasible rights that all government officials must protect for the benefit of all generations, even those yet to come.

Beyond leveling the playing field in contests between environmentalists and industry, constitutional amendments at the state and federal level promise to effect a broader cultural and intellectual transformation. Explicitly recognizing a right to a healthy environment would alter how people think about the environment and our relationship to it. The mantra "pure water, clean air, and a healthy environment" would take on the stature of an entitlement in people's minds, becoming far more than what it is now—a "nice idea." We would all take it personally when companies destroyed the forests and wetlands around us, or when they polluted our air or water. We'd feel outraged, perceiving that industry wrongfully took something of ours to which they had no right. And we'd feel more of an obligation to protect the earth for others. After all, we're not the only ones who possess a right to a clean environment—there is the next generation, and the generations after that. Constitutional amendments protecting the right to a clean environment have the power to change everything about how people interact with one another, with the world, with their decision-makers, and with future generations.

Enshrining environmental rights within a constitutional amendment and holding lawmakers accountable on the basis of those rights was a breakthrough for me and my colleagues in our fight against shale gas extraction. I'm writing this book to share this breakthrough with anyone who cares about human welfare and our natural world, but especially with environmental activists and advocates. My message is simple: *you can do this.* You might feel beaten down by the seemingly impossible battles you're waging, but take heart. You have a new strategy now to draw on—environmental constitutionalism. It is a winning strategy that will forever change the foundation upon which you pursue your advocacy.

No matter where you happen to live, and especially if you live here in the United States, I'm here to say that you should dramatically raise your expectations. You have a *right* to pure water, clean air, and a healthy environment. This right is inherent and indefeasible. It *belongs* to you. Many politicians rail against entitlements and dismiss millennials as an "entitled generation," but they've got it wrong. Entitlement is not a dirty word. It is a recognition of rights. And make no mistake, when it comes to the environment, you *are* entitled. When your right to a healthy environment is challenged, you should rise up as firmly and passionately in defense of that entitlement as you would rise up to defend your right to free speech, freedom of religion, trial by jury, and private property. Standing up for your environment doesn't hurt jobs or industry, as those profiting from environmental devastation often contend. As I'll show later in this book, your right to pure water, clean air, and a healthy environment actually *underlies* many other social goods, including a strong economy.

This book offers a brief but comprehensive look at the power of environmental constitutionalism to effect change from the point of view of an activist. In chapter 1, I argue that environmental perils have reached a crisis point, leaving our country on the brink of irrevocable ecological devastation. Legislative environmentalism has had its day, and the environment is still on the brink of catastrophe—we need a new way forward. Chapter 2 elaborates on the idea of constitutional environmentalism as a means of enhancing existing legislative approaches to activism. In chapters 3 through 8, I take a closer look at a series of critical environmental issues, including fracking, the construction of pipelines and related fracking infrastructure, contamination from industrial operations, and excessive real estate development. I relate how grievous the harms have been despite the existence of environmental laws and regulations, and I explain the difference a constitutional amendment might make. I close the book by suggesting what each of us can do to help obtain constitutional provisions that secure environmental rights, and more broadly, how we can each embrace the mindset of environmental constitutionalism to improve our lives, empower our communities, and save our earth.

You might question whether we'll ever have a Green Amendment to the US Constitution, enshrining a right to a healthy environment. Isn't that unrealistic? Not at all. With vision and commitment, we can get there. In Pennsylvania, we used an existing provision to secure a transformational change in the recognition and protection of environmental rights. While we have not stopped the devastation of shale gas extraction (yet), we have unleashed a wave of change in the state that will yield better environmental protection across a range of environmental threats, including drilling and fracking, which we intend to ultimately ban from the state. It is time for communities across the nation to enact provisions within their state's bill of rights that protect the inherent right to pure water, clean air, and a healthy environment for present and future generations.*

If more people in other states demand that their environmental rights be recognized, honored, and protected at the state constitutional level, a broader movement will develop in due course. State-level change will become regional change, which will in turn become a national movement. Legislators who won't support environmental rights won't be elected or reelected to office. A generational shift in mindset will emerge, galvanizing the electorate to enact a more sweeping constitutional provision at the national stage. A Green Amendment in every state and in the US Constitution: it can happen. But it starts with you. Right now.

It's so important that we all move quickly. Following my mother's death, my family continued to venture to Columbia County to enjoy the forest. But over a period of years, nearby shale gas extraction ruined this land. Pollution, noise, and the ever-present fear of increasing drilling intruded on our oasis. Eventually this all became too much. We sold the land to its original owner, entrusting him to protect it as best he could. Sadly, my family's story has been replicated throughout the region, the state, and the country. The culprit has not just been

---

* In situations where environmental degradation is implicated, Pennsylvania attorneys now routinely include a claim under article 1, section 27. As a result, in 2017 the Pennsylvania Supreme Court weighed in yet again to stress the power and importance of article 1, section 27 and to offer additional clarity on its meaning. The court confirmed its previous determinations that environmental rights are "inherent and indefeasible" and that article 1, section 27 places a limitation on the state's power to deprive people of these rights, either through direct government action or through the acts of others. As the court made clear, Pennsylvania's government is a trustee of the state's natural resources, obligated to preserve them for the people of Pennsylvania, including future generations. In order to fulfill its trustee obligations, Pennsylvania's government must not only prohibit the degradation, diminution, and depletion of natural resources, but must also act affirmatively to protect the environment.

shale gas extraction, but many other damaging industries, technologies, and forms of development. Our Columbia County story ended badly, but yours doesn't have to. Let's stand up for our right to a healthy environment. Let's take our country back from the industrial interests that seek to exploit our natural world for their own profit. Let's rise up together and demand our environmental rights. Let's change our constitutions to recognize that our right to life, liberty, happiness, and a clean and healthy environment far overshadows the rights of others to pollute for profit.

CHAPTER ONE

LIVING IN THE
SACRIFICE ZONE

Would you send your kids to school near a working oil refinery? Would you let them play tag or hopscotch amid giant smokestacks spewing out a witches' brew of chemicals? Of course not. That's crazy. Unthinkable. Yet that's exactly what Rosaria Marquina of Manchester, Texas, did each day. Her seven-year-old boy Valentín attended JR Harris Elementary School, which *USA Today* ranked as one of the nation's most polluted. When kids at JR Harris Elementary play outside during recess, their developing bodies ingest toxic levels of benzene, chloroform, and 1,3-butadiene issuing from the community's numerous oil refineries and petrochemical plants, as well as from the ships and barges that navigate the nearby Houston Ship Channel.[3] Valentín breathed that foul air every day—until doctors diagnosed him with leukemia.[4]

Rosaria pulled Valentín out of the school. But Valentín had a little sister, six-year-old Mónica. She still attended JR Harris

Elementary. Financially strapped, Rosaria had no choice but to live in this toxic neighborhood and enroll her children in its public schools. Imagine how hard it must have been for her to say goodbye to her daughter each morning when she dropped her off. "I don't know whether I am giving her an education or a death sentence," Rosaria said to a reporter.[5] Public officials reassured her that her kids were safe at school, that the community's pollution problems didn't pose health risks to her children. With constant exposure, they develop natural defenses within their bodies, she was told. "If that's true," she wondered, "what happened to Valentín?"[6]

In 2016, Manchester ranked among the country's most environmentally degraded places.[7] Children growing up there were over 50 percent more likely to develop acute leukemia than other American kids.[8] The pollution was obvious, palpable. Because of Houston's famous lack of zoning, children played on jungle gyms and ran miles on the school track with industrial compounds spewing pollution in the near background. The community's César E. Chavez High School is located within a mere *quarter mile* of three major oil refineries.[9] Small homes with tricycles and monkey bars bordered chemical storage facilities. Residents nursed lifelong coughs and endured unremitting noxious odors. They washed the accumulated soot off their cars each morning and were told that the fruit they grew in their yards was too toxic to eat.[10] This was simply part of the fabric of everyday life in Manchester, Texas.

But the story of Manchester's pollution didn't end there. In this city, industry didn't just engulf schools and houses. It penetrated *beneath* the community as well. Pipelines crisscrossed one another beneath the ground, transporting natural gas and oil to refineries. Jay Olaguer, director of the Houston

Advanced Research Center's air-quality science program, found the cancer-causing contaminant benzene leaching from these underground pipelines. Using cutting-edge tracking equipment, as well as CT scans and tests of human lung tissue, his study revealed dangerously high levels of benzene emissions within Manchester. Human lung cells begin to exhibit signs of asthmatic irritation and inflammation after just four hours of exposure to Manchester's oil facilities.[11] Imagine the fate of Manchester's residents, whose exposure to such contaminants was constant.

The New Sacrifice Zones

During the Cold War, experts coined a powerful euphemism to describe areas damaged irreparably by nuclear radiation. They called them "sacrifice zones."[12] These places were so devastated by the manufacture of nuclear weapons that they became inhospitable to life—humans, animals, plants. They were areas that the US government had literally sacrificed for the sake of the nuclear arms race. Since the Cold War, many communities have been knowingly sacrificed, this time not in service to national security, but to industry. Toxicity was so pervasive in Manchester that it had become a permanent health hazard. And so the people of this city were being sacrificed, knowingly, intentionally, and with the full blessing of the law, ostensibly for the sake of local and national economies.

Perhaps you don't live in a clearly identified sacrifice zone. Does that mean your area is safe? The available scientific data demonstrates that widespread environmental catastrophe is under way throughout the country and world. As former NASA researcher and professor of mathematics Dave Pruett observes, environmental degradation is so widespread that "We're All in the Sacrifice Zone Now."[13]

Most people believe that the United States of America is a nation made of laws, and that these laws are adequate to protect us from environmental harm. We have the Clean Water Act, the Clean Air Act, the Safe Drinking Water Act, the National Environmental Policy Act, to name a few. In fact, we have so many environmental laws that developers, industry representatives, and conservative politicians complain loudly about them. They take to the airwaves, contending that environmental laws are unnecessary and interfere with their ability to carry out their operations, manufacture their products, extract targeted resources, turn a profit, and create jobs.

This could not be further from the truth. Corporations are fully pursuing their operations and creating jobs, but our environment and health are not being protected. Environmental degradation of all forms is under way in every part of every community in the United States of America. We're loading our local water and air with pollution. We're allowing construction to take place in wetlands, old-growth forests, streams, and rivers. We're shattering the earth's geology and turning formerly bucolic areas into pollution-spewing industrial sites so as to extract every last drop of fossil fuel. We're changing our climate in deadly ways. All of this is occurring *despite* the Clean Water Act, the Clean Air Act, the Safe Drinking Water Act, the National Environmental Policy Act, and other environmental laws. It's occurring despite the existence of the federal Environmental Protection Agency and state departments of environmental protection. It's occurring despite elected officials who purport to act in our communities' best interests.

More Dangerous Than War

The general public tends to focus on environmental degradation at times of great emergency, largely forgetting about it once the emergency has passed. Many people thought a lot about petrochemical pollution in 2010, when the BP Deepwater Horizon spilled over four million barrels of oil into the Gulf of Mexico.[14] Heart-wrenching photos of brown pelicans coated in globs of oil flashed across television screens. Journalists conducted interviews with members of fishing communities devastated by the impact on their livelihoods. Witnesses saw swirling rainbows of deadly oil spreading endlessly across the water. While chemical contamination from that devastating spill continues to impact communities and environments, how much attention do the news media and the general public pay today? How often do most people think about the impacts of that spill?

Let's consider a few facts that get lost when sensational spills and other environmental calamities aren't claiming the headlines. We learned as schoolchildren that water is essential to life and that our bodies are comprised of over 60 percent water. Despite this reality, we allow sewage, industrial runoff, and unregulated pharmaceuticals to contaminate our limited freshwater supplies. In fact, we don't just allow this pollution to happen—we invite it. We *intentionally inject* contamination into our waterways, either as a way to dispose of contaminated waste, or because adding toxic chemicals to freshwater allows us to carry out industrial operations like natural gas extraction.

Surface water pollution adversely affects more than half of the world's population, causing millions of deaths every year. At least half the world's groundwater is so polluted that it is unsafe to consume.[15] Certain bodies of water are more polluted than others. Several Asian rivers, such as the Ganges in India or the Citarum in Indonesia, set world records for pollution, while China's relentless drive to develop has left its water supplies in a state of crisis.[16] In some Chinese cities, a scant 3 percent of the water is safe to consume, while in some areas of neighboring Bangladesh, one in five deaths are attributable to water-based arsenic contamination.[17] Few places are categorically safe. The United Nations estimates that by 2030, nearly half of the world will lack access to freshwater.[18] As environmentalists, scholars, and economists have predicted, freshwater is becoming so scarce that it will soon be the "new oil."

America's pollution levels track this global trend, with approximately half of our streams, lakes, and bays suffering significant pollution, and too many of our drinking water supplies laden with harmful, cancer-causing chemicals.[19] Though Erin Brockovich brought the dangers of one such chemical, chromium-6, to the national spotlight in 1993, the Environmental Protection Agency (EPA) has still failed to take the steps required to remove it from our drinking water. Chromium-6 now infects the tap water of over 200 million Americans and will cause approximately twelve thousand cancer deaths by century's end.[20]

The state of our air is no better. In October 2016, a UNICEF report revealed that around 2 billion children breathe air posing long-term health hazards, while 300 million breathe extremely contaminated air.[21]

The study directly linked airborne contaminants to 600,000 baby and toddler deaths every year.[22] Although better off than countries like China or India, America is hardly spared deadly air pollution. According to the American Lung Association's "State of the Air 2016" report, over half of the country's population inhabits regions with unhealthy levels of ozone or particle pollution.[23] Despite this dire situation, states across the nation are slashing their environmental protection budgets and cutting critical staff at their state agencies. As a result, state governments lack needed personnel and equipment to monitor, report, and regulate pollution levels. Some states have reduced or suspended antipollution programs altogether.[24] Federal environmental protection measures have fared similarly over the years.

Contrary to what the authorities in Manchester, Texas, may argue, our bodies don't develop "defenses" against air and water pollution. Instead, our bodies fall victim to it. They sicken. They die. Scientists have linked air pollution to major killers like heart disease, cancer, and asthma.[25] In 2013, the World Health Organization (WHO) International Agency for Research on Cancer (IARC) classified outdoor air pollution as "a major environmental health problem," responsible for increases in bladder and lung cancers.[26] In fact, an astonishing seven million people die annually from air pollution.[27] And think about this: every year, more people die from water pollutants than from all episodes of war and global violence combined.[28] That's right, pollution kills more people than *war.*

Air pollution might also be the key to unlocking the mysteries of neurodegeneration. Intriguing data from around the world are linking air pollution to dementia and Alzheimer's disease, two of the most devastating medical enigmas of our time and illnesses that afflicted my father and my grandfather. A 2017 University of Toronto study found that people living within fifty meters of a busy freeway or thoroughfare had a 12 percent greater likelihood of developing dementia.[29] Assistant professor Hong Chen, the paper's lead author, said, "Little is known in current research about how to reduce the risk of dementia. Our findings show the closer you live to roads with heavy day-to-day traffic, the greater the risk of developing dementia."[30] Seventeen studies published in 2016 also linked air pollution with dementia. Based on the research to date, Professor Caleb Finch, an expert on human aging at the University of Southern California's Leonard Davis School of Gerontology, said, "I think [air pollution] will turn out to be just the same as tobacco—there's no safe threshold."[31]

Among the many pollutants that harm us, the accumulation of heavy metals in our bodies is particularly worrisome. Inorganic arsenic consumption,[32] lead poisoning,[33] and mercury[34] harm human development and are correlated with increases in cancer, disease, and early death. A large nationwide academic study recently found that most women have pesticides in their urine and coursing through their blood.[35] Pesticide accumulations in pregnant women have been linked to higher rates of developmental disorders and autism.[36] It may be hard to accept, but our pollution is harming children in devastating ways before they are even born.

Indeed, over the course of the twenty-first century, the prevalence of childhood developmental disorders has significantly increased, with millions more reported cases.[37] Autism rates have continued to climb since 2000 (when specialists began tracking),[38] and the rate of attention deficit hyperactivity disorder (ADHD) has increased by between 33 and 52 percent (depending on the age and gender of the child).[39] While 8.7 percent of children were asthmatic in 2001, that percentage climbed to 9.3 in 2012.[40] Such disorders stem from many different causes, including genetics. Yet increasing exposure to pollution is playing a role. The latest studies analyzing the environmental determinants of disease demonstrate, according to health specialist Alycia Halladay, PhD, that exposure to chemical pollutants "can affect the developing brain in ways that may lead to autism."[41] According to the National Resource Center on ADHD, exposure to lead or pesticides is a potential cause of ADHD in children.[42] And a well-documented association exists between asthma, as well as asthma-related deaths, and air pollution.[43]

Cancer itself—whether linked to air pollution, other contaminants, or genetic predisposition—is also steadily becoming more prevalent. In 2016, the United States diagnosed approximately a million and a half new cancer patients, and about 600,000 Americans died of the illness.[44] Childhood cancer is also on the rise. In the early 1990s, there were about 150 to 160 diagnoses per million American children. By 2009, that number had increased to 175 cases per million.[45]

Cancer, autism, asthma, ADHD—these are but a few of many harmful effects that pollution has on our bodies. But we humans are not the only ones who have suffered thanks to the largely silent scourge of environmental degradation. When formerly pristine areas become transformed into sacrifice zones, our animal friends suffer, too. Over the long term, their suffering only intensifies and broadens our own.

Victims of the Anthropocene

By any standard, sturgeon are remarkable creatures. They've swum the world's oceans since the age of the dinosaurs, making them some of the most ancient fish in existence today.[46] Some species of sturgeon can live between 50 and 150 years and grow in excess of a thousand pounds.[47] The fish have made headlines for their famous (if sometimes frightening) habit of leaping into the air.[48] Scientists aren't sure why sturgeon adopted this curious tendency, but they believe it's part of a complex acoustic communication system. A quick look at these animals can convince you of their uniqueness. With bony plates accompanying their standard fish gills, they *look* prehistoric. As Dewayne Fox, a longtime researcher of the Delaware River population and professor at Delaware State University, relates, "Sturgeon in their present form look like they did 73 million years ago."[49]

The Delaware River is home to a genetically unique line of Atlantic sturgeon, one that is found nowhere else on earth. But in 2012, sturgeon became famous for another reason: Atlantic sturgeon, including our Delaware River population, joined shortnose sturgeon on the federal Endangered Species List.[50]

How did sturgeon become critically endangered after freely roaming the seas for 200 million years? Historically, the culprit was humans' taste for caviar. During the nineteenth century, the world transformed fish eggs, cured with salt, into a delicacy. The global caviar industry transported wild sturgeon eggs (roe), harvested from the Black and Caspian seas, throughout Europe. After years of overfishing, however, European sturgeon populations dwindled, and the industry moved west. The nineteenth-century Delaware River was so populated with sturgeon that it became the caviar capital of North America. The sturgeon of the Delaware River fueled a massive caviar industry, creating jobs and generating wealth for the region.[51]

At its height, the North American caviar and fishing industry helped power the regional economy. Many people earned a living by catching sturgeon and canning their roe for shipment and sale. By 1900, however, sturgeon populations dwindled, and they have flirted with extinction ever since.[52] Scientists estimate there are currently fewer than three hundred spawning adults left of the Delaware River's genetically unique line of Atlantic sturgeon. According to Erik Silldorff, an aquatic ecologist who specializes in the species, there are so few Atlantic sturgeon in the Delaware River population that some years there may be no females entering the river to spawn.[53] Shortnose sturgeon in the Delaware River have fared little better and are also found on the federal Endangered Species List.

Sturgeon haven't mounted a comeback over the past century—despite multiple regulatory and grassroots efforts—because of environmental degradation. Dredging and deepening of the Delaware River's main navigation channel to accommodate larger ships take a significant toll on the species. As Professor Fox explains, adult sturgeon swim up the river's navigation channel, where they fall victim to large ships: "some ships bump on bottom; you can see the scour marks. When you have two ships with twenty-foot-diameter propellers passing in opposite directions that takes 25 percent of the channel. We get a lot of animals cut in half."[54] Deepening also increases the inflow of water from the ocean, diminishing freshwater habitat essential for sturgeon spawning. Water diversion projects upstream, like those proposed to accommodate industrial drilling operations, and periods of drought, such as the one experienced in 2016, also reduce freshwater flows into the river, allowing the salt line to further advance. Other industrial activity, like nuclear power plants, which suck up river water for cooling purposes, make the Delaware River increasingly inhospitable to sturgeon.[55] As Silldorff laments: "Even when all the signs showed that we were continuing to inflict irreversible harm on a species well recognized as having suffered population collapse, when left to our own devices, we failed to take action to curb our behaviors and protect them."[56]

Similar challenges affect sturgeon populations all along the East Coast. In the Hudson River watershed, neighbor to the Delaware River, authorities are replacing the Tappan Zee Bridge, an important traffic conduit for New York City, with a new bridge. A major victim of this expansion is the Hudson River's sturgeon. Dead and mutilated carcasses have peppered the shoreline since the project began in 2012—the same year these animals were placed on the Endangered Species List.[57] Hudson River sturgeon also suffer from the increased presence of bridge construction boats, which slice and gash the fish in their propellers, and from the habitat harms impacting their populations.[58]

The Hudson River and Delaware River sturgeon are listed as endangered. Sturgeon in the Chesapeake Bay and the south Atlantic region are also listed as endangered, with the Gulf of Maine population classified as threatened.[59] Around the world, sturgeon represent the most imperiled of all species, according to the International Union for Conservation of Nature.[60] As Professor Fox explains, sturgeon species "have suffered population declines because of pollution, dams that block access to spawning areas, dredging, unintended by-catch during fishing operations, and vessel strikes."[61] In addition, having worked to protect Atlantic sturgeon for the last two decades, I can tell you that among the biggest threats to their future survival is a lack of strong regulatory protections and agencies willing to make conservation of the species a priority in their decision-making.

The loss of species, thanks to development, pollution, and other forms of environmental degradation, is hardly limited to sturgeon. Approximately 80 percent of the world's flora and fauna inhabit forests.[62] Without forests, these plants and animals perish, while climate change and greenhouse gas emissions increase, disrupting global water cycles and degrading our air quality.[63] Between 2001 and 2011, the United States destroyed nearly 17 million acres of forested land in the contiguous forty-eight states.[64] Though forests still account for approximately one-third of the world's surface area, every year we are losing forest cover for a landmass half the size of England.[65] The World Wildlife Fund calculates the loss as forty-eight football fields of forest every sixty seconds![66]

Between 2008 and 2011, we also destroyed nearly 24 million acres of grassland, scrubland, and wetland—a surface area larger than Indiana.[67] The combined surface area of destroyed land from 2001–2011 is roughly equivalent to the entire state of Idaho.[68] Wetland ecosystems are so diverse and valuable that they've been nicknamed "biological supermarkets," providing food to different plants, animals, and microorganisms, and ensuring that global chemical balances, like those of water and nitrogen, remain in balance.[69] Priceless ecosystems are disappearing before our eyes.

As a result of habitat destruction and pollution, most wildlife inhabiting the world today are under siege. According to a World Wildlife Federation 2016 study, 58 percent of the world's animals perished within forty plus years (1970-2012). By 2020, we can expect the demise of two-thirds.[70] In a recent study, Stanford biologist Paul Ehrlich demonstrated that extinction rates are the highest they have been since the disappearance of the dinosaurs 66 million years ago.[71] Indeed, the "species holocaust" we're seeing is so extreme that some specialists have seen it as marking a change in geologic time. The Holocene era, which encompasses the entirety of human civilization, has given way to the human-centered Anthropocene era.[72] One of Ehrlich's collaborators, Gerardo Ceballos of the Universidad Nacional Autónoma de México, offered a terrifying assessment of the fate of life on earth: "If it is allowed to continue, life would take many millions of years to recover, and our species itself would likely disappear early on."[73]

For now, of course, we humans are still here, and so are the last of the sturgeon. We still have an opportunity to reverse course and alter the devastating impacts we are inflicting. We need nature for more than just food, air, water, and space to live. We also need to bask in nature's majesty; for the sake of our psychological and emotional health, we need respite from our bustling lives. Unfortunately, our ability to enjoy the bounty of nature has also become a casualty of environmental degradation. We're paving over nature, with little thought as to how it might coarsen our lives.

They Paved Paradise and Put up a Route Extension

The city of Trenton, New Jersey, has seen more glamorous days. Since manufacturing left the area, jobs are few and crime and poverty rates are high. But this city once possessed riches you couldn't measure in dollars. It had free and easy access to the Delaware River. From anywhere in the city, you could navigate your way to a cluster of trees that marked the edge of an embankment. From there, you could descend to the cool, refreshing water below. Kids played in this area, swinging from tree branches into the water and frolicking along the shore's edges, while adults fished on the upriver portion. The local folks called this reach of my watershed "South Trenton's Jersey Shore." Many inhabitants didn't have the time or the financial means to visit the beaches of Cape May or other resort areas along the Jersey Shore's Atlantic Ocean. But they had the Delaware River.

Then the New Jersey Department of Transportation

(NJDOT) stepped in. As with the dredging of the Delaware River bottom to accommodate larger ocean vessels, the state transportation agency decided it needed to convert a two-lane scenic road into a four-lane highway. This would make it quicker, easier, and cheaper for large, heavy trucks to motor through the region rather than having to navigate the streets and bridges of South Trenton. To build this new highway expansion, NJDOT decided to tear down the stately corridor of sycamore trees along the river's embankment and fill in part of the Delaware River. Trucking in tons of fill for the river and its bank, the agency planned to perch the highway alongside the river, cutting the community off from its once free and easy access to the water's edge.

With this priceless community treasure in peril, the Delaware Riverkeeper Network voiced strong opposition. The state's plan was foolhardy to begin with. The Tri-State Transportation Campaign, headed by resourceful attorney Janine Bauer, identified a network of preexisting highways with sufficient capacity to accommodate truck traffic and orient it around the city.[74] The city, noted Bauer, was within its legal rights to ban trucks from scenic Route 29. NJDOT nonetheless insisted on walling off the city from its remaining waterfront. Janine and I organized against this new section of highway, the Route 29 Extension, as strongly as we could. Ed Lloyd, one of the state's most highly regarded environmental attorneys, joined the fight, bringing with him the legal resources of the Rutgers Environmental Law Clinic. Protecting this reach of river and its plants and animals was one of our major objectives, but we also argued against the expansion because this river belonged to the community, especially its youth. It was their oasis, something they deserved, a special place they were entitled to enjoy.

Sometimes, as with the overturning of Act 13, you score a major victory. As most environmental advocates and activists will attest, such victories are uncomfortably few. Even though we had all the ingredients necessary to achieve success—a solid transportation solution, important public interests that needed protection, environmental laws, and large-scale community, legal, and professional opposition—the state still decided to build that Route 29 Extension. Shortly after the final decision was made, I received a call from Ed saying, "Maya, you won!" I detected sarcasm, but over the phone I couldn't be sure.

"What do you mean we won?" I asked.

"Well, the state just called and told me so." Yes, Ed was definitely being sarcastic. The state had designated funds for a walkway running parallel to the river and adjacent to the highway. As the state attorney explained it to Ed, locals would supposedly be able to use this walkway, which would sit at least ten feet above the waterline, to view the river and cast lines for fish. There was also talk of a stairwell from the walkway that would take folks down to touch the water. "The state tells us it is a perfect compromise," Ed added. Of course, it wasn't perfect as planned, nor is it perfect as it currently exists.

Shortly before the expanded highway opened to traffic, the state banned large, heavy trucks from using it, confirming that Janine and the Tri-State Transportation Campaign had been right about rerouting the trucks all along.[75] Now the Route 29 Extension serves Trenton's workforce, who can flee the city and its problems a little faster once the workday ends. Homes that once enjoyed a view of nature now face a highway wall. Visitors to this once peaceful part of the Delaware River are now plagued by high-speed traffic zipping past and battering their ears. Breathing in exhaust and struggling to hear the sounds of nature, local residents can't begin to touch, feel, and enjoy the river water. South Trenton's Jersey Shore is dead. And guess what? For no good reason. Once there was a river here, and now there is a highway. To the benefit of nobody. To the detriment of an entire community.

What happened to South Trenton is happening, in one form or another, around the country and globally. Extensive habitat destruction is dramatically curtailing humanity's access to nature. More than 50 percent of the world's inhabitants live in either suburban or urban contexts and the United Nations Population Fund estimates that this number will skyrocket, with 5 billion of the estimated 8.5 billion total population living in developed areas by 2030.[76] Never in human history has our species been so urbanized, so removed from the countryside, from wilderness, from natural spaces.

Human beings evolved in natural contexts. Today, however, the artificial light and noise we confront thanks to anti-green development corrodes our happiness and health. In 2011, the World Health Organization determined that in Western Europe noise pollution resulted in 1 million deaths every year.[77] A 2010 study determined that those living near noisy airports were at a much greater risk of heart attack.[78] As for artificial light, our enhanced ability to generate it has had many positive benefits, including greater economic productivity and higher quality of life in urban areas. Yet it also takes a steep toll on human health. Whether coming from our smartphones, 24/7 industrial fracking operations, car headlights, or flashing street signs, excessive light exposure increases our risk of depression, breast cancer, cardiovascular disease, diabetes, obesity, high blood pressure, and mood disorders.[79]

As author Richard Louv observes, unchecked urbanization

might eventually sever our links with nature, or it could also lead us to reshape our relationship with the environment in positive ways. With the help of nature-conscious "biophilic designers," we could create nature-rich workplaces, schools, homes, and cities, which are proven to be more productive and happy places.[80] If we increase the biodiversity in our urban parks, we become psychologically healthier, experience less stress, have lower body mass indexes (BMI), and enjoy enhanced creativity. Louv's research demonstrates that even providing people with access to places like South Trenton's Jersey Shore can enhance human longevity and energize the human spirit.

As Louv understands, we risk more than disease and a lack of well-being by allowing ourselves to become distanced from nature. We risk dehumanization. Take our connection with the human senses. While we're taught as children that human beings have five senses, scientists believe we actually have as many as ten to thirty.[81] By spending so much time glued to our screens, we're blocking out these senses, not allowing ourselves to fully develop. When we don't allow ourselves exposure to the sensory cornucopia that nature provides, we're not fully alive. What kinds of artistic, cultural, and scientific innovations might we achieve if we venture into nature more, activating and tapping into these super-senses? If we don't stop degrading the environment, we'll never know.

Locked In

Dr. John Abraham, professor of thermal sciences at the University of St. Thomas School of Engineering, calls the years 2014–2016 a "three-peat." Globally, 2014 was the hottest year ever recorded. It was eclipsed by an even hotter 2015, with

2016 winning the heat trifecta, prodigiously outdoing the prior two years.[82] But what does that really mean? Climate-change deniers argue that just because the surface temperature of the earth increased exponentially in a single year or two or three, this doesn't *prove* that climate warming is accelerating. Temperatures fluctuate year to year as a result of normal weather patterns, they say.

I'm not here to argue with climate-change deniers, and I don't need to. The climate science is clear: humans have released an unprecedented amount of carbon dioxide, as well as other greenhouse gases, into our atmosphere. Those emissions threaten to produce widespread, irreparable changes here on earth.[83] Once levels surpass a certain threshold, a cascade of uncontrollable changes will occur. The earth's climate and the fate of its inhabitants will become, in the words of climate scientists, "locked in."

Other forms of environmental degradation, generally due to pollution and development, are becoming locked in as well. I have had the thrill of seeing one of the Delaware River's Atlantic sturgeon, but at the rate we are impacting this species with dredging, pollution, and other harms, my son, Wim, may never experience this thrill for himself. Likewise, my daughter, Anneke, and I joined Dr. Larry Niles and Dr. Mandy Dey on the beaches of the Delaware Bay, helping place scientific identification bands around the legs of red knots to help scientists track their population health (or lack thereof). This bird species has suffered devastating declines, largely due to the overharvesting of another species, horseshoe crabs, in Delaware Bay, as well as loss of habitat. As volunteers helping internationally recognized red knot experts, Anneke and I have sat together on a warm beach, helping to measure birds' beaks and wings, weighing them, affixing tracking bands to their legs, and enjoying the thrilling moment the birds are set back into flight. These creatures are so small you can hold them in one hand and admire their beautiful red plumage. Will Anneke's children have the same opportunity to witness their beauty and majesty?

By irreparably altering our environment, we're preventing future generations from enjoying and benefitting from nature. When we poison a stream, the damage might last for hundreds of years. Likewise, when we invest in fossil-fuel infrastructure like pipelines, power plants, and compressor stations, we create a situation with a surprising degree of permanency. We commit ourselves to *using* the infrastructure and the dirty fossil fuels it carries for decades. While industry will reap economic benefits from that infrastructure during the short term, as a community and nation we are subjecting our children, for generations, to its manifold costs. We are also preventing ourselves and our children from embracing a path fueled by clean, renewable energy.

Already at age eleven, Wim is confused as to why I am fighting gas drilling wells and pipeline projects, and why we had to lose our special forest in Columbia County. Upon learning that our own home is fueled by solar panels, he asks, "Why aren't we just putting solar panels on everybody's roofs?" Wim, like so many children I encounter in my work, asks the obvious. In truth, many of the young children and young adults I meet are not just confused. They are angry about the choices we are making for their future.

Other development choices we make are depleting water resources for future generations. An example is our tendency to treat rainfall as wastewater rather than a resource. Felling forests, filling wetlands, flattening our landscapes, and packing down soils for development prevent rain from soaking into the soil. As a result, that rain doesn't recharge groundwater, providing needed baseflows for our streams, and replenishing drinking-water aquifers and wells. Instead, common development practices send that rain rushing off the land in a torrent, through man-made systems of curbing and piping. It is then dumped quickly, directly, and unceremoniously into rivers and streams, causing flooding in communities downstream. The rush of rainfall also delivers all the pollution that exists in its path, like oil, trash, winter salts, and excess fertilizers, contaminating streams and rivers. While development methods and storm-water strategies exist that can alleviate or avoid most of these harms, the outdated management techniques provided for by most laws and used by most developers actually do worse damage to the environment. With each new development project that fails to protect our vital natural systems, we lock our children into worsening droughts, floods, and pollution in both our own neighborhoods and those downstream.

In addition to preventing our children from benefitting from nature, we're impoverishing their awareness and experience of it. America's children today are opting for technology over nature at staggering rates, with interest in the outdoors declining 50 percent between 1997 and 2003.[84] Other areas of the world have seen similar trends. Environmentalist George Monbiot considers children's seclusion from the joys of nature "a second environmental crisis" facing the world.[85] In addition to diminishing creativity and cardiovascular health and accelerating developmental disorders and obesity, this crisis will produce a generation of children who won't love nature, and who won't fight for it. As Monbiot observes, "Without a feel for the texture and function of the natural world, without an intensity of engagement almost impossible in the absence of early experience, people will not devote their lives to its protection."[86]

Our children will also likely experience diminished emotional and intellectual development as a result. Children are naturally curious about the world around them, fascinated about nature and how it works. In *Last Child in the Woods* (a must-read for all parents and educators), Richard Louv explores the rich body of research demonstrating that children learn better when they enjoy access to nature and the great outdoors.[87] Kids residing in the inner city or dense metropolitan areas, surrounded by cement, can't focus or learn as efficiently. Their creativity and imagination can falter, and with it their self-confidence. Even the ability to peer out of a classroom window and spot a tree enhances a child's capacity to learn.

In destroying the natural world, we've impacted our children's capacity to learn and grow. When kids aren't running around climbing trees and crawling through creeks, when they're confined to their backyards or playing mostly organized sports, when they spend too much time on their phones or tablets, they're unable to develop in a holistic, well-rounded way. As George Monbiot suggests, "Natural spaces encourage fantasy and roleplay, reasoning and observation. The social standing of children there depends less on physical dominance, more on inventiveness and language skills."[88] Our polluting habits and the continuing destruction of naturally healthy spaces rob our children of the carefree joy, the wonderful sense of discovery, and the important skills-development associated with unstructured play in nature.

The Old Weapons Aren't Working

In 2007, fed up with the pollution degrading their health and communities, people in Houston, Texas, finally had enough.

Concerned residents, environmental organizations, and honest municipal leaders demanded that the oil and gas industries be held accountable for pollution they had caused. Houston's city council got tough, devising a muscular set of environmental laws and enforcement mechanisms to halt pollution. Unconvinced by the industry's claim of healthy emissions levels, the city of Houston enacted a new regulatory regime, requiring emitters to purchase pollution permits, and criminally punishing industries that didn't comply with air quality and public health standards.[89] Fines levied against noncompliant plants and refineries ranged from several hundred to several thousand dollars per day.[90]

Unhappy with the new ordinances curtailing their power to pollute with impunity, the oil and gas industry took the city to court, appealing these ordinances to the state's highest tribunal.[91] In April 2016, the Texas Supreme Court faced a decision analogous to Pennsylvania's Court when debating Act 13. It could choose to rule in favor of individual and community health or to bow to powerful corporate interests. Sadly, the Texas high court opted to side with industry over democracy—the wealth of the few over the health of the many. On April 29, 2016, in an 8–1 majority ruling, the court delivered a landslide decision in favor of industry, overturning the city's health ordinances. Such a ruling was disappointing, but squarely in keeping with America's dismal history of legislative enforcement when it comes to the environment. In the United States, all the environmental degradation surveyed in this chapter has occurred *despite* an extensive regime of laws, regulations, and regulatory bodies in place to protect the environment.

Our existing legislative-based environmental protections have failed us. And they have failed us for a variety of reasons. As we'll see in later chapters, our elected officials have at times been in the pockets of industry. At other times, industry veterans have been appointed to lead regulatory bodies. At still other times, industry has exerted so much lobbying power that it has succeeded in changing the law to reduce environmental protections or do away with them altogether. Sometimes all of these factors have come into play at once, as was the case at the federal level following the 2016 presidential election. Overall, legislative-based approaches to stemming environmental degradation have left communities, activists, and others fighting environmental battles at a distinct and often overwhelming disadvantage against industry.

Bear in mind, existing laws *don't ban* pollution or development. Industries are perfectly able to pollute the air and water not in spite of, but *because of*, the Clean Air Act and the Clean Water Act—they simply need the right permits to do so. In the very act of purporting to restrict or regulate pollution, our laws legalize it. In addition, industry has had an easy time manipulating existing laws in their favor. They're amazing at working the system. And as a result, the rest of us are paying the price. The sturgeon are dying. We're building highways over our riverfronts. Rates of cancer, asthma, autism, and other illnesses are rising. Our children are losing touch with nature. Kids are going to school next to oil refineries. Pollution is threatening the peace, sanctity, and safety of our homes. Jobs that depend upon healthy environments are being lost. Jobs that would advance environmentally beneficial economic growth are going uncreated. Any way you look at it, we are losing. And so, too, are the generations to come.

Unless we're prepared to live—and die—in the sacrifice zone, our country must radically rethink its approach to protecting the environment. And activists everywhere must lead the way. In Pennsylvania, we didn't rely on legislative protections. We tried a different strategy entirely. We overcame industry's control over the legislative process by passing and then claiming our constitutional rights. Article 1, section 27 of Pennsylvania's constitution safeguarded our rights to a healthy environment. While it took more than forty years, Pennsylvania's constitutional provision is beginning to operate as it should have all along, as a constitutional check that protects people's rights to a clean and healthy environment.

I'm writing this book so that other states can seize the opportunity to create a robust amendment while avoiding the pitfalls that we encountered. In 2013, we took a massive step toward eradicating fracking from Pennsylvania for good. We continue to work toward that goal, but we already have fundamentally changed how decisions about our environment are made in Pennsylvania. As a result of our case, Jordan Yeager observes, Pennsylvania's decision-making must now be intentional and science-based; it must consider cumulative environmental impacts, and it must be tilted in favor of environmental protection. Our strategy itself was the true winner in court that day. By claiming a healthy environment as a fundamental liberty and ensuring that this right is recognized alongside other long-standing freedoms like free speech, freedom of religion, and the right to bear arms, people in states across America could better protect themselves, just as we have in Pennsylvania.

Constitutional provisions to ensure a healthy environment comprise the linchpin of a new environmentalism. Unlike its alternatives, this brand of environmentalism doesn't rely on government, environmental organizations, or wealthy green benefactors to affect change. It draws on an authority more powerful than corporations, laws, and governments. *This authority is the inalienable, indefeasible, inherent rights we all possess as residents of the earth.* Constitutional environmental amendments are our greatest hope for protecting the people of Manchester, the sturgeon, the people who are here today, and their future descendants. As I've experienced firsthand, constitutional environmental rights and protections afford all of us concerned about our environment, our health, our safety, our children, the quality of our lives, our economy, and our jobs newfound leverage against ineffectual or corrupt lawmakers and inadequate laws. Let's turn our attention now to constitutional rights—what this new weapon is and how it has evolved over time.

CHAPTER TWO

THE RIGHT TO A HEALTHY ENVIRONMENT

Author and outdoorsman David James Duncan has had a tumultuous relationship with rivers. In 1983, Duncan published *The River Why*, a novel about fly-fishing, young brothers, and coming-of-age in the great outdoors. He then purchased a home on an unspoiled Oregonian waterway, seeking a peaceful place to raise his family and find further inspiration for his art.[92] At first his home was every bit the idyllic natural oasis he'd envisioned. But then the logging industry stepped in. Clear-cutters decimated the temperate forests surrounding his home. They polluted his river and degraded the delicate habitat of the owls, salmon, and marshlands that had helped inspire his life's work.

Determined to raise his young daughters in an intact ecosystem, Duncan moved his family to Missoula, Montana.[93] Another waterway beckoned him there: the mighty and historic Blackfoot River. The Nez Perce and the Bitterroot Salish Indians had followed the Blackfoot during their buffalo hunts, and the explorers Lewis and Clark had used it to orient themselves during their famous expedition across the American frontier. More recently, the Blackfoot had inspired Norman Maclean's classic book *A River Runs Through It* (1976) which became a major motion picture starring Brad Pitt and Tom Skerritt. The river's plunging depths, picturesque vistas, and trout-filled waters provided endless recreational opportunities for fly fishermen, kayakers, and curious children. It also helped to sustain the region's thriving tourism and agriculture sectors.

But the Blackfoot watershed was also under assault. This time, the culprit was voracious metal prospectors. In 1989, Arizona-based Phelps Dodge and Colorado's Canyon Resources began scouring this Montana watershed for gold. Estimating that 8 million ounces of gold could be extracted from a mountain in the Blackfoot headwaters, the companies formed a venture known as Seven-Up Pete. Its purpose: to construct one of the North American continent's largest open-pit gold mines. Eager for new revenues and swayed by Seven-Up Pete's promises to protect Montana's pristine environment, state regulators approved the company's development plans and delivered the necessary permits.

Duncan sincerely hoped that Seven-Up Pete was committed to environmental preservation, and in 1996 he joined forces with graduate student Gus Gardner to scrutinize the venture and its activities. The two gentlemen were "shockingly disappointed" with what they discovered.[94] Seven-Up Pete planned to employ a controversial and sinister technique called "cyanide heap-leach mining." Along the butte of the upper Blackfoot, where elk calve and sandhill cranes nest their eggs amidst soaring pine trees, Seven-Up Pete would continuously detonate ammonium nitrate bombs until it removed the entire mountain, inserting in its place a gash in the earth as deep as the former World Trade Center buildings were tall.[95] Seven-Up Pete would deploy millions of gallons of cyanide-laced water to separate gold from rock, yielding a mere *one ounce* of product for every 245 tons of rock it processed![96] This was the lowest-grade ore that anyone had ever attempted to mine on such a monumental scale. As Duncan details in *My Story as Told by Water*, "The estimated 570 million tons of 'waste rock' excavated to create the pit will be sculpted into a coffin-shaped riverside mountain— larger than New York's Central Park, taller than the Washington Monument—from which heavy metals, sulfuric acid, and nitrates will leach into the Blackfoot watershed forever."[97] For the following twelve to fifteen years—the mine's estimated lifespan—Seven-Up Pete would "dewater" the pit, using 10,000 to 15,000 gallons of water every single minute, depressing the Blackfoot Valley's water table by over 1,000 feet, evacuating the surrounding wetlands, springs, and ponds of water, imperiling one of the few remaining US habitats of the river-dwelling bull trout, and returning *billions* of gallons of poisonous water into the Blackfoot.[98]

The community met such extreme exploitation with incredulity and defiance. A tremendous public battle ensued, pitting corporate mining against courageous residents. Realtors, religious leaders, vegans, taxidermists, nature lovers, regional artists, and celebrities like Robert Redford banded together to save the river. Emblazoning their cars with bumper stickers that read "The Blackfoot is more precious than gold," these residents did everything they could to protect the environment, their livelihoods, and their health against environmental degradation.[99] Filmmakers made documentaries, scientists donated their time to exposing the recklessness of the mine, hundreds of women donated antique gold jewelry to raise funds, whitewater and fishing guides agreed to host clients only if they wrote letters in protest, artists donated their products freely, musicians performed concerts to raise awareness, and environmentally conscious businesses like Patagonia organized community fundraisers.[100] As Duncan describes, "The flow of courage, perseverance, and self-giving this river has inspired in its human admirers has been as beautiful to watch as the river itself."[101]

All of their self-sacrifice wasn't in vain. The environment won. The Montana Environmental Information Center (MEIC) and Women's Voices for the Earth (WVE)—two environmental nonprofits like the Delaware Riverkeeper Network—filed an appeal, contesting the corporate mining venture's rights to send polluted water surging into the Blackfoot and neighboring watersheds.[102] They pursued a novel legal strategy: instead of fighting the mining venture by appealing to state legislation, national accords, or executive actions, they sought recourse through Montana's constitution. After all, they reasoned, the state's constitution reigns supreme in that jurisdiction, superseding any policy, regulation, and legislation.

In addition to article 2, section 3 of the Montana constitution's Declaration of Rights, which affirms the "right to a clean and healthful environment" as inalienable among all persons, article 9 further safeguards inhabitants' rights to a protected and improved environment. "The state and each person," article 9, section 1 reads, "shall maintain and improve a clean and healthful environment in Montana for present and future generations." In the breakthrough *MEIC v. Montana DEQ* (1999), the state supreme court ruled unanimously in favor of Montana's

environmental health, rescinding the rights of mining companies to irrevocably degrade the watershed.

As with our Act 13 victory in Pennsylvania, the *MEIC* case
produced an inspiring piece of jurisprudence that would continue to shape the state's environmental agenda for decades. Justice Terry Trieweiler, who wrote the court's opinion, stated the
case for the environment in stirring terms: "Our constitution
does not require that dead fish float on the surface of our state's
rivers and streams before its farsighted environmental protections can be invoked."[103] The environmental rights conferred by
Montana's constitution, stipulated Justice Trieweiler, were "both
anticipatory and preventative." Nonprofits and other concerned
individuals didn't have to wait until degradation was under way
to take legal action. The court empowered them to *prevent* environmental despoliation before it occurred.

As the *MEIC* decision demonstrates, constitutional provisions present an exciting opportunity for activists seeking to
preserve nature's bounty. Activists have long relied on legislation
to save our planet—all too often without success. Following the
MEIC and Act 13 cases, Montanans and Pennsylvanians interested in protecting the environment have resurrected a powerful tool. In Pennsylvania, we used the constitution to prevent
legislation forcing the approval of fracking within every part
of every community. Since that victory, we have deployed our
state's robust constitutional provision to wage other important
environmental battles. Our colleagues in Montana have done
similarly. What would happen if activists deployed this strategy
in all fifty states, and ultimately at the federal level? What would
happen if people everywhere began asserting their inalienable
right to a clean and healthy environment, rising up when industry and their political allies trample on that right?

A Brief History of Environmental Constitutionalism

Let's review the origins of this potentially fearsome weapon in the environmentalist's arsenal. As a strategy, environmental constitutionalism first emerged out of the political and social ferment of the 1960s. Rachel Carson's seminal book *Silent Spring* (1962) had raised public awareness about the perils of pollution and helped galvanize the modern environmental movement. Afterward, a series of media spectacles heightened fears among everyday Americans that industrial fecklessness, carelessness, and greed were ruining the country's natural resources. In 1969, for instance, a pile of trash and oil-laden debris caught fire off Cleveland's Cuyahoga River, leaving the impression that the river itself was on fire. *Time* magazine detailed the story to a horrified nation, describing the river as a waterway that "oozes rather than flows," because of rampant industrial pollution.[104] The Cuyahoga feeds into Lake Erie, which was also so polluted that throughout the 1960s it was frequently pronounced dead.

To blunt outrage over environmental degradation, the Nixon administration accelerated its planned establishment of the Environmental Protection Agency and began drafting the Clean Air Act. But by the 1970s, Americans were fighting back in other ways. They flocked to join environmental groups such as the Audubon Society, the National Wildlife Federation, the Sierra Club, and the National Parks Conservation Association. And they sought to claim their *right* to a healthy environment. Individual states began enshrining environmental protections in their constitutions. Over the next few decades, approximately one-third of America's states drafted or amended their constitutions to address environmental protection in some fashion.[105] Wisconsin senator Gaylord Nelson even proposed an environmental amendment to America's federal constitution, but his proposal was quickly shot down (as were subsequent efforts to pass such an amendment).[106]

Despite their proponents' laudable intentions, most state-level constitutional amendments in the United States have had little impact. Although sometimes rhetorically beautiful, these amendments have been largely ornamental—and certainly not strong enough to overcome the many inadequacies in our environmental laws. Virginia, for example, employs lovely language about environmental protection in its constitution, but then undermines that language by declaring environmental protection a mere prerogative of the state instead of a right of the people. Virginia's provision only *empowers* the general assembly to undertake protective action to ensure "clean air, pure water, and the use and enjoyment for recreation of adequate public lands, waters and other natural resources. . . ." (article 11, section 1). The Virginia legislature *can* but isn't *compelled* to enforce environmental protections. Michigan's provision is somewhat better, mandating that the state legislature protect natural resources, but still stopping short of defining an individual right: "The conservation and development of the natural resources of the state," reads article 4, section 52 of Michigan's constitution, "are hereby declared to be of paramount public concern. . . . The legislature shall provide for the protection of the air, water and other natural resources of the state from pollution, impairment and destruction."

Other states that stopped short of affirming a general enforceable right included provisions in their constitutions that allowed for protection of natural resources but for economic and recreational purposes. States like Idaho, Kentucky, Minnesota, and Vermont focused on preserving the right to fish, hunt, and trap as part of their communities' historic heritage. Notably, their provisions didn't even recognize how environmental degradation impacted these enumerated rights. As any fisher will tell you, it is one thing to be able to catch a fish, but quite another to know that you can safely eat it. And this is not a merely intellectual point. Recent studies suggest that pollution is making seafood increasingly unhealthy for humans to consume.[107]

Illinois and Massachusetts were among just a handful of states that granted people the explicit right to a healthy environment. Of these states, most vested protections in the legislature, rendering the constitutional promise of a healthy environment illusory. In Illinois, the legislature and the courts have worked in concert to *undermine* the constitutional promise of an environmental right.[108] In a case that involved tree felling and well testing, for instance, the Illinois Supreme Court ruled that the environmental provision in the state's constitution did not, by its terms, create a legal right that could be vindicated in court. According to the court, the environmental harms claimed by plaintiffs, absent a cause of action supported by another legal theory, weren't significant enough to merit constitutional protection on their own. In the court's words, the harms "amount to fear that the environmental attributes of the [ ] site will be despoiled and, in the process, that nearby wildlife habitats will be damaged. Such allegations of damage, however, even if true, *are not actionable* absent a cognizable cause of action."[109] The court thus limited the practical relevance of the state constitution's environmental provision in affecting legal outcomes.

During the 1970s, only two states, Montana and Pennsylvania, passed the strongest form of constitutional protection able to produce real environmental change. Both states located these environmental provisions within their constitution's declaration of rights, thus placing them on par with other cherished freedoms such as the rights to free speech, freedom of religion, and due process. Instead of simply using inspiring language to proclaim the right to a healthy environment, Montana and Pennsylvania employed muscular constitutional provisions ensuring this right to all state residents. Montana and Pennsylvania defined the right to a healthy environment as an inherent, indefeasible, and inalienable personal liberty.

Of course, bold declarations of rights mean nothing if plaintiffs don't ask courts to apply them in meaningful ways. In Pennsylvania, decades passed before constitutional environmentalism yielded tangible benefits, largely because early plaintiffs brought ill-considered test cases for the newly minted provision. In the early 1970s, a company contracted with America's National Park Service to construct a 307-foot observation tower overlooking the sprawling Gettysburg Battlefield in Pennsylvania. The Commonwealth of Pennsylvania challenged the permit based on article 1, section 27 of the constitution. The tower, the state alleged, would detract from the battleground's natural beauty and historic setting. The court found against the state, suggesting it hadn't provided sufficient evidence that the observation deck compromised "the natural, scenic, historic or aesthetic values of the Gettysburg environment."[110]

In this case, the lack of compelling facts inspired an outcome that undermined the state's recently passed constitutional provision. It is embarrassing that Pennsylvania's inaugural environmental lawsuit, fought on constitutional grounds, sought to prevent a relatively insignificant harm instead of protecting the state's priceless waterways, wilderness, or endangered species. The observation tower, the state alleged, represented "a despoliation of the natural and historical environment" which would "disrupt the skyline, dominate the [battlefield] setting from many angles, and . . . further erode the natural beauty and setting" that marked the place of an awful "brothers' war."[111] To site the construction of the tower (which by some accounts was well designed to be unobtrusive, aesthetically pleasing, and of "great educational value") as a violation of a constitutional right seems extreme by almost any measure.[112] As lawyers like to say, bad facts make for bad law. Because of lawsuits like *Commonwealth v. National Gettysburg Battlefield Tower*, which championed aesthetic concerns instead of environmental stewardship and protection, it took over forty years for Pennsylvania's environmental rights amendment to achieve a profound environmental victory in the court system.

The Gettysburg case carries a lesson for us: to overcome the present environmental crisis, we must remain laser-focused on protecting water, air, soils, plants, animals, and wilderness. If we interpret environmental provisions too broadly and use them where other legal means are clearly more appropriate, we're only handing our opponents ammunition to dismiss our cases in court. And in the process, we're damaging the legitimacy and effectiveness of constitutional environmental amendments.

A Compelling State Interest

Given the limited impact of constitutional protections to date, why should we think that they hold such promise? Well, just look at those few jurisdictions, both domestically and internationally, where we *do* have strong constitutional provisions. We've discussed the profound impact Pennsylvania's revived provision is having on decision-making in the state. In other locations with strong provisions, an emerging body of case law is similarly applying and refining the right to a healthy environment, transforming it from merely another good idea into a law of the land that provides genuine and meaningful protection. In 2001, just two years after Montana's supreme court rescinded its mining permits to Seven-Up Pete, the court reviewed the district court decision of *Cape France Enterprises v. Estate of Peed.* In this case, two family members, Lola Peed and Martha Moore, partnered to buy a piece of property upon which to build a hotel. Cape France Enterprises planned to subdivide its property in Bozeman, Montana, selling a five-acre parcel to Peed and Moore. To secure approval for the subdivision, Cape France needed to drill a well so as to confirm a viable water supply for the property. Preliminary investigations revealed that a neighboring dry-cleaning business might have contaminated the groundwater with perchloroethylene (PERC), a toxin that causes cancer and organ failure in humans and is poisonous to aquatic life. Drilling a well at the site would confirm the presence or absence of this dangerous toxin. But if the toxin was present, drilling could also flush it into the local groundwater system.

Concerned about the environmental impacts and its potential legal liability, Cape France Enterprises refused to drill the well. To further their development project, Peed and Moore sued. The case came before Montana's supreme court. Recognizing that drilling the well could expose people and the environment to dangerous toxins, and citing the state's environmental rights provision, the court found that no compelling state interest warranted the well drilling. The court determined the contract was thereafter null and void.[113]

While the *MEIC* and *Cape France* court decisions are a far cry from the copious body of constitutional jurisprudence defining a right like free speech, they represent an encouraging start. In these Montana cases, the court focused the state's two separate but related environmental provisions in several important ways. The court emphasized that the constitutional obligation to "maintain and improve a clean and healthful environment in Montana for present and future generations" applied to both the state and individuals. The court also clarified that the healthy environment was fundamental and "may be infringed only by demonstrating a compelling state interest."

A "compelling state interest" represents a significant legal threshold and qualifying metric. It affords us a clear test for evaluating whether the state might legally infringe on environmental rights while carrying out other duties. The state is, after all, fundamentally interested in enforcing contracts, like the one the Peed estate made with Cape France. Contracts represent the backbone of private property rights and other fundamental liberties. When balancing the fundamental liberty of a healthy environment and contracts in this dispute, the court sided with the environment, because it had no "compelling state interest" to act otherwise.[114] Strong constitutional amendments provide a basis for requiring such science-based decision-making and a consideration of the cumulative and holistic impacts of proposed projects. With these two cases, Montana is developing a sturdy foundation on which to build its constitutionally grounded vision for a healthy environment.

Countries throughout the world are likewise laying the groundwork for enhanced environmental protection. Globally, constitutional measures protecting the environment vary in scope, power, and breadth, but they tend to be stronger than most provisions in America's states. In Gambia, environmental stewardship is conceived as a matter of national policy alone—Gambian people have no recourse to the courts should their environmental constitutional rights be infringed.[115] In Portugal, the constitution treats a clean and healthy environment as a fundamental constitutional right, on par with other fundamental liberties. Portugal even allows victims of pollution or environmental degradation the right to seek compensation in court.[116] In 2008, Ecuador went even further, becoming the first country to grant protections to nature itself.[117] Instead of granting nature the status of property and endowing people with the right to a healthy environment, Ecuador's constitution vests nature (often referred to as *Pachamama*, an ancient Incan earth deity) with the right to exist and flourish.

The Toronto Initiative for Economic and Social Rights (TIESR) maintains a database on global environmental protections, rating them according to their vigor. Environmental provisions are either "absent" (as in the case of the United States and Canada), "aspirational" (a non-binding expression of ideals or aspirations intended to guide state policy but that cannot be legally enforced), or "justiciable" (enforceable in a legal setting). According to the database, the number of provisions that pass the justiciability test is low (i.e., 28 to 33 percent).[118]

Still, most countries in the world have recognized the importance of environmental protection. At present, 147 out of 193 of the world's constitutions contain explicit environmental provisions.[119] As David Boyd, one of the leading authorities on environmental constitutionalism, notes, "No other human right has achieved such a broad level of constitutional recognition in such a short period of time."[120] Just a relative handful of wealthy countries have lingered behind, including the one with the most political and economic power: the United States.

In many countries, environmental protections enshrined in

constitutions have yielded important environmental victories. In 1997, concerned Chileans mobilized against the Trillium Corporation, an American firm that secured a government permit to clear-cut 270,000 hectares (667,184 acres) of forest in the Tierra del Fuego wilderness. According to environmental and constitutional law professors James May and Erin Daly, "The Tierra del Fuego region of Chile contains some of the world's last remaining continuous stands of cold-climate virgin forests, known as 'dwarf trees,' . . . stands that were spied upon and written about by Magellan and Darwin."[121] As environmentally conscious Chileans argued in court, Trillium's project violated the country's national constitutional provision guaranteeing the "right to live in an environment free from contamination" (article 19, number 8). While the Chilean government had auctioned off these priceless old-growth forests to reap easy profits, Chile's judiciary deemed this decision unconstitutional. The *Trillium* decision represented a major victory for the environment of the Southern Cone—Argentina, Brazil, Chile, Paraguay, and Uruguay—and for global environmental jurisprudence.[122] Similar environmental victories have saved forests in the Philippines and Hungary, ensured the remediation of Manila Bay and Argentina's Matanza-Riachuelo River, protected the Ganges River in India and the Achelous River in Greece, safeguarded Africa's limited freshwater supplies, and prevented offshore drilling and saved sharks, sea turtles, and the endangered green macaw in Costa Rica.[123]

As encouraging as such environmental victories are, we need many more of them. And to obtain those victories, we need more constitutional amendments in states and countries that don't already have them, including at the federal level in the United States. Just as important, we need *better* constitutional protections in the vast majority of the states and countries that do have them. We need protections that are located in the bill of rights, that contain language explicitly granting environmental liberties to the people, and that frame such rights as inherent, indefeasible, and intergenerational.

A Personal Call to Action

In the United States, a constitutional approach seems especially promising and necessary when we consider how American juris-prudence has traditionally enabled environmental degradation. Supreme Court Justice Oliver Wendell Holmes is famous for prohibiting the false exclamation of "Fire!" in a crowded theater. But he also had something memorable to say about the environment. In the 1930s, New Jersey disagreed with neighboring states about water diversion policy. New Jersey appealed its dispute to the US Supreme Court, and in deciding the case, Justice Holmes declared that "a river is more than an amenity, it is a treasure." When I first read this quote, I felt proud, because the litigants were vying over access to the Delaware River. Clearly, Justice Holmes took inspiration from our mighty Delaware River and crafted a stirring call to honor and protect our country's precious water systems.

But then I took a closer look at the quote. It read: "A river is more than an amenity, it is a treasure. It offers a necessity of life that must be rationed among those who have power over it." My heart sank. Instead of issuing a rousing call to cherish and safeguard nature, Justice Holmes promoted an irresponsible and domineering view toward rivers and the environment. Indeed, *New Jersey v. New York* (1931) profoundly hurt the Delaware River and impacted everyone downstream. New Jersey petitioned the country's highest court to keep the Delaware river system intact, while neighboring states wanted to divert its water to quench the thirst of residents elsewhere, especially in the New York City metro area. In siding against New Jersey and in favor of diversion, the court inaugurated a sad chapter in the Delaware River's conservation history. The court's decision to *ration* the river represented another sad loss for the sturgeon, as well as for the watershed's other marine, plant, and human inhabitants.

The more I thought about Justice Holmes's words, the more I realized that they spoke to the central environmental problem I mentioned earlier in this book: pollution and environmental destruction are *not illegal* in this country. People are free to pollute, damage, and devastate the environment so long as they obtain government permits or licenses to do so. The DuPont corporation has secured numerous permits over decades allowing it to discharge PCBs and other cancer-causing substances into the Delaware River. Blessed with governmental permits, PSEG Nuclear LLC operates the Salem Nuclear Power Plant, killing over 14 billion eggs, larvae, and fish from the Delaware River every year, even though it could reduce those kills by over 95 percent with the installation of modern technology.[124] The US Army Corps of Engineers continues to deepen and dredge the Delaware River to accommodate larger tankers and container ships, introducing pollution into the water column and destroying precious wetlands habitat in the process. Sadly, government-issued licenses to pollute are rarely denied. The Delaware River lost at the hands of Justice Holmes's court, it lost to the South Trenton route extension, and it has lost to numerous dredging, nuclear, industrial, and development projects ever since.

But in 2013, the Delaware River and all of Pennsylvania's people and environments didn't lose. When we appealed to the Pennsylvania constitution for protection, the Delaware River-keeper Network, seven towns, and Dr. Mehernosh Khan (represented by three of the smartest attorneys I know) overturned a major pro-drilling and fracking law passed by Pennsylvania's governor and legislature. We scored a landmark, precedent-setting, environmental victory. As attorney Jordan Yeager (and one of the aforementioned smartest), remarks, "We had a legislature and a governor that passed a law . . . that would have ensured that fracking [would happen] in every zoning district, in every municipality where it could happen. It would have led to the wholesale mass industrialization of huge swaths of the state. . . . I don't think it's an understatement to say that [Pennsylvania's constitutional provision] saved a vast, vast amount of the community from being fracked."[125]

America desperately needs more of these kinds of victories. And it needs more states with stronger, more explicit constitutional provisions protecting the environment. Ideally, of course, we'd instantly catch up to the rest of the world by amending our national constitution with an environmental rights provision. But let's be realistic. Since the adoption of the Bill of Rights two centuries ago, the American constitution has been amended a scant *seventeen* times. Many of these amendments reflected epochal transformations in American society and culture. The thirteenth amendment abolished slavery, the sixteenth instituted the federal income tax, and the nineteenth extended voting rights to women. While environmental protections merit a federal amendment, this will only become possible after a grassroots transformation has occurred across the nation and in the individual consciousness of our people.

The place to start is at the state level. State constitutions are more dynamic documents than the federal constitution. (The state of Massachusetts, for example, has altered its state constitution one hundred and twenty times.[126]) Furthermore, under the Bill of Rights, state governments have a constitutional responsibility to act where the federal government is silent. Given the federal constitution's deafening silence about the environment, and given the country's lax enforcement of environmental laws discussed in chapter 1, state constitutional action is not just logical but imperative. State constitutions provide individual states with the means to grant the environment the highest possible protection, that of a recognized right, within their jurisdictions. Until we have a federal constitutional right that protects everyone equally, state action is the way to go.

As local charters, each state's constitutional provision about the environment reflects local needs and values. My home state of Pennsylvania adopted what I consider a minimum standard of environmental protection. Pennsylvania's constitution succinctly and elegantly ensures that "the people have a right to clean air, pure water, and to the preservation of the natural, scenic, historic and esthetic values of the environment. Pennsylvania's public natural resources are the common property of all the people, including generations yet to come. As trustee of these resources, the Commonwealth shall conserve and maintain them for the benefit of all the people." Pennsylvania's provision recognizes environmental rights as inherent, indefeasible, and generational. The provision is self-executing (meaning no further state action is necessary to give it legal life). It provides individuals with the legal right to enforce it. And it places a clear obligation on all government officials to protect our environment and natural resources.

In 1972, when Montana considered enacting its environmental provision, delegates to the constitutional convention strongly believed they needed powerful language and comprehensive protections. Drawing on America's Bill of Rights, Montana's state constitution similarly declared environmental protections to be "inalienable." Montana's provisions place strong emphasis on the future, suggesting that each Montanan is responsible for not only preserving and protecting the environment but also for *improving* it for *future generations* to come. While several other state constitutions make passing reference to future generations, and while Illinois also vests individuals with the duty to protect the environment, Montana clearly articulates and prioritizes all of these safeguards. It is little surprise that this state joins Pennsylvania on the vanguard of contemporary constitutional environmentalism in America.

Pursuing a Green Amendment on the state level affords a unique opportunity to hold public conversations about a state's unique values, goals, and needs. Hawaii generates significant tourism revenue, and its statewide conversation in the 1970s, while falling short of an ideal amendment, explicitly protected the island chain's scenic beauty. In contrast, given its northern location and the increasingly warm planet, Alaska's statewide conversation might reference climate change in place of its current focus on resource exploitation. Whatever the emphasis or priorities, each state can arrive at its own vision and articulation of environmental protection.

Regardless of the final outcome, such conversations tend to promote better grassroots appreciation of environmental activism, with important consequences for activists themselves. Industry representatives and their political allies often try to shame activists with labels such as "radical," "extremist," or "ecoterrorist."

They try to represent our perspectives as naive or antibusiness. Over time, these attacks can take a psychological toll.

With a constitutional amendment in hand, activists can more easily withstand such attacks and bolster their morale. By passing a progressive environmental rights amendment, the community publicly affirms its understanding that the environment isn't something inert that industry can rightfully destroy. It affirms its understanding of nature as worthy of safeguarding for ourselves and future generations. The playing field shifts; now it's industry that has become marginalized, and government that must explain its lassitude in protecting the environment. As Jordan Yeager so beautifully explains, "When we start getting people to think about their environmental rights, […] there are ripple effects from that. I think it can reshape the way people think about what government is doing to them. It shifts the burden onto government to say, 'You've got to establish that what you're allowing to happen isn't going to hurt us before you allow it to happen.' I think that's just a very powerful concept."[127]

It's about time that we stand up for what truly is ours, that activists feel empowered to fight on the public's behalf, that industry should no longer possess unfettered access to the levers of power, and that government feels obliged to protect people. It's about time we took our environment back, providing it the defense, protection, and restoration it so desperately requires.

In my own public conversations, I see firsthand the deep emotional impact that constitutional discussions can have. I meet with many communities up in arms about impending pollution—an ill-conceived development project, a drilling operation, a plan to discharge sewage sludge on a nearby farm, a scheme to fill a wetland and thus destroy a habitat. These people often feel frustrated at how little protection the law or their elected representatives provide. But when we talk about environmental rights, the room becomes electric. It dawns on people that they should have these rights and that government and industry should honor them. Audiences become incredulous upon realizing that these rights in most instances go unrecognized and unprotected. After I gave a talk about Green Amendments in New Jersey, for example, Julia Somers of the New Jersey Highlands Coalition was so enthusiastic that she immediately followed up to see how we could help make this happen in her state. She was excited to learn that an effort was already under way and to see how her organization could become an integral part of it.

In Oregon, an audience member told me that he was certain he had the right in his state to expect clean water. When I disabused him of this fact, he shook his head and exclaimed, "How is that possible?" People just can't believe that an industrial operator with a permit can gain the right to pollute, while residents living nearby can't count on a right to breathe clean air or drink clean water. The anger that this realization prompts leads people to want to hear more—and often, to take action.

In urging these people on, I alert them to an especially important feature of state-level constitutional protections: their stability. In the United States, history has taught us that the government's commitment to the environment is subject to change. Our presidential and congressional representatives serve two-, four-, and six-year terms. A visionary environmental policy agenda during one congressional session or presidential cycle can easily turn into an "anti-environment" policy agenda the next. To rectify our present environmental crisis, we must elevate the environment above partisan politics. We can only do this if every state and the United States recognize a constitutional right ensuring every individual and every generation a healthy environment. The first step toward achieving this noble goal is to generate state-level awareness and enthusiasm. And that's an accomplishment that *all* of us can help bring about.

As I like to remind people, environmental progress begins with concerned individuals like David James Duncan, who joined forces with his fellow Montanans and prevented an environmentally catastrophic mining operation. By starting with local communities, we build momentum toward the ultimate goal—Green Amendments in our state and federal constitutions, safeguarding the right of every person who lives in America to a healthy environment. We also make incremental progress on a range of specific environmental problems that are putting us all in the sacrifice zone. Shale-gas fracking, oil and gas pipelines coursing through our communities, industry's legal (and illegal) release of pollution into our air, water, and soils, and unchecked real estate development—these all threaten to devastate our local ecologies, economies, and health. As we will see in the following chapters, Green Amendments, starting with the states, can better enable us to beat back each of these specific threats, succeeding where even the most elaborate and well-intended legislation has failed.

CHAPTER THREE

FRACKING AWAY OUR FUTURE

In 1988, Terry Greenwood gave up his career as a truck driver and mechanic and purchased a small twenty-acre farm in Daisytown, a sparsely populated borough in southwestern Pennsylvania's Washington County. It seemed, overall, like a great move, and for the next two decades, it was—Terry thrived as one of America's small independent farmers. Then in 2007, the Dominion Resources energy company knocked on his door. Engineers had advanced the hydraulic fracturing—fracking—technology necessary to access natural gas contained in underground shales. Terry's fields happened to reside over plenty of shale gas just waiting to be tapped. Dominion wanted to build wells on his land and exploit the gas resource.

Although Terry wasn't interested in having an energy company drill on his family farm, he had no choice. Dominion wasn't *asking* him to grant access to his land by signing a lease in exchange for royalties, as energy companies often did. Instead, the company simply brandished a lease it already had on the property that dated from 1921.[128] As many residents of Washington County would soon discover, they owned their homes and properties, but not the "mineral rights" to their land.[129] Dominion informed Terry that it would site two industrial fracking wells on his farm. Construction would begin immediately, and there was nothing he could do about it. Terry begged the company to drill as far away from his cattle, hayfields, and home as possible, but the company refused. The gas wells, Dominion informed him, would operate a mere four hundred feet from his groundwater wells, and three hundred feet from his pond. To compensate Terry and his family for any inconvenience, the gas company provided a scant $400 a month in energy royalties.

Drilling on Terry's property began in December 2007. Week in and week out, Terry watched as the company transformed his peaceful, quiet, and bucolic oasis into an industrial site. The company paved over his six acres of hayfields, clearing land for industrial gas rigs to drill and construct gravel roads. Terry reported that the company treated him disrespectfully, throwing garbage on his property, and carelessly erecting an electric fence, which stunned one of his horses, removing the skin from its legs.[130] When Terry tried to remove the garbage, not wanting it buried on his property, the energy company accused him of using the garbage to block the road, which he did not do. The company even took Terry to court.[131]

Unfortunately, such harassment and land destruction were the least of Terry's worries. By early 2008, a few months after fracking operations began, Terry noticed changes to the water on his property. The surface-water pond where his cattle drank turned a bright, brackish red. It was so obviously contaminated that Terry cordoned it off to protect his animals. He also appealed to the Pennsylvania Department of Environmental Protection (DEP). Surely it would help. After all, reining in industrial contamination was its job, right?

To Terry's surprise, regulators claimed the water was "good" and then refused to conduct any soil testing. As they told Terry, the water on his property came from a pond and wasn't intended for human use.[132] Under these circumstances, there was nothing they could do. Terry countered that humans *would* be consuming the water. Cattle ingested it, which meant that anything present in the water would enter human bodies once people consumed the cattle. The Pennsylvania DEP declined to comment on this point.

In a sense, Terry was wrong. Humans wouldn't consume his cattle any time soon. That's because his cattle started *dying* at unprecedented rates. In a typical year, Terry lost one or two animals to disease or accidents. In 2008, however, eleven of his animals perished. Four became blind, one developed a cleft palate, and some were stillborn. Photographs of these creatures reveal that their eyes were bright blue and white, likely evidence of toxic chemical exposure. At least one stillborn calf was so mangled that its mother didn't bother to clean it off after birth, but instead discarded it like rubbish. Terry contacted the Pennsylvania DEP, but inspectors showed little sympathy. "That's a farmer's luck, losing cattle," an inspector told him.[133]

Terry knew that it wasn't farmer's luck. Dominion stored industrial wastewater in rickety pits on his property, and Terry had observed water gushing from these pits into his farmland, right where his animals roamed and drank.[134] He contacted the Pennsylvania DEP once more. Investigators conducted an inquiry and concluded that "there was no spill and no natural gas drilling contamination of Greenwood's pond water."[135]

Dr. John Stolz, a professor of environmental microbiology at Duquesne University, who studied Greenwood's case, strongly disagreed with the Pennsylvania DEP's assessments.[136] Terry's photographs of the pond water clearly showed Stolz that spills had occurred.[137]

A Pennsylvania DEP inspector also told Terry he shouldn't worry because the gas industry disposes of its fracking wastewater elsewhere. "They dump it on the fields in West Virginia," the inspector assured him.[138] Terry knew for certain that this wasn't true. When his wife left for work in the mornings, the ground beneath her tires was often completely wet, even though it hadn't rained. One day, high in the mountains, Terry's brother witnessed fracking fluid streaming from an industry vehicle into the wilderness. When his brother confronted the industry representative, alerting him of his crime, the man objected, saying that it had been an accident—a valve on the truck had somehow come open.[139]

In addition to contamination of his pond, Terry also had to contend with poisoning of the water he and his family used for drinking, cooking, and washing. The well water on Terry's land became so contaminated that it resembled "iced tea." The energy company told him and his family to stop drinking it immediately. A few months later, the well water disappeared altogether. Dominion initiated five attempts to access freshwater, puncturing holes in Terry's farm until the company finally struck liquid. While Pennsylvania's DEP insisted that this newly accessed well water was perfectly safe, it had a briny taste, and Terry suspected that it was laced with fracking chemicals.

With his water sources decimated and his animals sick and dying, Terry's property values and annual revenues plummeted. In 2011, his bull became sterile—a result typical in cases of toxic exposure. Instead of siring two dozen offspring, the once virile animal produced no new calves, and Terry was forced to sell him. Terry dreamed of abandoning this nightmare and moving, but he couldn't afford to. Who would purchase a farmstead studded with gas wells and containing no reliable water? In the first four years of drilling on Terry's property, his son tabulated $50,000 in losses.[140] That didn't include his $125,000 farm, which had lost all its value.[141] As Terry gazed around his once idyllic community, he eerily noted additional catastrophes under way: "There's been dogs died, goats died, and people sick. You put the sick people and the animals together and you have a big problem. There's been more stillborn [human] babies around here too."[142]

The United States of Arabia

Little did Terry Greenwood and his neighbors realize, their county had been swept up in America's new energy boom. Beginning in the late 1990s, the oil and gas industry began eyeing Pennsylvania's Marcellus shale, zeroing in on the area where Terry's farm was located.[143] Harvesting natural gas from America's great shale deposits, such as the Marcellus, located below the Appalachian Basin, and the Bakken, resting below the northern United States and central Canada, had been an energy pipe dream for decades. But the twenty-first century marked a bold new energy era based on fracking.

Armed with innovative techniques and proprietary chemical concoctions, America's drilling and fracking industry promised to lead the country into a brighter, more independent, and lucrative future. Beginning in the early 2000s, media headlines proclaimed the end of "dirty coal," which polluted the earth, and the rise of natural gas, which was allegedly much cleaner. By the end of the 2000s, domestic fracked gas was also heralded as our ticket out of the global recession and our difficult relationships with volatile Middle Eastern states. According to news reports, natural gas promised to make the United States "energy independent" within decades.

The oil and gas industry allocated millions to lobbying efforts and marketing campaigns, funding studies about the merits of fracking and lining the pockets of local, state, and national politicians to ensure their support for fracking projects. As I described in this book's introduction, they also began knocking on the doors of rural Americans, asking them to sign leases for gas exploration on their land. If local landowners agreed to the drilling, the energy companies promised, they'd become rich. As for any risk of environmental damage, well, that was nothing to worry about—fracking for gas was absolutely safe, industry representatives claimed.

These sales pitches caught Americans off guard. As rural America struggled to stay solvent in the late 2000s, during the worst economic crisis since World War II, energy companies were promising them a front-row seat in America's lucrative clean-energy future. Meanwhile, few independent studies existed to shed light on fracking's economic, environmental, or health impacts. Organizations like the Delaware Riverkeeper Network worked hard to document early instances of devastation unleashed by fracking, but we had a lot of ground to cover, and the industry had a huge head start. Tracy Carluccio, the Delaware Riverkeeper Network's deputy director, spent countless hours with me researching the latest science, seeking out experts, and talking with victims of the fracking industry. Grassroots organizations like Karen Feridun's Berks Gas Truth were founded and began to raise awareness and sound alarm bells.

For the most part, however, people heard from the well-funded industry and their elected representatives that fracking was both safe and profitable. In fact, fracking seemed like a no-brainer. Why *not* allow it on your land or in your community?

More Dangerous Than It Looks

If you scrutinized the industry sales pitch, however, as my colleagues and I did, there was ample reason to suspect that fracking posed serious problems, especially as far as water was concerned. A traditional natural gas well (what regulators term a "conventional well") requires approximately 100,000 gallons of water to drill. A fracked shale gas well (or, as regulators call it, an "unconventional well") requires a stunning 3 to 5 *million* gallons (and even more for wells with longer well bores). That's 10 million gallons of water for the two wells on Terry's twenty acres of farmland alone. That water isn't simply used and then recirculated. It's infused with proprietary mixtures of chemicals, including toxins and carcinogens. These chemical-laden fracking fluids are then injected, at extreme pressures, through a borehole drilled deep into the earth, where they mix with naturally occurring but no less dangerous substances, including barium, strontium, benzene, toluene, and naturally occurring radioactive materials (NORM). After passing through the earth's geology as the result of drilling and fracking, the already toxic frack fluid becomes even more contaminated and dangerous.[144]

It's not just the actual drilling and fracking that inflict so much harm. Shale gas extraction is an industrial operation that requires significant modification of the landscape. Every well that is fracked requires heavy and polluting industrial equipment as well as access roads to accommodate thousands (yes, thousands) of trucks loaded with sand, chemicals, and waste-water. Each industrial shale gas extraction site, known as a well pad, requires up to five acres of land for the pad itself, but when you add in the access roads, pipelines, vast wastewater storage pits, and other infrastructure needed to support the drilling and fracking operations, each pad really requires the development and degradation of approximately seventeen to twenty-three acres of land, much of it forests, wetlands, and other natural habitats.[145]

As we consumed whatever scientific research we could on fracking, the constantly emerging stories of damage wrought by fracking confirmed our worst suspicions. Jenny and Tom Lisak had lived happily on their land since 1983. An organic farm they ran provided them, their three children, and the wider community with delicious fruits, nuts, vegetables, and berries. In 2009, when drilling in the Marcellus commenced in their township, the Lisaks soon noticed their water going bad. As they peered in their cistern, they noticed it looked a grisly orange and smelled oily, with bubbles rising and white chalky matter floating on top.

The Lisaks were horrified. Believing that the drilling company, their elected representatives, and the Pennsylvania DEP would be equally upset to learn about what was happening, Jenny began making phone calls. When she reached the drilling company, employees there denied any wrongdoing but offered to buy her bottled water anyway. Officials from the Pennsylvania DEP came and tested her water but then went silent—Jenny didn't hear anything back for months. As for her call to State Senator Joe Scarnati, Jenny shakes her head and simply reports that he offered "no help."

Unable to rely on the water at their home any longer, the Lisaks repurposed a large water tank they had for irrigating crops. Every day or so, a member of the family drove the tank in their pickup truck to a neighbor's house and filled it up with a garden hose—a two-hour process. It was hard living like that, but the Lisaks didn't know what else to do.

The Pennsylvania DEP finally called back with test results, informing the Lisaks that their water problems weren't caused by the drilling. So what did cause it? The DEP couldn't say. The Lisaks weren't at all reassured. "I knew that there was nothing else happening in the area," Jenny recounts, "and nothing between the gas well and our water."

Meanwhile, Jenny learned that her neighbor, an absentee landlord who owned an adjacent plot of three hundred acres but actually lived in Colorado, had leased her neighboring property for fracking. While the drilling company could have situated their drilling site anywhere on the property, they decided that the best spot was right outside Jenny's kitchen window next to her garden. She couldn't believe it. "A whole 300 acres and they decided right by my home was the best spot. Naively, I thought this was a mistake—they just didn't realize that someone lived right next door and that there were several other families close by." Jenny eventually learned she was wrong, it wasn't a mistake at all. Jenny visited State Senator Joe Scarnati's office, not realizing that he was pro-drilling (in fact, he was a primary mastermind behind the now infamous Act 13 described in chapter 1). Again, she received no help. Eventually, a legal clinic filed papers to help Jenny challenge the drilling permit on her neighbor's land. Later, for reasons unknown, the drilling company pulled their permit application.

Although that immediate threat was gone, still other horrors continued to mar the Lisak family. Under the guise of trying to suppress dust, trucks rumbled over the local dirt roads, spraying water. The trucks ventured down an unpaved road that ran right by the Lisaks' house. Jenny's collies, who enjoyed investigating the freshly sprayed roads, would come home and "lie around on the front porch, licking their paws." Within a few months, the male dog died of cancer at age five, and the female lost a litter of puppies. Jenny and Tom soon learned that the water sprayed was frack wastewater.

Over this same period, the Lisaks had been trying to decide whether to send their fifteen-year-old son away for school. A particularly smart kid, he had a chance to enroll in an early college program. For Jenny, the choice was clear: "In the end, I realized that I had to send him away in order to keep him safe. I wasn't sure what would be best for him, but I wanted him safe. I knew I had to let him go."

The parade of horribles continued. More wells were drilled in the township, their toxic emissions carried by the wind and fouling the air on the Lisak property. A well in nearby Clear-field County blew out. Who knew what toxins the Lisaks and their neighbors had been exposed to? Horrendous traffic, day in and day out, disturbed their once-quiet community. Walking and driving around their property and the surrounding lands, the Lisaks passed massive impoundments filled with toxic frack wastewater. On one occasion, Jenny's throat seized up. She hurried away, coughing and wheezing. For three days, the coughing continued, accompanied by a sore throat.

Month after month, my colleagues and I came upon stories like these. It seemed obvious that the fracking industry was impacting every aspect of people's lives—their health, their peace of mind, their ability to sell their land and move away to safer spaces. It was ruining their present and compromising their future. And still the politicians supported it. And still the industry claimed it was safe.

The Scientific Consensus Against Fracking

Today we know beyond any doubt that fracking isn't safe. Between 2009 and 2015, scientific research on fracking's health and environmental effects exploded, with at least 685 research studies appearing in peer-reviewed journals.[146] The evidence is damning. A few years after fracking ruined Terry Greenwood's farm, a research study was conducted in Washington County, Pennsylvania, home to Pennsylvania's highest concentration of fracking wells. "Within 1 kilometer of a gas well," the 2014 study found, "residents had up to twice the rate of health problems per person compared to those who lived 2 kilometers away or further."[147] These include "higher rates of skin, respiratory, neurological and gastrointestinal problems among people living near gas wells." People residing within the one kilometer radius of fracking and drilling had *twice as many* health problems as those living outside this danger zone.

Another 2014 study found increased cancer risks among those inhabiting the gas lands. Testing fracking sites in Arkansas, Ohio, Colorado, Wyoming, and Pennsylvania, researchers documented the presence of eight toxic chemicals in the air with levels significantly surpassing federal limits. In some of the samples, the concentration of the carcinogen benzene tested at 770,000 times over normal levels.[148] Inhabitants of the drilling areas under study reported sudden adult-onset asthma, cognitive impairments, and other health problems. Dr. David Carpenter, the lead scholar on the study, lamented that only time would tell how truly bad the impacts were. "Cancer has a long latency," he explained, "so you're not seeing an elevation in cancer in these communities. But five, ten, fifteen years from now, elevation in cancer is almost certain to happen."[149]

Subsequent research has confirmed that fracking's impact

on our air not only boosts cancer rates but also contributes to climate change. Numerous studies show high levels of volatile organic compounds (VOC), greenhouse gases, and other airborne toxins emanating from drilling sites, degrading the air quality of the entire North American continent.[150] An April 2016 study found that North Dakota's Bakken shale oil and gas field operations emitted a stunning 2 percent of the world's ethane.[151] Until 2009, ethane emissions, among the world's top three sources of human-generated climate change, were decreasing; but since America's shale gas explosion they have increased, putting the world at greater risk for an imminent climate-change catastrophe. Likewise, between 2002 and 2014 we have seen a 30 percent increase in US emissions of methane, a deadly greenhouse gas that over the span of two decades has been eighty-six times more potent at trapping heat in the environment than carbon dioxide.[152] Shale gas extraction, and the infrastructure that accompanies it—like pipelines—might well determine our planet's fate.

As frightening as these air pollutants are, water contamination is equally scary. Between 2005 and 2013, the shale gas industry consumed approximately 250 billion gallons of water, treating it with 2 billion gallons of toxins.[153] The sheer volume of waste that results threatens to contaminate many of our country's water sources, imperiling everyone's access to one of the most important elements of human survival. Numerous studies confirm that fracking operations contaminate surface-water streams and groundwater supplies with lethal carcinogens, human endocrine disruptors, and other harmful chemicals.[154] Let's not forget radioactivity. Frack wastewater contains lethal amounts of radium, which according to recent studies has been measured "as high as 3,600 times the United States Environmental Protection

Agency's (EPA) limit for drinking water."[155] Other radioactive materials such as radon have become increasingly prevalent in Pennsylvania's communities since the onset of the fracking boom.[156] Such substances are also migrating throughout the country, traveling to wherever Marcellus shale gas is transported. Of the 5 million gallons of freshwater sacrificed for every fracking well, approximately 4 million is lost underground. Not only is this 4 million lost for future human or ecological use, but it continues to circulate through the earth's geology, where it can, in time, contaminate additional underground water supplies. The other million returns to the earth's surface. This water is so toxic that generally one of three things happens: the water is further diluted and blended with toxic chemicals so it can be used for the next fracking operation; it is hauled away to be disposed of through injection deep into the earth; or it is stored in surface water impoundment pits, where it threatens the health of people and wildlife alike. Leaks, spills, off-gassing, or damage to the impoundment pit linings can spread these toxins to wildlife, farm animals, and people. Wildlife who see these wastewater impoundments as another innocent body of water to drink from, swim in, or gather food from become unwitting victims of its contamination.

Frack wastewater disposed in the earth via underground injection causes yet another set of destructive harms: earthquakes. On November 6, 2016, a 5.0 magnitude tremor seized Oklahoma, ruining homes, canceling school, and causing widespread evacuations near Cushing.[157] Though such earthquakes are historically unknown in this region, the state now has so many earthquakes that in 2015 Oklahoma overtook California's status as the nation's leader in seismic activity.[158]

Oklahoma's earthquakes clearly owe much to the injection

of fracking wastewater, a practice that has been increasing in Oklahoma in recent years.[159] The subterranean frack fluid, explains geophysicist George Choy, is the culprit as it "fills pores in dormant faults, causing them to slip and unleash the quakes."[160] These earthquakes threaten to do much graver harm than disrupting school and compromising buildings. That's because Oklahoma is our country's major energy storage and transport center. Barrels of above-grade oil storage containers stud the landscape around the small town of Cushing, and beneath the surface a maze of pipelines crisscross one another, creating one of the largest confluences of underground energy pipelines in the country.[161] It is only a matter of time before a larger earthquake causes catastrophic damage. Oklahoma, and Cushing in particular, notes Johnson Bridgwater, director of Oklahoma's Sierra Club, has "the potential for producing one of the worst environmental catastrophes in American history."[162]

Scientific evidence is increasingly documenting what those living near the shale fields and working on this issue already know: fracking is a widespread public health nightmare. The use of frack water in California's Central Valley has compromised soil quality, exacerbated drought in the region, and threatened to endanger the food in one of the most agriculturally prolific areas in the world.[163] Fracking jurisdictions have experienced increased rates of hospitalization, car accidents, reproductive health and childhood development problems, and cancer risk.[164] The 24/7/365 exposure to light and noise disrupts community peace, and as we explored in chapter 1, has a detrimental effect on health. Contrary to widely circulated industry claims, fracking is bad for the economy and erodes the fabric of our communities. While a few make money, entire towns are left to suffer. Fracking operations are correlated with "steep increases in rates of crime, including sex trafficking, sexual assault, drunk driving, drug abuse, and violent victimization."[165] Though women disproportionately bear the brunt of such public health nuisances, Terry Greenwood also suffered routine harassment and intimidation. No one is safe.

Along with the Delaware Riverkeeper Network and other environmental organizations, Karen Feridun has helped spearhead the fight for a ban on fracking in Pennsylvania. As she has observed, the people of Pennsylvania and other regions where fracking occurs are "test subjects in a live laboratory experiment." To Karen, the results of this experiment are painfully clear: "Fracking has been devastating Pennsylvania communities for well over a dozen years. You simply cannot make it safe; there is no law or regulation that can make it safe."[166] Karen is right. Of the 685 peer-reviewed studies mentioned above, none argue that fracking is good for public health or the environment. After surveying this vast body of research, the Concerned Health Professionals of New York and Physicians for Social Responsibility concluded that there exists "no evidence that fracking can be practiced in a manner that does not threaten human health."[167] All together, they find that fracking "poses significant threats to air, water, health, public safety, climate stability, seismic stability, community cohesion, and long-term economic vitality." Such catastrophic harms, they suggest, cannot be solved through "regulatory frameworks."[168]

The Fracked-Up Legal Landscape

Given the widespread scientific and medical consensus, not to mention the personal tales of destruction that activists like me hear about daily, one might wonder how fracking could possibly be legal. Sadly, fracking isn't merely legal: the fracking industry actually enjoys special exemptions from many of the environmental laws governing industrial activity in the United States. In 2005, George W. Bush enacted the Energy Policy Act. This bill was a boon to conventional energy, providing tax incentives and other kickbacks to the nuclear and fossil fuel energy sectors. The bill also contains the infamous "Halliburton loophole," which allows the oil and gas industry to keep its chemical fracking recipes secret and grants them exemption from the Safe Drinking Water Act's requirements.[169] The Halliburton loophole has hastened America's fracking-based energy boom, in the process contributing to the grievous injuries suffered by the Terry Greenwoods of our country.

Witnessing the cascade of harms from this boom/bust industry, many US municipalities, cities, and states have responded by enacting moratoriums or outright bans on shale gas extraction and fracking operations. The Delaware Riverkeeper Network was one of the first groups to secure a moratorium against the industry. As I related earlier, we secured a *de facto* moratorium on drilling and fracking within the confines of the Delaware River watershed in 2010. Vermont, a leader in environmental protection, banned fracking in 2012.[170] Democratic Governor Andrew Cuomo followed suit in 2014 with a ban on fracking in New York. In 2017, when signing a bill that banned fracking permanently in the state of Maryland, Republican Governor Larry Hogan announced, "because of Maryland's position in the country and our wealth of natural resources, our administration has concluded that possible environmental risks of fracking outweigh any potential benefits."[171] Other American cities and municipalities in Florida, Ohio, California, and elsewhere have similarly enacted outright bans or moratoriums on unconventional methods until science can confirm that they do no harm.

Europe is also boldly headed toward a frack-free future. The European Parliament heralded fracking's decline at the end of 2015, when it issued a report confirming that unconventional drilling contributes to climate change. Germany issued a fracking moratorium, as have Scotland, Wales, Northern Ireland, and Castile La Mancha.[172] France and Bulgaria have gone farther and banned fracking outright. The fate of the rest of the world hangs in the balance. Marcellus-sized shale deposits lie beneath Argentina, China, Poland, and other countries. Only time, the vagaries of the global energy market, and the determination of people in those countries to protect themselves will decide whether these countries will also become swept up in the fracking boom.[173]

In the United States, the weakness of regulatory regimes coupled with industry's immense power are leaving many vulnerable, even when public opposition to fracking is strong. Consider the city of Denton, located just north of Texas's sprawling Dallas–Fort Worth metropolitan area. In 2015, residents in this fossil-fuel-friendly state decided to wage their own grassroots opposition effort against fracking. As Dr. Adam Briggle, a professor of environmental studies at the University of North Texas, explained, "There are nearly three hundred wells in the city limits of Denton, but this neighbourhood was sandwiched by two gas well pad sites. It was when people saw this and how close to homes they were drilling that we realized we had to look after each other here."[174] Professor Briggle joined a chorus of concerned locals, donning "Frack Free Denton" T-shirts. Confronting the oil and gas industry head-on, the Denton community amassed enough signatures to force a vote on whether fracking should be banned locally.

The industry put up stiff opposition, but that was nothing compared to the resolve of local residents. In 2014, Denton became Texas's first city to enact a ban. "It felt like vindication," Dr. Briggle said, "an indication that grassroots democracy can still work in this country."[175] And yet Denton's victory proved temporary. Industry representatives filed lawsuits at the state's capitol immediately following the victory. In May 2015, the industry did more than overturn Denton's ban on fracking. It also used this opportunity to preempt similar actions in the future. There now exists a functional *ban on banning* fracking within the Lone Star State.

Denton's story has been replicated throughout our country. Concerned communities have joined together to enact moratoriums and bans, only to have those very protections overturned or undermined. Consider what happened in Colorado, another national energy leader. In 2016, the state's supreme court overturned one local fracking moratorium, citing its incompatibility with state law. Another municipality's ban was also overturned because, the court claimed, the ban "materially impedes" state authority.[176] On still other occasions, anti-fracking measures were stifled by procedural and bureaucratic obstacles. After the Ohio counties of Meigs, Athens, and Portage sought to strike down fracking in the 2016 elections, Jon Husted, the secretary of state, eliminated their anti-fracking ballot initiatives for technical reasons.[177]

The fracking lobby also influences local legislatures and municipalities to do its bidding. This was immediately apparent to Brian Coppola, who was a Robinson Township supervisor in Washington County as the first wave of fracking swept his region.[178] He watched as the industry infiltrated the area, promising his constituents economic windfalls. "You've got ten acres of land, you're going to make millions," he recalls industry spokesmen proclaiming. He then watched as frequent industrial accidents in the area contaminated the water tables, compromised soil quality, and destroyed the quality of life for the residents of his community. As people began realizing that fracking wasn't the clean, safe operation the industry had promised them, they descended upon Brian and his colleagues, complaining that they now inhabited an industrial wasteland. Brian tried appealing to the Pennsylvania DEP, only to find the government agency filled with industry apologists. They treated his constituents with the same condescension they had shown Terry Greenwood and his family.

Coppola similarly recalls what happened when legislative proposals that would soon become the infamous Act 13 began appearing in both houses of Pennsylvania's legislature. Joining other elected officials in the county, he went to the capitol for the first time to lobby every representative and senator in Harrisburg to vote against it. Yet most of Pennsylvania's elected officials hadn't even read the legislation. When Dave Ball, a councilman and kindred spirit from Peters Township, joined with Coppola to challenge their legislators on the substance of the bill, legislators merely recited industry talking points and were clearly ignorant as to the critical substance of the law.[179] They were also unwilling to conduct any further research. Brian, Dave, my organization, the Delaware Riverkeeper Network, and I managed to overturn the most dangerous and damaging parts of Act 13 with our legal challenge, but we are all still fighting the industry, with Brian and Dave leading the charge on behalf of municipalities and their governing rights. Since losing at the state level, the industry has switched tactics, making new efforts to influence local municipalities. The industry convened its leaseholders and told them to pool their influence to remove uncooperative officials from office, including in Brian's Washington County. The industry contended that this was the only way residents would see any profits. Because of this industry onslaught, Brian was voted out of office. Now, many townships within Washington County are run by special interests that simply ignore the Act 13 legal victory and allow drilling almost anywhere they choose. The best way to explain it, says Brian, is that "Some of those communities have been turned into third-world countries, with the gas company as dictator."[180]

The landscape across the United States thus remains highly uneven. Some jurisdictions have promulgated outright bans, while others have fragile moratoriums that can be overturned on a partisan whim or on technical grounds. Industry lawyers and lobbyists are constantly challenging the Delaware River watershed's moratorium.[181] As this book goes to publication, we are fighting yet again to prevent our river and communities from losing this protection. The industry has big plans for Pennsylvania's Marcellus and Utica shales. As of July 2017, an astonishing 10,553 wells have been drilled, and operators have secured permits for 18,512.[182] In coming decades, the fracking industry would like to install upwards of 63,000 wells in interior sections (the richest gas-producing areas) of the Marcellus.[183] If you include the entire Marcellus shale region, that number could rise to around 100,000, according to industry projections.

Rather than invest in clean-energy technologies, many states like Pennsylvania are pushing for the construction of pipelines and fracked gas power plants, arguing that fracked natural gas comprises the best alternative to coal. This is false, and we've known it for years. It's worth taking a slight detour to recount *how* we know it.

One fateful fall afternoon in 2009, Dr. Anthony Ingraffea, a professor in Cornell's engineering college, and Dr. Robert Howarth, an earth and atmospheric scientist, met for lunch at Rulloff's Restaurant in Ithaca, New York.[184] For over twenty-five years, the two scholars had shared the same university, but they had never run into each other on Cornell's sprawling campus. This lunch was the beginning of an extraordinary collaboration that would have wide-ranging implications for climate change research and American energy policy.

As a natural gas engineer, Tony knew that methane (or CH4) joined carbon dioxide (or CO2) as one of the main greenhouse gases on the planet. Such gases were famous for producing the "greenhouse effect," in which heat is trapped in the atmosphere, warming the earth's surface. From his background as a structural engineer in the gas industry, Tony also knew that methane formed whenever plant and animal matter decomposed, making it the main ingredient in natural gas, which people had just begun fracking from shale to make America "energy independent." As a specialist on the topic, Bob had a much more precise understanding of methane. He had spent years considering why, beginning around 2007, the methane thresholds in our atmosphere had skyrocketed. Bob suspected that the globe's increased methane concentrations were the result of heightened fossil fuel emissions following the advent of shale fracking in the United States. "Let's test the hypothesis," Tony and Bob agreed during the meal, "that shale gas is better for the climate than coal."

In 2009, questioning this hypothesis was almost outlandish. Everyone from President Obama to the major green organizations like the Sierra Club and the Environmental Defense Fund (EDF) embraced natural gas. In order to meet the country's needs for electricity generation, they all believed that we should close dirty coal-powered power plants and substitute natural gas. Natural gas, after all, produces less carbon dioxide than coal. Carbon dioxide is the world's leading greenhouse gas, trapping energy in the atmosphere and leading to climate change. Seeking a reduced carbon footprint, Barack Obama, Hillary Clinton, and the major environmental organizations banded together, declaring natural gas to be the "bridge fuel" to a cleaner, safer, and more sustainable future.

Bob and Tony noticed a flaw in the logic of the clean-energy natural gas party line. What about methane? The entire "bridge fuel" argument was based on the presumption that all methane pumped from natural gas wells was burned. Bob and Tony suspected that an unknown quantity was actually being released into the atmosphere. Such fugitive emissions were responsible, they deduced, for higher concentrations of global methane in the atmosphere.

The question of fugitive methane emissions has dramatic implications for climate change, but to appreciate this we need to understand how methane differs as a greenhouse gas from carbon dioxide. Ultimately, to have any hope of halting catastrophic climate change, we must reduce our emissions of carbon dioxide. Some of the carbon dioxide we emit today will continue to influence climate and warm the planet for hundreds and perhaps even a thousand years into the future. But methane is an important part of the problem, too. While it only remains in the atmosphere for a decade or so, methane is a more potent greenhouse gas than carbon dioxide in the short term. Over a ten-year period, when comparing an equal weight of the two gases, methane is 100 times more powerful in trapping heat in the Earth's atmosphere. There is substantially more carbon dioxide in the atmosphere than methane—more than 200 times—and so carbon dioxide is the major driver of climate warming even though methane is 100 times more powerful. But importantly, the Earth's climate system responds more quickly to changes in methane emissions. By reducing methane emissions today we can slow the rate of global warming, while it will take thirty years or more for the Earth's climate to respond to reductions in carbon dioxide emissions. Society must reduce emissions of both gases, but only the reduction of methane can slow global warming in any meaningful way between now and 2050.

The two scholars agreed at lunch to test the hypothesis that shale gas was better than coal by tracking methane's entire life cycle, from the time it is released from the ground at the shale well to its final end use. "Let's track how much of it doesn't get burned, and from that, let's figure out what impact that amount has on the climate," said Tony. The two scholars were perfectly suited to do this. Having spent twenty-five years of his career working with the oil and gas industry, Tony was an expert in much that happened with hydrocarbons below the earth's surface. Bob was a specialist in everything that happened above the ground in the earth's atmosphere. As Tony memorably stated, "We were a match made in hell" (for the industry, that is).

Over the following two years, both scientists discovered that no one had ever measured fugitive methane emissions from the fracked gas life cycle in a comprehensive or systematic way. The two scholars surveyed all available literature on the topic, ran the numbers, and compared the climate-changing potential of shale gas, non-shale gas, coal, and oil. In 2011, the prestigious journal *Climatic Change* published their paper and its startling conclusion: natural gas, harvested from shale, was worse for the climate than coal.[185]

These two scholars were the first to advance such a politically unpopular conclusion, and they were lambasted in the media and across academia. Bob's computer was hacked as the paper made its way through the peer review process. Someone from the shale gas industry received a copy of the stolen article draft, and it circulated through back channels. The *New York Times*'s Andrew Revkin and the former director of Pennsylvania's Department of Environmental Protection John Hanger published open criticisms of the paper before it was even published or finalized. The torrent of accusations and slander culminated in 2013, when Steven Chu, former US Secretary of the Department for Energy and a Nobel Prize laureate, secured a copy of the paper prior to giving a keynote address at a shale gas conference. While touting the many economic benefits of shale gas and its nearly pristine safety record, he dismissed the study in the following terms: "There was a very famous Cornell report which we looked at and decided it was not as credible as it—well, we didn't think it was credible. I'll just put it that way."[186]

While the blowback to the paper surprised the scientists, it began an important conversation. In the years following the publication, scientists from around the world began taking methane measurements, making our knowledge on the topic more precise. Dozens of peer-reviewed papers on the topic have followed, and the emerging consensus firmly supports the conclusion of Tony and Bob's 2011 paper: *natural gas is not a bridge fuel to a cleaner future.* It is, rather, exacerbating global pollution and climate change. As Bob warned the White House in 2016, "Although we should reduce carbon dioxide emissions, reducing carbon dioxide alone will not slow global warming on the time scale of the next few decades. The climate system responds much more quickly to reducing methane emissions."[187]

Toward a Frack-Free Future?

The research is clear: fracking cannot be made safe. No set of regulations can address the wealth of harms that fracking inflicts. It must be stopped. For that, we need the Constitution. At the federal level, a Green Amendment could well have prevented the fracked gas and oil boom from sweeping America in the first place. If the right to a clean, healthy environment were enshrined in the Constitution, the 2005 Halliburton loophole might have come under judicial review and been found unconstitutional. Without this piece of enabling legislation, along with others implemented at the state and federal levels, significant portions of our wild, forested areas could have remained unfracked, allowing biodiversity to flourish and curious children and adults to explore. Our air and water quality would be better, and we might not have to worry about an earthquake rocking Oklahoma, causing the equivalent of the *Exxon Valdez* disaster on land. We would be contributing far less to global climate emissions. Absent local sources of natural gas, the country might have focused instead on creating long-lasting and well-paying jobs, putting people to work in the renewable energy sector.

Green Amendments at the state level could also have made a substantial impact. Perhaps they wouldn't have provided an instant panacea, but they at least would have provided us the tools we needed to secure protection and exercise more caution (e.g., waiting for the scientific and anecdotal evidence to accumulate before granting drilling permits). A state amendment wouldn't guarantee that fracking won't exist, but state constitutional amendments similar to Pennsylvania's would have assisted the grassroots anti-fracking struggles in states like Texas, Colorado, and Ohio. If activists had mobilized for environmental amendments early, back when the gas industry was first taking shape, they would have enjoyed significantly more success. Had the courts recognized the legal power of article 1, section 27, from its outset, Pennsylvania also would be a far different picture.

Think of what an environmental amendment would have done for people fighting in Denton. Armed with a constitutional right to a healthy environment, they wouldn't have simply won their case. They would have spread the message that everyone in Denton, everyone in Texas, and everyone in the country are *entitled to a healthy environment.* The anti-fracking movement would have gained more visibility and helped to create a new environmental awareness and consciousness in America. Even at this late hour, the enactment of Green Amendments at the state level could still allow us to transform our communities and our mindsets. Denton's mantra should be our own: we are all entitled to a frack-free future. Constitutional environmental amendments are the winning strategy we need to get us there.

Terry Greenwood would have liked to have seen such victories. Yet he never will. In 2011, he abandoned his life as a farmer and became a full-time anti-fracking activist. He joined forces with his good friend Ron Gulla, who signed one of the first fracking leases on his property in Pennsylvania, and then just like Terry proceeded to lose his water quality, peace of mind, and livelihood. The energy industry tried settling with Terry and Ron as they did with so many others—paying them off for an undisclosed amount, and including nondisclosure agreements as part of the settlement to prevent them from speaking out. Both disillusioned farmers refused to be silenced, and they devoted their energy and resources to educating others about the perils of fracking. Whether Terry was testifying before a regulatory body or speaking to a small group of concerned individuals at a local community event, he always flashed pictures of his dying animals and orange metallic pond in the hopes of preventing a similar fate for other farmers and householders.

Terry and Ron's humility and courage transformed countless people, including Briget Shields, who attended a fracking awareness event at which they spoke. Because of Terry and Ron's expertise in the fracking movement and passion for helping others, they fielded requests from community groups and traveled around the region to speak about fracking. In the late spring of 2014, Briget (by then an experienced fracking opponent herself) accompanied Terry and Ron to Coshocton, Ohio, where they agreed to facilitate a conference. A grassroots group in this Midwestern city had just begun organizing against the industry and needed help from seasoned veterans. Earlier that year, Terry had contracted an aggressive brain cancer, and he had been in and out of the hospital for treatment. This diagnosis was shocking and painful. Those close to him say that nothing in his genetic history suggested he was predisposed to such an illness. Terry nonetheless joined his two collaborators, brandishing the pictures of his harmed animals and empowering those in the neighboring state to stand up for themselves and combat the industry. A week later, on June 8, 2014, Terry succumbed to his illness. He was sixty-six.

We can't prove that exposure to fracking-based toxins caused or hastened Terry's death. But members of his community have little doubt. Within a ten-mile radius of Terry's home, located squarely within Pennsylvania's fracking epicenter, aggressive glioblastoma brain cancers like Terry's have become strikingly common, according to locals. Still, doctors won't designate a cancer cluster. Because the chemicals used by the fracking industry are proprietary and closely held as trade secrets, doctors can't definitively link local cases of brain cancer to fracked gas exposure.

Terry's family and friends look back fondly on his love for motorcycles and auctions, as well as the red-and-blue-striped suspenders he wore with pride. But perhaps Terry's greatest legacy was his commitment to the environment. I myself remember that when I was in Terry's presence, I felt inspired by his passion and powerful words of concern, as well as by his conviction that we could win this battle. I'll never forget Terry's personal mantra: "Water is more important than gas."[188]

Since Terry's passing, other champions have arisen to combat the industry and protect communities. Jenny Lisak has become an outspoken advocate against fracking, spearheading the "List of the Harmed" inventory, which documents the impact of the industry on diverse communities.[189] Although not a fracking victim, Karen Feridun, founder of Berks Gas Truth, has traveled across the country, learning about the people devastated by this industry and giving them the tools to speak up and fight back. Tracy Carluccio, the Delaware Riverkeeper Network's deputy director, has put her vast knowledge and years of organizing experience to work fighting fracking. Cornell University professors Tony Ingraffea and Robert Howarth have used their scientific expertise and industry background to provide the data, research, and teaching needed to help us document fracking's many dangers. Jordan Yeager, John Smith, and Jonathan Kamin put their powerful legal minds to work, helping Dave Ball, Brian Coppola, me, the Delaware Riverkeeper Network, and seven towns win our inspiring and unprecedented legal victory that defeated Act 13. Without the dedication of these skilled attorneys, we wouldn't have prevailed over the efforts of industry-supported legislators like Senator Joe Scarnati. We wouldn't have restored municipal and environmental rights to everyone in the Commonwealth of Pennsylvania. We wouldn't have inspired a conservative supreme court to recognize that environmental rights are inherent and indefeasible and deserving of the highest regard we can provide in the US legal system.

As powerful as they are when working together, these extraordinary people and countless others cannot affect change on their own. The industry is more powerful. We need effective and well-written environmental amendments in every state and in the federal constitution. Knowledge of environmental provisions allows individuals to speak out, become involved, and defend their right to a healthy environment, even against powerful corporations falsely promising wealth and safe energy. Such amendments also provide environmentalists and concerned people with a powerful tool for preserving their farms, communities, and wilderness from destruction. But constitutional amendments do even more. As we'll explore in the next chapter, they can help us forestall the damages caused by *conveyors* of fracked energy. The proliferation of pipelines is an immensely harmful threat to the environment. Our greatest hope for combating it isn't more legislation and regulation. It's Green Amendments.

CHAPTER FOUR

THE PERILS OF PIPELINES

During the summer of 2011, artist and farmer Asha Canalos noticed something curious around Minisink, a rural town in upstate New York about an hour from Manhattan.[190] On her neighbors' front lawns and by the side of the road, signs began cropping up reading, "Stop the Minisink Compressor Station."

Asha wasn't familiar with compressor stations. As she was new to town, she began introducing herself to her neighbors and asking them for information. It turned out that many of her neighbors were 9/11 first responders who had moved to Minisink for its natural beauty, relaxed pace of life, healthy air, and clean environment. These police officers and firefighters, whose health had been devastated by airborne toxins from the World Trade Center site, suspected that compressor stations had something to do with fracking. After all, New York was prime energy real estate. Like Pennsylvania, it sat atop the coveted Marcellus shale deposits.

But New York was supposed to be safe. Unlike Pennsylvania,

New York developed a robust and influential anti-fracking movement early on, before the industry took root and grew. The Delaware Riverkeeper Network joined with grassroots community efforts spearheaded by Wes Gillingham of the Catskill Mountainkeeper, Jill Wiener of Catskill Citizens for Safe Energy, and David Braun's New Yorkers Against Fracking, among others. Grassroots community efforts were so successful that they garnered the support of celebrities like Yoko Ono and Mark Ruffalo, who partnered with CNN anchors to spread awareness.[191] On November 29, 2010, six months before Asha purchased her farm in Minisink, the New York State Assembly instituted a moratorium on shale gas fracking within New York State so that state agencies and experts could investigate its ramifications.[192] Four years later, New York would become among the first states in the nation to ban fracking indefinitely.[193]

But as New Yorkers would come to discover, you can ban fracking itself, but not the interstate infrastructure supporting it.[194] Pipelines and associated compressor stations are a major component of the shale fracking industry. Once the industry fracks natural gas from underground shales, it transports the contents around the country through a vast network of pipelines. Compressor stations are the engines that power these pipelines, ensuring that gas is "compressed" or pressurized enough to course its way across vast swaths of real estate beneath our country.

The Millennium Pipeline Company, which proposed the new compressor station project in Minisink, assured Asha and her neighbors that the facility itself wouldn't disrupt community peace. Low profile and shrouded in attractive green landscaping, the facility would resemble a barn or industrial warehouse, with a series of tubes protruding from the ground and several innocuous-looking smokestacks. The plumes emanating from the compressor's silos would be nothing to worry about, a Millennium pipeline representative said. They consisted of "mainly water vapor."[195]

Residents were skeptical. After conducting their own research, they discovered that even in the best of circumstances, compressor stations release hazardous pollutants into the air, including hormone disruptors, volatile organic compounds (VOC), and other human carcinogens. Such pollution rates only increase when pipes leak or when they naturally degrade, releasing fugitive emissions into the air. Emissions also skyrocket during venting or blowdown periods, which release even more gas from the facility.[196] Beyond these emissions, compressor stations, as Asha and her neighbors learned, degrade the quality of life in a variety of ways in communities where they operate. A quick Google search revealed that people who live near compressor stations complain about noxious odors and noise disturbances. Like the pipelines they powered, compressor facilities had a history of accidents, leaks, and even explosions. Asha was disheartened to learn that facilities in Sissonville, West Virginia, and Artemas, Pennsylvania, run by NiSource energy, Millennium's corporate owner, had recently experienced fires.[197] Victims of such accidents can suffer dismemberment, chronic disease, and even death. Ominously, Millennium planned to situate the compressor station in the *middle* of Minisink, which was agriculturally and residentially zoned. This was a well-populated area. Nearly two hundred homes would be located squarely in the danger zone should an explosion occur, with some residences a mere six hundred feet from the slated facility.

As plans for the compressor station solidified at the end of 2011, concerned residents in Minisink banded together to

100 THE GREEN AMENDMENT

stop it. They began by spreading awareness throughout the town, uniting the science and community data demonstrating the harms facing residents and the environment. Armed with this information, they tried to convince government officials and agencies to deny approval of the compressor station and protect their community. As Asha explained to staff from the Federal Energy Regulatory Commission (FERC), the federal agency regulating interstate fracked gas pipelines, the new compressor station imperiled her home, her business, and her whole community. As Asha detailed, she and her husband had already plowed over two of their eleven acres of farmland, constructed greenhouses, and grown some impressive seedlings, along with forty different heirloom vegetables and blueberries. All of their hard work would come to nothing if the compressor station began spewing toxins across her land.

In media interviews, the first responders shared how the compressor station's contaminants would exacerbate their already compromised immune systems. NYPD officer Nick Russo had developed stomach problems and difficulty breathing after four months at Ground Zero. "So I move up here, next to the beautiful cows and farms," he explained to reporters. "And now here I am fighting a compressor station on farmland right down the road."[198] Ultimately, the Minisinkers feared what might happen to them if an accident occurred at the compressor station. "There are several things that keep all of us awake at night," Asha said. "The most frightening of all is the possibility that the facility could blow up and kill people."[199]

Unfortunately, the evidence residents provided of imminent harm yielded no results. So they planned to reach out directly to the FERC commissioners, the five individuals who would actually decide their fate. The community of Minisink organized a trip to the nation's capitol to express their concerns. This was the first time that an American community traveled to a FERC commissioners' meeting in DC to lobby against a compressor station project. Asha fondly remembers how the diverse band of residents piled into chartered buses, galvanized to defend their community on Capitol Hill. Parents with strollers and small kids sat shoulder to shoulder with retirees, staunch liberals alongside Tea Party conservatives. Many people on the buses were 9/11 first responders, fighting to preserve their fragile health and the future of their community, including the healthy environment that attracted them to the upstate New York region in the first place.

Imagine how startled this group was when, upon arriving in DC, it encountered Homeland Security officers in full body armor. As residents later discovered through a Freedom of Information Act request, Millennium had followed their organizing activities on social media and notified FERC that a group of "environmental protestors" would be arriving. Asha wondered if the officers in riot gear knew that they were confronting 9/11 first responders, as well as teachers, farmers, and artists only interested in preserving their idyllic rural community. But residents were even more shocked to learn that during meetings when FERC commissioners decided the fate of communities like Minisink, they showed little interest in community concerns. Commissioners offered no opportunity for public comment at these meetings, and they rebuffed residents' efforts to speak to them informally before or after meetings. Undaunted, the people of Minisink showed up at meeting after meeting. Wearing T-shirts and holding small signs, they delivered their message: *don't* approve the Minisink compressor! Ignoring residents' pleas, FERC issued its approval of the Minisink compressor station on

July 17, 2012. Short of litigation, there was nothing the residents could do to stop the project. The people of Minisink filed suit, funding their costly court battle entirely out of their own pockets. Sadly, and characteristically for FERC, while the residents awaited their day in court to appeal the decision, FERC allowed Millennium to begin construction. On October 1, 2012, pipeline industry workers descended on the town to clear trees, move earth, and drill bedrock. The construction activity was nonstop, producing "a terrible grinding noise" throughout the day and night, which Asha described as "relentless and maddening." It seemed like nothing would stop Millennium, not even Mother Nature. When Hurricane Sandy struck in late October 2012, most residents lost power and found themselves stranded upstate, unable to drive to their families in New York City. Millennium appeared unfazed by the superstorm, trucking in enormous generators to the town, lighting up the site like a football field, and continuing its work at breakneck speed.

In June 2013, just nine months after construction began and nearly a full year before the town of Minisink's scheduled court date, the compressor station began operating. When emissions peaked during venting periods, residents smelled disturbing odors. Asha described one of the many smells emanating from the site as something approximating "a bathroom in a gas station," with a citrus deodorizer masking more noxious, underlying odors. Residents began reporting scores of medical problems including nosebleeds, rashes, sore throats, and headaches. The 9/11 first responders were among the afflicted, their preexisting respiratory issues flaring. For the first time since moving to Minisink, Asha found it difficult to go outside. She suffered intense nausea and dizzy spells, muscle pain and weakness, insomnia, and fatigue. As time passed, her illness worsened. In 2013, doctors diagnosed her with fibromyalgia, and she and her husband made the heart-wrenching decision to stop farming. When Asha sought care at a local medical facility, doctors didn't link the compressor station to her health problems. Asha found that strange, as she suspected there was a connection. She had read the work of Wilma Subra, an acclaimed chemist and member of two EPA advisory councils who won a MacArthur "Genius" Award" for helping communities understand and redress environmental perils.[200] As Asha was chagrined to learn, the symptoms Subra painstakingly catalogued in polluted areas mimicked those of people in the groundbreaking documentary *Gasland*. But as Asha later discovered, the health-care facility where she sought care had partnered with CPV, a company building a giant fracked gas power plant in a town bordering Minisink. The medical facility had, very simply, a financial stake in the expansion of industrial fracking in the region. Some quietly wondered how this might impact the thinking of those working at the health-care center. Admittedly, the findings of Dr. Subra and others on the health impacts of fracking had not yet penetrated the vast majority of health practitioners' awareness and practice. It would be years before the medical establishment convened medical conferences and wrote manuals on the topic. Regardless, Asha became sicker, and the community's lawsuit dragged on.

On August 15, 2014, the United States Court of Appeals for the District of Columbia finally rendered a decision in the Minisink case. Residents felt optimistic that they would prevail in their appeal of FERC's decision to grant Millennium a license for this compressor station. After all, the residents had both evidence and moral standing on their side. In addition, their lawyer,

Carolyn Elefant, hadn't merely objected to the project; the community had advanced an alternative for the compressor station. The Wagoner Alternative plan, which the Minisink community had meticulously crafted and researched, contained a far more sensible proposal. The pipeline running beneath Minisink was old and decaying, leaving residents at risk of explosion. The Wagoner Alternative involved replacing an antiquated seven-mile stretch of pipeline (thereby reducing the threat of explosion) and moving the proposed facility to a location that was industrially zoned, where no one inhabited a danger area in case of an explosion, and where a pre-existing compressor station had previously operated for years. The people of Minisink were not looking to foist this industrial monstrosity on another community. They were advocating an alternative that would not locate it near *any* local neighborhood. Richard Kuprewicz, a pipeline safety specialist with decades of field experience and expertise, attested to the viability and value of the residents' less damaging alternative plan. One of FERC's commissioners had even called the Wagoner Alternative plan "superior." A victory in the court would require FERC to take another look, one that included other options, including the alternative plan the community had devised. It also meant the community would live to fight another day, and maybe even stop the project altogether, which is what many who were part of the battle were seeking to do.

Despite the evidence, the judge ruled against the residents, telling them, in essence, to buck up and deal with it. "Given the choice, almost no one would want natural gas infrastructure built on their block," he wrote in his decision. "'Build it elsewhere,' most would say. The sentiment is understandable. But given our nation's increasing demand for natural gas (and other alternative energy sources), it is an inescapable fact that such facilities must be built somewhere."[201] With these words, the nation's second-highest court decided to leave FERC's licensing decision in place, thereby cementing Minisink's fate as one of America's many sacrifice zones.

The news hit the town hard, and residents began fleeing. Some in the community began recanting negative testimony that they had provided to media outlets and published in blogs. They needed to sell their homes and leave, and they believed that their complaints about the compressor station and pollution were depressing property values. Deeply disappointed by the outcome of the compressor station, Asha and her husband moved to New Mexico. Her health has improved and she has merged her activism with her art career, completing a residency at Santa Fe Art Institute as an activist-artist, and working with environmental groups to amplify stories of those on the front lines of fracking. But many families in Minisink were unable to move and start over somewhere else. Consider the fate of the heroic 9/11 first responders, who survived the most horrific disaster inflicted on their country, only to deal with another one their country inflicted on them a decade later. "We fought the terrorists after 9/11," notes now retired officer Russo, "and now I'm fighting my own government to save my home."[202]

Pipeline Politics

You don't have to live in Minisink or near the fracked gaslands to understand how controversial pipelines, compressor stations, pumping facilities, and their access roads are. The Keystone Pipeline System, which transports crude oil from the infamous tar sands in Alberta, Canada, to refineries throughout the United States, received international attention in 2012. That year James Hansen, one of the world's most acclaimed environmental scientists, declared that if the tar fields were thoroughly exploited for their oil reserves, the result would be "game over for the climate."[203] In the waning years of President Obama's second term, Keystone came to symbolize this environmental struggle, and when the president's administration rejected the pipeline's extension in 2015, many considered this a defining environmental victory. In 2016, another grassroots movement formed in opposition to the Dakota Access Pipeline project. Running beneath the Standing Rock Indian Reservation, the pipeline threatened ancestral burial grounds and water supplies for Native Americans. At the height of the protests, 10,000 concerned opponents descended on North Dakota, facing off against officers in riot gear and publicizing their struggle on social media using the #NoDAPL hashtag.[204]

Outside of these iconic pipeline struggles, I suspect that most in America pay little attention to pipelines and the compressor stations that power them. As someone who works full-time on environmental advocacy, I myself hadn't thought much about pipeline infrastructure until 2010. I still remember the day that Faith Zerbe, monitoring director of the Delaware Riverkeeper Network, came into my office, wanting to talk about the Northeast Upgrade Pipeline Project. The project, she explained, an expansion of an existing pipeline system, involved twenty-five additional miles of pipeline, threatening 450 acres of land, ninety bodies of water, and at least 136 wetlands. It also required an additional twenty-nine access roads, constructed through pristine wild lands and residential communities in our watershed. Faith believed the pipeline constituted a grave environmental threat. After a relatively short conversation, I gave her permission to begin work on the issue and then quickly returned to the emails, files, environmental reports, and project deadlines on my own docket for that day. At that moment, I understood these items as more visible and dangerous threats to my watershed and left the pipeline issue in Faith's eminently capable hands.

As an organization, we gradually began working on the issue. Faith gathered data and trained community monitors as watchdogs for pipeline harms. Ed Rodgers, our video reporter, began documenting the pipeline threat on film. Aaron Stemplewicz, who would soon become our legal expert on pipelines, began to master the intricacies of pipeline law and litigation. Community photographs and Ed's videos showed me the devastating harms pipelines inflicted on our watershed.

In 2012, I set aside other issues I was working on to join Faith on a trip upriver so I could view the recently laid Tennessee Gas Pipeline Company's 300 Line and understand firsthand its impact on fragile wetlands and forest ecosystems. I remember how our long, peaceful drive through Pennsylvania's beautiful Delaware State Forest was brutally shattered as we confronted a hundred-foot open cut in the tree canopy. A previously constructed section of pipeline lay directly underground here. Vegetation over the pipe was spotty, struggling to grow back through the unnaturally compacted soils above the pipeline. The Craft Brook creek at the bottom of the hill was entirely exposed to the elements, no trees on its banks to provide shade, habitat, or pollution protection.

We traveled to another part of the public state forest over a once-narrow gravel road that had been widened to accommodate large trucks for the pipeline. When we finally arrived at a construction zone, where a pipeline extension was underway, I shuddered at the massive, open-cut wound through the wilderness. The red of the exposed soil made it look like the forest and wetlands were bleeding to death.

We parked on the side of the road and walked down a hill to survey the surrounding creeks and wetlands. I'll always recall the pools of shrinking and muddied water with spring peepers, wood frog tadpoles, and other critters struggling to survive in the burning light of the sun and the warming turbid water, no longer shaded with a healthy and mature tree canopy. The eyes of a green frog peered out of the muddied pool, surveying the landscape and trying to understand the hostile new environment. We would then travel on to see the forests, wetlands, and rivers that the Tennessee Gas Pipeline Company's Northeast Upgrade Project (NEUP) would soon attack. In Milford, Pennsylvania, we met with concerned residents to talk strategy over the proposed section of expansion. Their fear and anger were palpable. They were facing the same environmental and personal-property destruction that would soon engulf many more communities from the expansion of fracked gas pipelines across the United States.

This trip was a turning point in my career and life. In the years since that day in 2012, I've witnessed the way that pipelines and other fracking infrastructure destroy farms, families, businesses, homes, communities, and nature. Like so many of the pipelines now crisscrossing our country's watersheds, wild areas, farmlands, and residential communities, the NEUP that Faith was so committed to stopping wasn't necessary for the region's energy supply at all. That's because there is in fact no real gas shortage in our nation and no need to extend existing pipelines or build new ones to provide energy. After much research and scrutiny, we found that the only good any of these pipelines served was to pad corporate profits.

The profits created by the pipeline projects came at a soaring cost. NEUP destroyed vast swaths of land, including forests, streams, and steep hillsides just north of the Delaware Water Gap National Recreation Area—a national park in an area vital to both ecological protection and the region's ecotourism industry. Like the community of Minisink, we challenged this project's approval in the US Court of Appeals for the District of Columbia. Unbelievably, we won our case. The court found that in reviewing and approving NEUP, FERC had failed to consider cumulative impacts and had allowed the pipeline company to break its larger pipeline project into smaller pieces for review, thereby masking the full extent of its devastation. But by the time we won, the pipeline was already built and in the ground. FERC used a legal loophole that prevented us from getting into court in time to make a difference for the NEUP. And so, in setting a legal precedent for cumulative impacts and segmentation, we assisted future pipeline plaintiffs but sadly did not help our Delaware River communities.

After we lost the battle to prevent the NEUP pipeline extension, we shifted our efforts to monitoring the pipeline company's compliance with environmental protection laws. Like most pipeline projects we've surveyed in the years since, this project's environmental record was dismal, with flagrant violations reported at every turn. By the time the Tennessee Gas Pipeline Company finished constructing this relatively short section of pipeline, community monitors and federal agencies recorded forty-three instances of silt-laden water entering streams, wetlands, and other environments off the pipeline's designated right-of-way; fifteen instances of failure to properly install erosion controls or use best-management practices to adequately protect resources; nine instances of failure to properly install and maintain erosion controls, resulting in adverse environmental impacts; six

instances of erosion and disturbance resulting from stormwater discharges off the right-of-way; and at least two instances
of in-stream work conducted during fishery restrictions. In
December 2014, the Pennsylvania Department of Environmental Protection fined the project $800,000 for environmental
harms.[205] Unsurprisingly, however, FERC declined to issue any
civil penalties for these violations. Further, upon learning of the
violations, FERC did nothing to ensure that the harms were
rectified before allowing Tennessee Gas Pipeline's construction
to continue. As you might expect, such administrative passivity
serves to normalize and even incentivize these types of sloppy,
environmentally destructive business practices.

On account of the devastation that pipelines, compressor stations, and related infrastructure unleash every day, they
now form a centerpiece of my work at the Delaware Riverkeeper Network. My battles focus on the pipelines transporting
fracked natural gas, instead of major oil pipelines like Keystone and Dakota. All of these pipelines have similar impacts,
but the body of laws governing them is starkly different. Like
shale gas fracking itself (see chapter 3), fracked gas infrastructure is exempt from many environmental protection laws that
govern other industries. While the battles against Keystone and
Dakota, furthermore, have rightfully captured the imaginations
of the public and the attention of politicians and the press, the
growing number of battles against fracked gas pipelines have
not garnered nearly as much publicity. As a result, people like
Asha Canalos and towns like Minisink and Milford lack the
national spotlight as well as the tremendous financial resources
required to challenge pipeline companies and their henchmen at
FERC. That's tragic, because the natural gas infrastructure projects threatening these overlooked communities pose significant

and irreversible harms to our environments and everyone who inhabits them.

Like fracking operations, pipelines and compressor stations devastate forests, waterways, and wild lands. Approximately eighty-four acres of forest are lost or irreparably damaged for every mile of pipeline laid through these natural areas. Streams and wetlands are literally carved out to make pipeline paths, permanently robbed of healthy vegetation, protective soils, tree cover, and water supplies. As we saw in chapter 1, such degradation creates a series of locked-in environmental harms. Rainfall—once absorbed by leaves and forest beds—now runs off the land, carrying pollution and causing erosion, while the loss of natural forest and healthy soils also robs wetlands and streams of the groundwater needed to sustain them. The nature of pipeline construction and maintenance further exacerbates these built-in harms in two ways. First, construction crews using herbicides and other techniques prevent any substantial vegetation from growing in significant areas immediately surrounding a pipeline. In addition, construction crews compact the soil in what are supposed to be *temporary* construction work zones near pipelines. These areas end up being so damaged that the forest often struggles to regrow. Forests, fragmented for pipelines, lose the continuity needed to keep out invasive plants and animals, as well as to sustain the many flora and fauna that require an unbroken forest home. Ultimately, pipelines and other fracking infrastructure permanently degrade natural environments.

Pipelines are just as devastating for watershed businesses. In community forums throughout my state, I've seen farmers testify that crop yields plummet once pipelines are laid under their property. Soil compaction and improper landscape restoration reduce farm yields, farmers' production capacity declines, and according to numerous firsthand accounts, it never recovers. At one public forum at which I spoke in the fall of 2014, convened to discuss the PennEast Pipeline Project, a large, strong gentleman came forward. Introducing himself as a farmer from West Amwell, New Jersey, he said, "I have two pipelines that already run through one of my farm fields and for years I have been monitoring the crop yield with an expert's help. What I can show you now," he said, holding up a colorful picture of his farm fields with bright red areas signaling where a pipeline lay, "is that the pipeline in my field causes a 30 percent reduction in crop production."

Stories like these are typical of those I've heard on the lecturing circuit and witnessed in my travels throughout the region. Every day I also hear from householders forced to live near a pipeline or compressor station, unable to move away to secure a safer life for themselves. Mark and Alycia Egan bought their dream home in Sullivan County, New York. It was their refuge and their respite from bustling New York City, where they lived and worked full-time. But then the Millennium Pipeline Company proposed to expand its existing line, including constructing yet another new compressor right near their home. This one would have nearly twice as much horsepower as the one in nearby Minisink. The Egans quickly joined forces with the community to try and stop the impending doom. But they also realized the odds were stacked against them and tried to put their self-described "dream home" up for sale. After a year on the market, this fabulous house, located in a bucolic forest, on the bend of a beautiful stream whose running water makes soothing sounds day and night, still had no interested buyers. In fact, when the Egans accidentally left a map of the proposed compressor station on their kitchen table, one buyer who came to see the house took one look and immediately left, telling the realtor that she "loved the setting" but couldn't possibly take the risk. Many homes and farms proximate to pipelines languish on the markets like this, selling for fractions of their pre-pipeline values, if they can sell at all.[206] Ecotourism-oriented and seasonal businesses, dependent on fishers, hikers, and bed-and-breakfast enthusiasts, are all adversely impacted.[207] And when property values and local businesses decline, so, too, does the tax base upon which towns and cities rely.

Today's pipelines (including their compressors) pose manifold threats. They degrade fresh water and wild lands, pollute our communities, contribute to climate change, pose public health and disease risks, and exact an economic toll. Their footprints are greater than those of past pipelines, as is the level of damage and harm they inflict. Whereas once they might have been out of sight and out of mind, they are no longer.

Accidents Happen

Sometimes the harms wrought by pipelines are especially acute, immediate, and undeniable. On April 29, 2016, James Baker was at home in Salem Township, Pennsylvania, nursing an ankle injury. Shortly after his wife left for work, his house exploded. Literally exploded.[208] James couldn't maneuver too quickly, but he managed to hobble outside. A Good Samaritan spotted him from a distance and dragged him away from the nightmarish scene. James's clothes were burning, irreparably damaging his skin. Toxic smoke he inhaled caused his insides to burn as well. He suffered extensive damage to every part of his body.

James's tragedy seemed even more poignant in the following days, when, in reading the news reports, we all learned that his wife was pregnant. Unlike other expectant fathers preparing for parenthood, Baker's concerns were now of a different order. Only a charred shell of his house remained, surrounded by burnt trees. Where would he raise his newborn child now? When doctors prepared to amputate his ear, badly damaged during the fire, they unwrapped the bandage to discover that it had fallen off all by itself. People across Pennsylvania, including me, worried about James and his family as we read about his ongoing and painful saga.

For years, James and his wife had no idea of the industrial infrastructure in their small, peaceful township in Pennsylvania's Westmoreland County.[209] Sure, they saw an unassuming pipe surfacing from the ground with a little tag on it, but it looked innocent enough.[210] Little did they know that a company called Spectra Energy ran an interstate pipeline below their home, connecting a nearby compressor station with facilities all the way in New Jersey.[211] James and his family certainly didn't know that in 2012 Spectra had examined the pipeline and found alarming rates of corrosion.[212] Nor did they know that the company used unreliable tape—tape!—to cover the pipeline's imperfections.[213] Overlooking the unprecedented amount of pipe decay they found in 2012, the company decided to take no action until 2019, the date of its next scheduled pipe inspection.[214] Repairing the aging infrastructure would have cost time and money. Spectra was no more willing to voluntarily assume added costs than Millennium Pipeline company was in Minisink, New York.

As it turns out, damage from the explosion and its aftermath will cost between $75 and $100 million to correct.[215] In the wake of the blast, the company discovered an astounding 625 pipeline problems (or anomalies, as the industry calls them) in 263 miles of that pipeline.[216] We clearly cannot rely on pipeline companies or the regulators overseeing them to prevent calamities like this. But even if we could, gas pipelines are eminently hazardous, and catastrophes will occur. Energy companies claim that their pipelines are getting safer, but the safety record speaks for itself. In the span of almost two decades (1997–2016), the Pipeline and Hazardous Materials Safety Administration, the safety regulator for natural gas, hazardous liquid, and liquefied natural gas pipelines, recorded 5,679 "significant" pipeline incidents (i.e., resulting in $50,000 or more in costs), 310 fatalities, 1,301 injuries, and nearly $8 billion in costs and damages. That works out to an average of 284 incidents (including explosions) every year, 65 annual injuries, 16 deaths a year, and nearly $390 million in annual costs and damages.[217] Recent research suggests that the rate of accidents and explosions is not improving; in fact, it's growing worse. The latest generation of natural gas pipeline has an annual average incident rate exceeding that of pipelines installed prior to 1940.[218] With industry poised to install countless more miles of fossil fuel pipelines, these safety concerns grow increasingly scary. Unless something drastic happens, there will be many more James Bakers in the future.

Is the Constitution Pipeline Constitutional?

In addition to inflicting irreparable harm on our environment and acutely threatening our lives, energy companies trample on our private property rights. Consider archaeologist Megan Holleran, who learned one spring day in 2014 that the Constitution Pipeline Company planned a pipeline project underneath her family's homestead.[219] Though caught off guard, the Hollerans joined forces with many of their neighbors, adamantly resolved to block the company from undertaking the surveys needed to get federal permission to build their project. Despite their efforts and manifold objections, a federal judge granted the Constitution Pipeline Company the power of eminent domain in February of 2015, giving the company broad control over much of the Holleran family lands.[220]

It's hard to imagine the federal judge's rationale, given that the company hadn't even secured all the permits needed to construct its interstate fracked-gas pipeline. New York officials were still scrutinizing the proposal to determine whether the pipeline company was entitled to Clean Water Act approval, which it would need before breaking ground in the state. FERC and the courts disregarded these environmental procedures entirely, and Constitution Pipeline wasted no time making use of its newly secured eminent domain authority. It informed the Hollerans that they'd be by any day to clear their forest in preparation for the pipeline. The Hollerans, whose property was located along the Pennsylvania portion of the proposed pipeline, pleaded with federal agents and company employees to wait, explaining that they relied on their trees for a family maple syrup business, and that they were in the middle of their harvesting season. Besides, they reasoned, New York State hadn't yet approved the project!

Ignoring their pleas, the company sent crews to begin cutting the trees. The Hollerans protested, committed to protecting their trees. They were joined by neighbors and environmental advocates from both the greater Pennsylvania region and the project's New York portion. The Constitution Pipeline Company turned to the courts, arguing that the protesters violated the company's rights to the Holleran property. The court sided with the pipeline company and issued an order empowering US marshals and police to arrest any protesters who attempted to block the tree cutting. The courts also warned the Holleran family that it would be held responsible for the costs incurred from project delays if they were found to be coordinating, or in any way supporting, the nonviolent protests.[221]

Victorious in court once again, the company returned to the Hollerans' property with a dozen armed US marshals. Donning bulletproof vests and helmets, the officers patrolled a 150-foot "safety buffer" around the trees, their fingers curled around the triggers of their AR-15 guns. A photographer at the scene shot an iconic image of a yellow school bus filled with young children driving through the marshals' machine-gun-lined blockade. The Holleran family watched in horror, and from a distance, as men with chainsaws cleared approximately 558 maple, ash, cherry, and hickory trees. Over the course of three days, they littered the family property with dead, mangled tree limbs, draining the land of its ecological health and of the financial productivity that the healthy maple trees supplied. They also destroyed three generations of sentimental value.

As predicted, this tree clearing was premature. New York State ultimately denied the company its Clean Water Act Water Quality Certificate. Absent this approval, it was illegal for the Constitution Pipeline Company to lay any pipe for this project in New York.[222] But as senior pipeline litigator Aaron Stemplewicz notes, FERC's hold on the Holleran estate is still in force, despite the company's failure to secure essential environmental permits.

While litigation over the Constitution pipeline winds its way through the courts, people like the Hollerans are in legal limbo. They have no idea what rights they have to their own property. If the pipeline never gets approved in New York, will the Constitution Pipeline Company be allowed to use the Holleran land for other purposes? All the Hollerans know for sure is that their maple syrup trees are lost, and the sanctity of the forest and natural landscape they enjoyed for generations is gone, permanently. Megan's uncle Mike, a farmer, is allowed to use a regular tractor on the property. But if he wants to operate more heavy machinery or install a roadway, over which trucks can repeatedly cross, he must negotiate with the Constitution Pipeline Company, receiving its blessing first.

The Hollerans currently inhabit a nightmare similar to that of Terry Greenwood (see chapter 3). In Terry's case, the energy company seized access to the land based on a prior lease that Terry hadn't known about. In the Hollerans' case, the pipeline company seized the land through the power of eminent domain, a constitutional police power that is only supposed to be exercised for the *greater public good*. The Greenwoods and Hollerans owned their land and were liable for insuring it and paying all taxes. But despite fulfilling all of their property obligations, they lost the value and enjoyment of their lands as energy companies intruded—with the full blessing of federal officials and US law.

Cases like those of the Hollerans and the Greenwoods are hardly unusual. As I've discovered over the course of my work throughout the region and the country, pipelines and other infrastructure routinely deprive people of the full use and enjoyment of their property. Aaron Stemplewicz finds pipelines to be subject to "one of the most complicated regulatory regimes I have ever encountered." If Aaron, a lawyer in this field, continues to find it so complicated, despite his professional expertise on the topic, how do you think members of the general public feel? Overwhelmed, confused, and sorely abused.

Like fracking itself, pipeline activity exploded on the landscape, with lawmakers, litigators, environmental rights proponents, and residents only now beginning to understand the complexities involved. But while the intricacies are disputed in the courts (for instance, questions of jurisdiction, states' rights versus federal rights versus people's rights, the legitimacy of eminent domain, and the viability of government approvals in an array of complicated scenarios), people's rights hang precariously in the balance. Householders can't plant a tree or build a shed once pipeline companies claim their land. Farmers' crop yields decrease, property values plummet, and health problems grow. Pipelines deprive households and communities of peace, tranquility, and security. People wonder (and worry) if they will experience a heart attack, if their children will be diagnosed with leukemia, or if a pipeline accident will reach into their homes with explosive force, as one did with James Baker's. They are right to worry. Accidents, injuries, and explosions irreparably diminish the quality of people's lives and the landscapes they inhabit. In every instance, the health of the environment declines. Forests are felled, wetlands are damaged, wildlife is harmed, streams are cut, and methane and other forms of pollution are discharged into the air and water.

FERC or the Constitution?

Given the extraordinary level of devastation that fracked gas pipelines inflict, you would think that FERC, the agency overseeing their review and approval, would exercise excessive caution and relentless vigilance. Certainly, it stands to reason, FERC complies with every environmental and community-protection regulation, demonstrating a healthy respect for our country's most precious resources.

Unfortunately, this is far from the truth. As we've observed, once FERC approves a fracked gas pipeline, it allows the pipeline industry to seize private property, public parks, and other community lands with impunity. Most farmers, homeowners, land trusts, schools, and park managers currently menaced by pipeline companies are just like the Hollerans: they have no interest in granting an easement for a pipeline right-of-way that will permanently degrade the value of their homes, the productivity of their farms, the safety of their families, the sanctity of their schools, or the beauty of natural lands long safeguarded at taxpayers' expense. But their desires don't matter, because once these pipelines are approved, energy companies are entitled to seize these lands and exploit them for their own profit.

In fact, FERC routinely exploits a legal loophole to deny the public the right even to challenge approval of a pipeline project[223] before it allows pipeline companies to seize property rights via eminent domain, and before pipeline construction begins, including cutting trees and inflicting irreparable environmental harm. FERC uses tolling orders to put people, property owners, and environmental organizations like mine in legal limbo. As a result, they cannot challenge FERC pipeline approvals for an undetermined amount of time—sometimes for over a year—until the tolling order is lifted. During this hiatus, FERC routinely approves a pipeline project's exercise of eminent domain and construction. Through this legal maneuver, as we have seen with Minisink and the NEUP, FERC allows pipeline companies to advance their projects, seize property, and begin construction before impacted communities have the opportunity to challenge the project in court, let alone before a court can render a decision in their cases.

Given the safety problems and the widespread damage to communities, households, and businesses, you might also think that FERC scrupulously vets all pipeline proposals, only granting approval once it has considered all possible contingencies and eventualities. Wrong again. Misinformation, incomplete information, and "alternative facts" abound in the environmental review reports FERC issues for each project it considers. As I have come to learn, accurate facts are not a high priority for FERC. Getting pipelines built is. Since 1986, *FERC commissioners have only once—just once—denied a pipeline project placed before them*! That singular denial came in 2016 after the Delaware Riverkeeper Network filed a federal lawsuit, challenging the FERC approval process and using its *then* 100 percent approval rate as evidence of indefensible agency bias. Unable to refute or defend this simple and obviously outrageous fact, FERC Commissioners denied one pipeline project within ten days of our filing. As the Delaware Riverkeeper Network is currently arguing in court in multiple cases, and as we have experienced time and again, FERC works as an arm of the pipeline industry it is supposed to be regulating. Under federal law, the commissioners must give careful consideration to environmental and community harms before approving pipeline projects. But this never truly happens. FERC shamelessly adopts the biased claims and outright falsehoods articulated by pipeline companies in their proposals.

In the case of the Transcontinental Pipeline Company's Leidy Southeast Pipeline Expansion Project, FERC issued an approval, citing company data asserting that only seven exceptional value wetlands were affected. It refused to budge from its decision after later learning, largely sparked by evidence the Delaware Riverkeeper Network generated, that the project imperiled thirty-one exceptional value wetlands. FERC also relied on the pipeline company's data when it misidentified the type and quality of the vegetation that would be irreversibly lost following pipeline construction. The pipeline company asserted that in critical wetland locations, forests or trees didn't exist. We proved that they did. Even when provided with incontrovertible evidence of its mistakes, FERC did nothing to address the errors. Despite a wealth of data demonstrating to FERC that the information it had relied on from the pipeline company was incorrect, FERC decided to grant approval.

The PennEast Pipeline is another sad case in point. In April 2017, the US Army Corps of Engineers went on record stating that the application materials it received for the proposed pipeline were so incomplete that the Army Corps would be unable to even consider the project for wetlands approval, let alone render a decision. Among the deficiencies was the need for a "complete delineation of waters and wetlands, mitigation plans, cultural resource surveys, Tribal coordination, threatened & endangered species surveys." On April 26, 2017, the New Jersey Department of Environmental Protection (NJDEP) issued a finding that the PennEast application materials were, similarly, so incomplete that NJDEP would also be unable to consider the project for approval. Among these deficiencies was critical information regarding the presence of and impacts to freshwater wetlands, transition areas, and open waters, as well as an archaeological survey report investigating the proposed alignment for the PennEast Pipeline in New Jersey. In its final environmental impact study issued on April 7, 2017, even FERC identified dozens of areas where information was missing or deficient. And yet, based on the same information the other agencies had, and its own recognition of deficiencies in project documents, FERC announced that the PennEast Pipeline would not significantly impact the environment and would therefore receive its approval.

This whole-cloth adoption of pipeline company facts is only

compounded by the "revolving door" that exists between FERC and the energy industry. FERC hired Douglas Sipe, from an engineering firm with a $1.8 million stake in the Spectra Energy Pipeline Project, to be its outreach manager on energy projects. During his tenure at FERC, Mr. Sipe served as the environmental project manager for the Spectra Pipeline Project.[224] Maggie Suter, a FERC official tasked with reviewing the Cove Point and Atlantic Bridge projects, is married to Phil Suter, a paid consultant for the related Access Northeast Project. When Maggie Suter told her supervisors at FERC of the potential conflict, she was allowed to remain in her role of reviewing the Atlantic Bridge Project, and during her tenure she reviewed many others in which her husband and his colleagues had a significant financial stake.[225]

Such conflicts extend to the entire pipeline review process. FERC routinely hires third-party consultants who simultaneously consult for pipeline companies seeking FERC approval for their projects. For example, third-party contractor National Resource Group (NRG) prepared FERC's environmental assessment for Spectra Energy's Atlantic Bridge Project, while at the same time NRG was serving as a public outreach consultant on the PennEast Pipeline Project, of which Spectra is a significant part owner. In addition, the PennEast and Atlantic Bridge projects are physically connected, further entrenching the conflict of interest.[226] How can NRG objectively evaluate Spectra's Atlantic Bridge Pipeline for FERC when it has a significant financial stake in its outcome, and when it is working for the company's owner?

Currently, no governmental body or regulatory mechanism exists to check FERC's power. Per federal law, FERC is a self-financed agency that relies entirely on the industries it regulates for its whole budget.[227] While Congress technically has the right to constrain FERC's budget, there is no incentive for Congress to carefully review or limit the agency's budget request each year, because FERC raises every penny it spends from industry. The more pipelines, gas-delivery, and compressor facilities FERC approves, the more resources FERC can draw on to support its budgetary needs. As such, FERC has a direct pecuniary interest in approving natural gas pipeline projects under its regulatory purview. The president can only remove a FERC commissioner by demonstrating inefficiency, neglect of duty, or malfeasance in office. This sets a very high bar, and we have never seen a president inclined to pursue it. And, sadly, the courts have so far removed themselves as a needed check on power, seeming to bend over backward to give FERC undue deference in all of its decision-making.

As of this writing, two hundred organizations representing communities in thirty-five states across the nation joined with the Delaware Riverkeeper Network to call for congressional hearings into FERC's abuses and failure to protect communities and natural environments. But no congressional hearings have taken place. Indeed, we've only seen regulatory setbacks and proposed legislative rollbacks.

Support for fracking and fracked gas infrastructure is unfortunately a bipartisan affair. During his first hundred days in office, Republican President Donald Trump wholeheartedly embraced fracked gas and fossil fuel infrastructure. During his first week of office, he signed executive orders recommending work on the controversial Keystone and Dakota Access pipelines. He also moved to facilitate all pipeline projects, removing what his administration understood as *burdensome* and *unnecessary* environmental regulations that supposedly hamper such projects.[228] Sadly, his predecessor, Democratic President Barack Obama, similarly supported all facets of fracking, including its pipeline infrastructure. Legislators at the federal, state, and local level on both sides of the political spectrum have done similarly, touting the environmental benefits of fracked gas as a "bridge fuel," and greenlighting the expansion of pipelines and the compressor stations that keep the industry fracking.

Asha Canalos has a message for these politicians:

> Go visit these communities that are feeling increasingly under siege all over New York, in Pennsylvania, and across the country. Go take a good hard look at how it is to live up against this infrastructure, which is growing like a terrible cobweb at lightning speed. Go look at people's water wells, now brown and spitting with methane. Go look at farm animals dying and children getting sick in increasingly disturbing patterns near compressors and pipelines. Go look at plants that won't grow from the dust and acidity released, and farms being shut down near drilling wells due to contamination. Go look at that horrible, sad mess in its entirety. Then tell me it's worth it.[229]

Constitutional environmental protection could have made a world of difference for the people and communities profiled in this chapter. The extension of the Constitution pipeline and the expansion of the Millennium pipeline (the latter of which included the Minisink compressor station) are primarily regulated by federal law. With a federal Green Amendment in place, I believe the people of Minisink could have thwarted the compressor station's construction. Constitutional environmental rights would have forced an evaluation of the science and the project's cumulative impacts, exposing the true harms threatening the people of Minisink and its environs. Asha and her husband might still have their organic produce farm, and many 9/11 first responders could have received the protection we owe such heroes. With a federal constitutional right in place, the Hollerans likely would still enjoy free use and enjoyment of their property, selling maple syrup at weekend farmers' markets. FERC would not have license to pollute the country with impunity. Pipeline projects would have to withstand an analysis that weighed their overstated and often elusive benefits against our inalienable rights to a clean and healthy environment. Because they are inherently destructive for all the reasons I've outlined in this chapter, a federal amendment would certainly curtail the pipeline proliferation currently under way. In the process, it would also allow us to enjoy a more robust economy, creating more opportunities for Americans to work in the clean energy sector.

We at the Delaware Riverkeeper Network are still exploring the impact of state Green Amendments in the case of fracked gas pipelines under FERC's jurisdiction. When it comes to interstate pipelines and infrastructure, federal law preempts all state and local laws—the latter simply don't apply. But this does not mean the states have no role to play. As we discussed in the case of the Constitution pipeline, the states can say no to a pipeline. They get that right by virtue of federal law, including the federal Clean Water Act, which requires that individual states certify that a project complies with state water-quality standards before securing approval. State water-quality standards are just that—state standards. In interpreting, implementing, and applying state standards, a state is bound by its own constitutional provisions. Thus, even if a state determines that a pipeline complies with the requirements of its standards, it should not issue an approval if a construction project violates an existing constitutional right to a healthy environment.

As Aaron Stemplewicz and Jordan Yeager explain, just because you have complied with the specific mandates of a state regulation or permit does not mean you have also protected constitutional environmental rights. Perhaps your state requires landfills to be constructed on slopes less than twenty-five degrees and not within fifteen feet of an "exceptional value" waterway. What happens when a permit holder builds a land-fill on a twenty-four-degree slope that sits twenty feet removed from a pristine water source? While this permit holder has technically complied with the "four corners" of the state regulation, there's still a likelihood that the project will violate the state's Green Amendment. Stemplewicz and Yeager have had success employing these arguments in court, defeating several danger-ous projects, including an overturning of the DEP's approval for spreading sewage sludge on fields that drain into the Del-aware River. Real promise also exists for fighting back against federal fracked gas infrastructure. Even if a pipeline complies with applicable state standards, if it can be shown to violate the right to a healthy environment included in a state's constitution, the state may have both the opportunity and the obligation to say no. And if it doesn't, the people can take the state to court and challenge its findings.

With a federal Green Amendment in place, and/or an effective provision in the New York Constitution's declaration of rights, my life might be different, too. Remember in the introduction, when I told you about the inheritance my mother left me: sixty-eight beautiful acres of forest in the Susquehanna

River watershed? Since the fracking industry damaged our ability to enjoy that special place, I sold the property to the original owner, who planned to rejoin it to neighboring lots he owned and thus protect it forever. (In fact, the property had once been part of his family's homestead, which the family sold for financial reasons to my mother, but was now able to repurchase and restore to the original land heritage.) Meanwhile, my husband, Dave, and I set out to explore other places to buy land. After investigating properties for weeks, Dave announced one evening that he had found the perfect spot!

We contacted a local realtor and arranged to travel to New York to see the site. The following weekend, as we pulled onto the mile-long drive that took us to the property, we were excited but braced for disappointment. The seasonal gravel road led past idyllic forests, much of which were protected state wildlife lands. We came upon a small clearing with a dilapidated little house in the center. Our hearts sank a notch, but we knew there was land with the property, and that was really what we had come to see. We told the realtor she should go to her next appointment, for which we had already made her late, and that we would meet her back at the parking spot in an hour. After she left, Dave and I, along with our young son Wim, took a walk. We discovered a little trail behind the house and quickly found ourselves in a forest filled with beautiful trees, massive rocks, and acres of natural huckleberry and blueberry bushes, as far as the eye could see. As we continued to walk along this path, we saw off in the distance a mama bear with her two babies. Wim screamed at the sight, simultaneously exhilarated and frightened. It was a wonderful family experience, and in that moment we knew that we had found the perfect place to bring my mother's ashes and relocate our family. Three weeks later, we signed the papers, and this special forest was all ours. We returned my mother to the earth that day with song and prayer, hugs and tears.

When we purchased the property, I knew that the Millennium Pipeline ran through a portion of the forest located some distance down the road. It was admittedly a big mental hurdle to overcome, and I researched and analyzed the possible drawbacks at length. After considering the possible blast radius of an explosion, the environmental threat to our parcel, and the psychological effects of having this fracked gas pipeline proximate to our family's new sanctuary, we decided it was far enough away. We were wrong. Within eight weeks of signing the papers, we learned that Millennium had a new project planned for the area, including a new compressor station slated for construction in our new town, a mere five miles as the crow flies from our forest home.

I now find myself engulfed in a personal struggle like that waged by Asha Canalos, Megan Holleran, Terry Greenwood, and other families described in this book. But I don't just fight for my own family and my mother's memory. I fight for all the victims of the gaslands, for the Delaware River, for the land above the Marcellus shale, and for the future of the earth. I fight to protect our nation's air and water quality, two priceless and threatened commodities. Now more than ever, it's time to fight. And it's time to pass Green Amendments affirming the rights of each and every one of us to pure water, clean air, and a healthy environment.

CHAPTER FIVE

WASTED

In the early 1950s, the DuPont corporation began using a chemical called perfluorooctanoic acid (PFOA) at its Washington Works chemical plant in Parkersburg, West Virginia.[230] Belonging to the family of perfluorinated chemicals (PFCs), PFOA became popular among industrial producers because of its ability to keep surfaces smooth and free of moisture. In particular, the chemical served as the key ingredient in Teflon, DuPont's highly lucrative, trademark product. Companies also used PFOA in many other consumer products requiring a nonstick surface, including Stainmaster carpets, food wrappers, microwave popcorn bags, and the surface coating of eyeglasses.[231] As PFOA became part of the fabric of everyday life in the United States and beyond, DuPont grew into one of the world's largest, most profitable conglomerates.

There was a dark side, though. PFOA was toxic—and the company knew it. Within a decade of using the substance, one of DuPont's scientists judged PFOA so dangerous that people had to handle it "with extreme care." The company's in-house scientific studies linked the toxin to genetic mutations, organ malfunction, cancer, and death in animal subjects. In 1962, DuPont experimented with human subjects, asking study participants to smoke cigarettes laden with PFOA and report their symptoms. These subjects became acutely ill, suffering diarrhea, chills, and body pain. Over the decades, DuPont's factory workers also exhibited a variety of short- and long-term health ailments. Colds were so prevalent among DuPont factory workers that the afflicted referred to their routine nausea, dizziness, chills, headaches, and fever symptoms as the "Teflon flu." These workers also suffered from higher rates of cancer and birth defects in their children. As peer-reviewed articles have since confirmed, PFOA is indeed extremely harmful to human health over the long term. Even infinitesimally small levels of exposure have been linked to kidney and testicular cancers, thyroid disease, high cholesterol, pregnancy-induced hypertension/preeclampsia, ulcerative colitis, and decreased birth weight.[232]

Given this evidence, you would think that DuPont would have pulled Teflon off the market and notified workers of the risk. But the company didn't do that. Instead, it kept quiet about the risks and *increased* the volume and scale of its PFOA-laden products. As a result, DuPont employees and the public at large were exposed to the contaminant in even greater volumes. DuPont workers and chemists handled the substance every day. They even took it home to their families to clean vehicles, wash dishes, and take sudsy showers. DuPont disposed of PFOA waste by dumping it straight into the Ohio River, where the Washington Works facility was located. Alternatively, the company loaded it onto boats and disposed of it in the open ocean. During the 1980s, the company acquired land from a West

Virginia farmer and disposed of 7,100 tons of the chemical by dumping it in a landfill. The farmer became so sick from contamination that he had to discontinue cattle ranching.

After environmental attorney Robert Bilott decided to take on this humble cattle farmer's case in 1998, he became the DuPont Corporation's worst nightmare, exposing the company's decades-long cover-up and winning what was, at the time, the most lucrative settlement in the history of US environmental law. Based on information he revealed, the EPA sued DuPont for maliciously concealing the dangers of PFOA for decades. A court fined DuPont $16.5 million, the largest penalty ever secured by the EPA for a case of this kind. Still, the fine represented less than 2 percent of the company's PFOA-based profits in a single year.[233] In 2006, the EPA acknowledged the grave risks that PFOA posed, creating a stewardship program and encouraging leading companies to reduce and eventually eliminate PFOA from their emissions and products.[234] As of this writing, no companies within the United States manufacture this toxin. Meanwhile, DuPont still faces over 3,500 personal injury lawsuits. Environmental journalist Sharon Lerner christens PFOA "the tobacco of the chemical industry."[235] Big tobacco and DuPont both aggressively marketed their products for decades, knowing that as they reaped massive financial windfalls, they were poisoning and killing their consumers. Both now stand as enduring and hateful symbols of corporate greed.

The story of PFOA doesn't end there. In 2005, Tracy Carluccio, deputy director of the Delaware Riverkeeper Network, became aware of the chemical and its dangers to human health and the environment.[236] Having read about PFOA in West Virginia, she wondered whether it posed a danger in our watershed. Tracy was especially worried about DuPont's Chambers Works facility located on the banks of the Delaware River in Deepwater, New Jersey. This large manufacturing plant, which treated hazardous waste and manufactured Teflon, had discharged other toxins into the Delaware River. In fact, DuPont was one of the largest emitters of toxic compounds in the entire mid-Atlantic. And it wasn't all that long ago that the Delaware Riverkeeper Network had fought and defeated a proposal concocted by the US Army and DuPont to receive and dispose of VX nerve agent waste at one of DuPont's Delaware River facilities, essentially treating the highly toxic waste through dilution in the river. Was the Chambers Works facility discharging PFOA into the river and nearby water supplies? We were determined to find out.

Exercising her characteristic vigilance and meticulousness, Tracy read every piece of science she could find about PFOA. Then, joined by her husband Paul, and operating under the guidance of a tort attorney who specialized in environmental toxins, she traveled to Deepwater, New Jersey, and went door to door to collect tap-water samples. Having heard rumors of contamination, many families were eager to have their water tested. They pointed Tracy to their cupboards, where they had stockpiled gallons of water. The Delaware Riverkeeper Network sent the samples Tracy amassed to a Canadian laboratory, one of the only scientifically reliable labs not connected to DuPont in any way. It may seem incredible, but most US-based water-testing facilities issued specimen containers lined with Teflon! The Canadian facility found measurable traces of PFOA and related chemicals in the New Jersey tap-water samples. As we could thereafter prove, PFOA exposure wasn't limited to West Virginia, but had spread to the Delaware River and our watershed state of New Jersey.

Eager to combat this threat, the Delaware Riverkeeper

Network notified residents, the New Jersey Department of Environmental Protection (NJDEP), and local water companies. Several New Jersey–based environmental organizations joined us in a working coalition, including key statewide leaders David Pringle with Clean Water Action and Jeff Tittel with the Sierra Club. The United Steelworkers union at the DuPont facility eagerly joined the cause. Some employees at the Chambers Works factory had experienced frequent illnesses and were undergoing blood tests to reveal how much PFOA coursed through their veins. Tracy also contacted the attorneys involved in the Washington Works lawsuit in West Virginia. They traveled to the Delaware River watershed and held a town meeting at a local high school gym. Tim White, chief innovation officer for the Delaware Riverkeeper Network, led the organization's online effort to publicize the event, peppering the region with advertisements and notifying our members and community leaders. With the support of other environmental organizations and Delaware Riverkeeper Network staff, Tracy lined the town with flyers. Hundreds of concerned residents showed up. Our organization and partners would go on to host many more living-room-style organizing meetings, sharing information about the latest water-quality samples and spreading awareness about the dangers of PFOA. All of this attention spurred the NJDEP to investigate. What they found caused great concern: most of the sampled water supplies in New Jersey contained PFOA! In 2007, the NJDEP established a PFOA drinking-water guidance level of forty parts per trillion (ppt).

By 2009, the water experts and scientists at the New Jersey Drinking Water Quality Institute were deep into their study of PFOA and its health consequences. NJDEP conducted another round of water sampling and awaited the institute's findings so that it could propose the adoption of the "maximum contaminant level" and begin mandating the removal of the toxin from all drinking water supplies. When the Drinking Water Quality Institute met in late 2010 it was expected to issue its PFOA recommendation to the NJDEP. It issued no report, however, and the NJDEP wound up taking no action.

How could this be? The answer is politics. Nine months before the Drinking Water Quality Institute convened, Republican Chris Christie became governor. He had already indicated that he wouldn't approve any new environmental regulations and held true to his word. As if that wasn't enough, Christie went so far as to shut down the Drinking Water Quality Institute. It wouldn't reconvene for another four years.

Tracy was shocked but not defeated. At the Delaware Riverkeeper Network, we redoubled our efforts, submitting numerous public information requests for the PFOA study and water sample data that the institute should have issued. We finally secured the data and publicly exposed its findings: there was evidence of contamination in drinking water! One startling discovery was an astronomically high level of another member of the perfluorinated compound family, PFNA or C9, in the borough of Paulsboro's water supplies. Indeed, we couldn't find a record of a higher quantity of PFNA anywhere else in the world. We rang the alarm bells and notified Paulsboro, afterward discovering that a large plastics conglomerate, Solvay Specialty Polymers, had employed and emitted more PFCs than any other company in the country. Like DuPont, Solvay took no responsibility for contaminating local water supplies. Nonetheless, it temporarily paid for bottled water for some in the affected communities and they settled with Paulsboro by paying for the installation of a carbon filtration system on the borough's water supply to remove the toxins after special counsel Bradley Campbell sent the company a Notice of Intent to Sue.

But for many, the damage was already done. To this day, residents who drank contaminated water for years worry about whether their children or family members might get cancer or contract some other debilitating or deadly disease. Many towns have become aware of the dangers posed by PFOA and other chemicals in its family, and they have demanded that their drinking water be tested and remediated. Local and state authorities have begun to act. In addition, in 2014, after succumbing to public pressure, including from my organization, the Christie administration finally reconvened New Jersey's Drinking Water Quality Institute. Its members in turn decided to recommend safe drinking water standards and remove PFCs from the state's water supplies.

While all of this is encouraging, the danger lingers. PFOA is still in the environment, accumulating in our groundwater, soils, vegetation, environments, water supplies, food, and bloodstreams. As it lingers, we must confront an uncomfortable fact: legislative and regulatory tools like the Clean Water Act, the EPA, and state agencies, have an abysmal record of protecting our water. Corporate interests are simply too strong, the lure of profits too great. Members of the public—you and me, our friends and families—are left to pay the price. We'll need bigger guns—Green Amendments—if we are to protect our communities from the next PFOA.

The Great American Dumping Ground

PFOA represents just one industrial chemical. What other substances might be poisoning us unawares? The answer is, quite a number of them. In addition to fracking and its related infrastructure, toxic waste products from industrial operations are ruining our water, land, and air, despite powerful legislation designed to curtail them. Consider air pollution. Following Richard Nixon's historic Clean Air Act (1970), air quality improved dramatically in our country's cities and communities. By 1990, this national air quality legislation had prolonged 205,000 American lives, preventing 672,000 instances of chronic bronchitis, 21,000 instances of heart disease, and 18 million childhood respiratory problems.[237] In 1990, George H. W. Bush bolstered the Clean Air Act, putting in place even more rigorous emissions standards. In the two decades that followed, the nation saw a 41 percent reduction in the six most hazardous airborne toxins; also down are emissions of volatile organic compounds (31 percent), carbon monoxide (46 percent), and sulfur dioxide (51 percent). In 2010, the EPA celebrated the fortieth anniversary of the Clean Air Act and was proud to reveal that since 1990, there had been nearly 2 million tons fewer hazardous industrial pollutants in American communities, dramatic reductions in diseases related to air exposure (like skin cancer and cataracts), less acid rain, and some 50,000 lives saved from particle pollution.[238] And yet, as gratifying as these improvements are, they obscure a more important truth: our air is still terribly polluted. According to the American Lung Association, over 50 percent of Americans are exposed to unhealthy levels of particle pollution or ozone.[239]

As the PFOA story highlights, by-products of industrial activity are also polluting our water. Nick Patton, a senior attorney with the Delaware Riverkeeper Network, observes that "water pollution doesn't just impact the water we drink, but it also impacts the water we enjoy for swimming, boating, and fishing. Despite the enactment of the federal Clean Water Act in 1972 and the state environmental laws focused on water, nearly half of our nation's rivers and streams are impaired and are not clean enough to support their designated uses, like fishing and swimming."[240] By impacting fishing, water pollution in turn poisons the food we eat. In the United States, people used to expect that you could eat any fish caught in our nation's waterways. Not anymore. The rate at which industrial toxins accumulate in fish—a process called bioaccumulation—makes them increasingly dangerous to consume. Sometimes toxins even affect the physical development of fish. Few things are scarier for anglers than hooking a great catch only to find it physically deformed and riddled with unnatural growths. On second thought, here's something scarier: most chemicals don't produce visible physical effects. Unlike food going bad in your refrigerator, most industrial toxins found in fish—including some of those most hazardous to human health—are undetectable in terms of color, smell, and texture.

State agencies now routinely issue fish advisories, notifying people about which fish are safe to consume and in what quantities. Consumers of sport fish in Pennsylvania, for example, are often advised to consume no more than one eight-ounce serving of fish per month so as to allow enough time for the body to naturally purge contaminants. Many fish harbor bioaccumulated toxins of some sort and should be consumed rarely, if at all. Bottom-dwelling carp and American eel in Pennsylvania's Schuylkill River are so laden with industrial chemicals that the state of Pennsylvania recommends never consuming them.[241] In New Jersey, the state has issued "Do Not Eat" advisories in the Passaic River for all finfish, shellfish, and blue crab. Depending on the body of water, you might also find "Do Not Eat" advisories for American eel, largemouth bass, chain pickerel, yellow perch, or other fish species. Additional advisories urge people to limit their consumption of a variety of species over the course of a week, month, or year in order to prevent contaminants from threatening their health.[242]

Recreational anglers—as people who fish for fun are called—have the luxury of throwing back fish that are the subject of a toxic fish advisory rather than taking them home for dinner. But not everyone is so lucky. For subsistence anglers—people who rely on fishing to supplement their diet—much more is at stake. They often must either feed their families contaminated fish or go hungry. As I've seen along the Delaware River and its tributaries, language barriers and cultural habits compound the problem by limiting understanding of and compliance with fish consumption advisories. A 2003 Delaware Estuary fish consumption survey revealed that subsistence fishers who fished from shore (as opposed to boats) were African American, Vietnamese, Cambodian, Puerto Rican, and white.[243] While white and African American anglers were most knowledgeable about fishing advisories and tended to cook their food in compliance with safety regulations (i.e., removing belly and back fat, where chemicals concentrate), anglers of other ethnicities consistently consumed more than the recommended amounts of wild fish.[244]

Such problems are hardly limited to the Delaware River. In the Donna Reservoir and Canal System, located on the mighty Rio Grande, which separates Texas from Mexico, people are catching and eating toxic fish.[245] Aware of the water's contaminants for over two decades, municipal water suppliers in the Donna system treat the water before pumping it to local families and businesses. In 2008, the Donna system was elevated to Superfund status (i.e., the EPA deemed its toxicity so great that it dedicated federal funds for special remediation). The water from the Donna system is considered safe to drink; it is the reservoir's fish that are the problem. The bodies of the fish contain lethal amounts of polychlorinated biphenyls (PCBs), a group of known carcinogens. Fishing advisories warn passersby on the beaches, and in 1994 the Lone Star State instituted a "fish possession" ban (the only such ban for any Texas waterway). Fishing became a misdemeanor crime, punishable by fines. Yet recreational and subsistence anglers, either unaware or disbelieving, were undeterred. They continued to flock to the region and cast fishing lines along the miles of beaches, either consuming catches themselves or selling them to local restaurants and neighbors. The EPA was so desperate to stop fishing that from 2008 to 2012 it periodically electroshocked the water to kill off toxin-laden fish.

Like so many environmental perils facing us today, the real problem plaguing the Donna system is a troubling lack of enforcement. Although fishing in this area might be against the law, the Texas Parks and Wildlife Department employs only one person to monitor several hundred acres of this vast reservoir system. The department rarely levies fines, and signs alerting anglers to danger are routinely vandalized. Even grassroots community efforts to educate people are disregarded. Local resident Sandra Carrillo sees the warning signs as wholly ineffective—like a parent wagging her finger and warning her children against eating too much candy. Carrillo echoes the desperation of everyone involved, from local residents to the EPA: "We need someone with authority" to spread awareness and prevent people from poisoning themselves. I wholeheartedly agree. Of course it would be better if the toxins weren't in the fish to begin with.

Just because you aren't fishing on the Donna doesn't mean you're safe. In 2009, a national EPA study of lakes found the presence of noxious toxins—including mercury and PCBs—in fish sampled at all five hundred randomly selected locations nationwide.[246] PCBs cause cancer, liver damage, and birth defects. They're so harmful that Congress officially banned them in 1979. Like PFOA, they don't easily degrade, and as a result they now persist widely in freshwater fish. The rest of these toxins are similarly dangerous, increasing one's risk for cancer and other disease. Mercury, which is present in most US waterways, is especially harmful for babies and nursing women, adversely affecting fetal and childhood development.

And as Captain Paul Eidman can attest, pollution and environmental damage also extends to the oceans.[247] In the mid-1990s, Paul organized a group of fifteen people to work as professional fishing guides. Paul has since operated Reel Therapy, a catch-and-release angling company in the New York Bight, a geographical expanse in the Atlantic Ocean extending from Cape May in New Jersey to the eastern end of Long Island. To find ideal fishing locations, Paul must consider the ocean's clarity, color, temperature, pH, and oxygen levels every day. And of course he must contend with pollution. Over the course of his career on the water, Paul has witnessed the increased presence of multimillion-dollar waterfront homes. He appreciates how people are attracted to the view. But when these estates' expansive, fertilized green lawns directly abut the water, they release harmful nutrient contamination every time it rains. Such waterfront residences also require more coastal bulkheads, or retaining walls, to reduce property degradation and beach erosion. Cumulatively, this coastal development has wreaked havoc on aquatic grass environments where waters are oxygenated and filtered and where fish forage for food. Paul considers weakfish, for example, to be the proverbial canary in the coal mine of such ecosystem destruction. As juveniles and adults, weakfish once feasted on the grass shrimp that live and thrive in the native *Spartina alterniflora*, or smooth cordgrass. Paul has witnessed these vital, intertidal wetland grasses vanish, taking the shrimp and weakfish along with them. The weakfish populations in the New York Bight and off the Jersey shoreline are a mere fraction of what they used to be.

Rain signals even more catastrophic runoff as well. Every time one to three inches of rain fall in the Bight, stormwater runoff releases fecal matter, nitrogen, and other pollution into the ocean. "Just send a drone up after a rain and it's plain as day," notes Paul, referring to the discolored water issuing from municipal pipes and flowing directly into the rivers and ocean. Power plants compound such problems. As Captain Paul observes, following cold temperatures, warm-water discharges emanating from power plants also affect biodiversity. Striped bass fail to migrate southward and instead gravitate to these warm-water releases. When the plants shut down in midwinter, they subject the bass to the much colder ambient water outside the artificially warmed ocean pockets. The fishes' immune systems weaken, creating health conditions that lead to disease.

Surfers and swimmers along the New York Bight suffer just as much from ocean pollution, contracting eye and ear infections. On any given day, Paul casts his fishing line and at times finds tampon applicators, pill bottles, latex condoms, or other detritus dangling from his lure. Surfers similarly paddle through surfing lanes to find garbage bags and other floatables atop their boards. "It really throws a wrench into the whole experience," Paul laments. Towns all along the Bight have pipes discharging contaminated runoff into the ocean. Surfers, swimmers, and anglers know not to fish or swim on the outbound side of these pipes after it rains.

Such contamination has led to the increased presence of "Frankenfish" inhabiting the waters. Occasionally, Paul hooks fish with body lesions, bleeding ulcerations, and suppurating, cottage-cheese-like growths.

"Oh, that must be a Hudson River fish, because it looks like that," some anglers say.

"Oh, it has three eyes. It must come from the Raritan River," note others, referring to one of New Jersey's major watersheds, which empties into the Atlantic. Striped bass with offset spines, locally known as humpies, are an unfortunately frequent occurrence as well. So are pug-nosed bass. When fish have this genetic condition, their faces don't connect with the bottom of their jaws, leaving their lower jaws unnaturally and precariously distended.

Altogether, these conditions have taken a toll. Though Paul started with fifteen colleagues, each of whom embarked on this career for love of oceans and angling, he is one of the few remaining. Such high attrition has owed to many factors, including the Great Recession of 2008. But pollution makes finding good water and fish much harder. Paul nonetheless remains staunchly committed to responsible catch-and-release angling as well as to ecosystem conservation. He's actively involved in Washington politics, advocating responsible forage-fish ecosystem conservation. "These forage fish are the linchpin of the whole East Coast ecosystem," he explains to his clients and congressional representatives alike. Without these fish, eagles, striped bass, dolphins, and humpback whales can't have dinner. These forage fish also filter water. Seeing how the commercial fishing industry has ravaged the ecosystem, Paul has advocated a catch cap on the overall volume of Atlantic menhaden (also known as bunker) that companies can harvest from the sea each year. He and his team won a victory in 2012 when the federal government implemented a catch cap, conserving thousands of metric tons of fish.

Regional marine biodiversity has since flourished, with places like coastal Rhode Island, once bereft of major fish and forage bases, teeming with life. Following this victory, the deep-pocketed fishing industry began lobbying for higher catches, once again imperiling the very habitats on which large fish rely. I think how much easier Paul's conservation efforts would be if New Jersey had a constitutional amendment to a clean, safe, and healthy environment.

The Making of an Industrial "Accident"

Industrial contaminants are not simply present in our environment because companies and municipalities deliberately and legally dumped them to avoid expensive waste disposal. They're also there because industrial actors of various kinds have adopted a dangerously cavalier attitude toward disposing of and handling these chemicals. The "accidents" that result threaten both our safety and the ability of future generations to enjoy a safe and healthy environment.

On the morning of November 30, 2012, Trisha Sheehan was preparing to receive guests at her Woodbury, New Jersey, home, when she received a frantic call from her mother. "You need to turn on the news. There's been a bad chemical spill," her mom said.[248] A train had derailed in nearby Paulsboro, an industrial town with a marine port and a large oil refinery located southwest of Philadelphia. Unfortunately, the derailment occurred while the freight train was crossing a bridge, sending several of its cars plummeting into the Mantua Creek below, releasing approximately 20,000 pounds of vinyl chloride into the atmosphere.

Vinyl chloride is the primary ingredient in polyvinyl chloride (i.e., PVC), which is used to create plastics, wire coatings, vinyl floors, and automobile parts. A colorless, highly flammable toxin, vinyl chloride causes neurological problems, respiratory illness, and cancer in human beings. Trisha's family lived downwind from the spill, her home abutting the tidal Mantua Creek where the train cars lay, half submerged. While most parents would shudder at the thought of their children's exposure to such a chemical, news of the spill inspired terror in Trisha, because her children have chemical sensitivities.

When Trisha first discovered that her children were sensitive to allergens, she wasn't particularly alarmed or anxious. You don't have to be a scientist or public health expert to know that skin, food, and respiratory allergies are on the rise.[249] Most schools and restaurants are aware of the increased prevalence of environmental irritants and offer an assortment of gluten- and nut-free menu options, nondairy foods, and chemical-free soaps. But in 2009, Trisha began realizing that her case might be unusual. Her sister had just recarpeted a new home. As Trisha left her sister's house after an impromptu housewarming celebration, she was stunned to find her toddler unconscious in his car seat. As she learned from her pediatrician, there were chemicals in rugs and carpeting that were toxic to her baby. For most children and healthy adults, everyday exposures to chemicals in consumer products and environmental toxins have little effect. But for chemically sensitive children and immune-compromised adults, such exposure is immediately debilitating, and if left untreated, even deadly. When Trisha welcomed her second son in 2011, history seemed to repeat itself, as he also exhibited similar signs of sensitivity.

With two chemically sensitive children to care for, Trisha began learning all she could about environmental toxins, allergies, and irritants. When cleaning agents caused her children to break out in rashes, she made her own laundry detergent. She installed air purifiers in her home and spent hours at the grocery store, studiously reading the labels of all food items to ensure they were toxin- and allergen-free. Parenting her children sensitized her to the larger environment and the role that certain airborne exposures had on her children.

In 2010, Trisha joined the West Jersey/Philadelphia chapter of the Holistic Moms Network (HMN), a national nonprofit organization that helps parents avoid chemicals and take a holistic and varied approach to health. As Trisha's parenting experience had taught her, human health is so much broader than regular doctor visits, dental hygiene, and our vitamin and mineral intake. Our health has larger environmental determinants, like the air we breathe and the chemicals to which we are exposed in our homes, workplaces, and communities. Trisha used HMN to empower her community and other parents, giving them access to nontoxic cleaning supplies and food recipes, as well as to the camaraderie of other parents facing similar child-rearing challenges.

On the morning of November 30, Trisha was preparing for an HMN gathering at her home, and she felt empowered. She had taken her knowledge of environmental toxins and transformed her home into a protective cocoon, free of all toxins and irritants that might harm her children. But after news of the accident that morning, Trisha felt stunned and helpless. She sprang into action, canceling her plans and her children's playdates, taking every safety precaution and following every protocol to the letter. The nearby community had not been encouraged to evacuate, but were instead instructed to shelter in place. Trisha followed the advice of the government agencies and professionals charged with protecting her community. She locked her doors, fastened her windows, and kept her children close. But Trisha intuitively knew that there was nothing she could do to protect them from an accident of this magnitude. And she was right.

For even healthy individuals with no allergies or sensitivities, short-term vinyl chloride exposure is dangerous, causing eye and throat irritation, difficulty breathing, dizziness, lack of consciousness, and death. Occupational studies on long-term exposure suggest that the substance accumulates in workers' livers, heightening their chances of developing lung cancer, a rare type of liver cancer (hepatic angiosarcoma), brain cancer, leukemia, and lymphoma.[250] Given that most vinyl chloride exposure results from workplace conditions, most research is focused on adults who work in PVC facilities or other heavy industries. There was little study indicating what Trisha's children, as well as the larger community in Paulsboro, should have expected following such an extreme vinyl chloride exposure. According to the guidelines of the federal Occupational Safety and Health Administration (OSHA), the highest level an industrial worker should be exposed to is five parts per million, for no more than fifteen minutes of time. Following the accident, exposure rates were in the thousands of parts per million! A visible cloud of vinyl chloride encased the community, posing long-term health concerns to everyone there.

The derailment wasn't merely a tragic accident—it was the result of shortsightedness and negligence. As the freight train bearing toxic chemicals approached the movable bridge that November morning, the light was red. A red signal indicated that the rail lines weren't properly aligned and locked into place. As the National Transportation Safety Board report indicates, "The conductor inspected the bridge and erroneously concluded it was properly locked to prevent movement."[251] But the conductor lacked the expertise or qualifications to make such an assessment. On his command, the train barreled through the red light on misaligned train tracks and predictably swiveled, sending several freight cars plummeting into the water below.

The public health and safety response following the derailment was just as negligent as the original accident. Emergency response protocols dictated, for example, that following an accident of this magnitude, all people residing within a half-mile radius of the crash must be evacuated. The actual evacuation area was a mere fraction of the prescribed area. People residing in most parts of the contaminated zone weren't asked to leave. Believing the toxins had largely dissipated into the air or perhaps weren't that serious in the first place, the elderly tended to their gardens and children played outside and walked home from school, with no breathing apparatus or other precautions. First responders were told they didn't need to take special precautions in dealing with the airborne toxin and worked without hazmat suits or breathing apparatus. On a street running parallel to Mantua Creek, police and health officials offered protective gear on one side only. If you crossed the street, you had to put on a mask, but if you stayed on the other side, you didn't. It was as if a detoxifying curtain ran down the middle of the road, acting as a barrier preventing toxins from migrating to the other side. Of course, that wasn't at all true.

Even downwind in a neighboring town, shuttered in her home, Trisha and her family began exhibiting the telltale symptoms of vinyl chloride exposure. "We were vomiting, our eyes were watering, and it felt like there was a band around our head, the pain was so severe," she recalls.[252] After the spill, people around Paulsboro coughed and wheezed for weeks. Local

Paulsboro residents visited their local health providers for relief and were consistently told they had seasonal colds or allergies. "You have bronchitis. It's that time of year. It's seasonal," was a typical response. Trisha repeatedly called a nurse's hotline, asking for relief from her nausea, vomiting, and migraines. "You can go see your family doctor or go to the hospital and they will treat you," the hotline nurse told her. After a week of ongoing symptoms, Trisha left her home to seek care at her family doctor. But she also fundamentally didn't understand what was going on.

Community air quality notices in the area showed that toxicity levels were well under safe thresholds. Environmental attorney Mark Cuker, who represents over a thousand people affected by the accident, confirmed that exposure levels advertised on the Paulsboro Response website were completely false. The website indicated that the highest detected levels were "hundreds of times lower" than what the EPA deemed to be harmful. In actuality, the levels were dangerously high. To make matters worse, air quality was inconsistent. Approximately 5,000 pounds of vinyl chloride remained submerged in one of the freight train cars in the Mantua Creek. In the two weeks following the accident, first responders and emergency professionals tried to dislodge the car from the creek. Each time this occurred, there would be an "evacuation" of vinyl chloride. Trisha recalls that each time this chemical evacuation happened (without warning to the community), her sore throat and respiratory symptoms flared. The repeated eruptions caused dizziness and confusion as those two weeks wore on. One evening when Trisha's husband returned from work, he looked at her blankly and asked, "Have you been drinking?" Trisha was intoxicated and delirious, but not from recreational alcohol consumption. That evening she passed out, only to wake up later, vomiting and with a migraine.

The Consolidated Rail Corporation (Conrail), which owned the train and the malfunctioning bridge, took action to shield itself from legal liability. Immediately after the spill, railroad representatives visited doctors, telling them that the train derailment couldn't possibly have caused the physical complaints they were seeing in the community. Medical officials heeded this "expert advice" and told clients like Trisha that they had a seasonal cold or bronchitis. Many of Mark Cuker's current clients were misdiagnosed for this reason.[253] Conrail also hosted meetings with pizza and soda, offering families $500 vouchers in exchange for signing a waiver promising they wouldn't sue the company. If you were in the small evacuation zone, the company offered $2,500 a head. Many in this hardworking, largely low-income community took the money out of need, perceiving it as a windfall. Local families collected these checks for themselves and on behalf of their children. If they ever develop angiosarcoma of the liver or any of the long-term respiratory conditions that Mark's clients have, they can never sue.

As time passes, more side effects of vinyl chloride exposure manifest themselves. In the spring of 2013, about six months following the accident, Trisha's youngest son began suffering dangerous nosebleeds. As she later discovered, these were the same symptoms that the children who had walked through the vinyl chloride plume were exhibiting. Vinyl chloride thins the delicate membrane lining the nose, so any environmental allergen or fall to the face can cause a massive bleed. In 2016, a kindergarten teacher said to Trisha, "Do you know your son has short-term memory loss?" A public health policy expert later informed her that memory loss was one of vinyl chloride's many side effects.

The chemical sensitivities of Trisha's children did not make them uniquely susceptible to the hazards of a vinyl chloride spill.

It just meant Trisha was more aware when things went awry, and that her family suffered the effects more acutely and quickly than others. Many people exposed that day suffer now and will continue to suffer in the future. Mark's clients are experiencing a wide array of harms, with some exhibiting reactive airway dysfunction syndrome (RADS), an unusual disease causing long-term, severe respiratory problems. Many of the first responders that Mark represents have RADS and other chronic respiratory illnesses. And now it's just a waiting game for even greater hardship and disease to manifest itself. Concentrations that day were so elevated that we can expect angiosarcoma in the decades to come. "Cancer is big on my mind, and whether or not we will end up with the rare form of liver cancer that vinyl chloride causes," Trisha said. "I shouldn't have to worry about my three-year-old getting cancer from a chemical that was released nearby that he breathed in, in his own home."[254]

The Paulsboro train derailment should never have happened. The conductor should never have crossed the red light, and Conrail officials responsible for managing the bridge should never have acted with such nonchalance, elevating the cancer risks and long-term respiratory illnesses for community residents and first responders. The negligent company took advantage of the rampant misinformation, falsely reassuring the public and shielding itself from liability. Government officials failed to take adequate precautions. Health officials, firefighters, police officers, and school administrators weren't told that astronomical levels of vinyl chloride had erupted into the atmosphere, and were therefore unable to protect the long-term health of the larger community.

Now you might read about the Paulsboro story and think, "How awful! But at least *my* community is safe." But is it? What kinds of industrial operations exist in and around your community? And what kinds of chemicals do these operations handle? According to one estimate, about 9 million Americans, disproportionately including people of color, "live in neighborhoods within three kilometers of large commercial hazardous waste facilities." But "thousands of additional towns are near other major sources of pollution, including refineries, chemical plants, freeways and ports."[255] Paulsboro is part of the heavily industrialized Philadelphia corridor. When oil refineries set up shop in a residential town, with toxin-laden freight trains and cargo ships traversing the region many times a day, people nearby become more vulnerable. Assemblyman John Burzichelli conceded that point after the Paulsboro accident, remarking, "When you live between two oil refineries, you have a sense that these things can happen."[256] Millions of Americans live in the midst of industrial operations. But as we explore throughout this book, you don't have to be located in an industrial corridor or in close proximity to hazardous facilities to be at risk. Given how lax industry is in handling these chemicals and how lackadaisical government has been in regulating industry, such incidents might well happen in your community one day.

Foaming Up Our Water Supplies

I've pointed to the gross failure of government and our laws to prevent pollution, but it's important to understand that in some cases, government itself is the polluter. An important example is perfluorooctanoic acid (PFOA), the Teflon toxin, and perfluorooctane sulfonate (PFOS), one of its chemical cousins in the PFC family. In the mid-1960s, the 3M Company partnered with the US Navy to engineer an ingenious product that would help suppress airplane fires, making military personnel safer while fighting wars abroad.[257] They created aqueous film-forming foam (AFFF), which the US military has stockpiled in large quantities since the 1970s. While airplane crashes are rare, AFFF is used frequently when conducting military foam testing exercises. During these drills, the military simulates an emergency, creating a huge fire on one of its bases and marshaling copious amounts of foam to suppress it. These exercises often take place in cavernous indoor airplane hangars, which become filled with AFFF from floor to ceiling. During these drills, military personnel constantly release the foam until the fire is suppressed. Then they rinse it away, sending it down the drain and into the environment. This doesn't just happen once or twice in a year. As of 2014, firefighting foam exercises may have taken place at upwards of 664 identified military sites in the United States.[258]

They happen near where I live, and for years, most residents were oblivious to the risks. Children residing just north of Philadelphia, near military bases located in Warminster, Horsham, and Warrington, used to look forward to the days when magical foam, resembling spools of white cotton candy, trickled down from the sky. As it accumulated throughout the town, children spent the day frolicking in the substance, staging mock foam battles, and using it as lubricant to slide down sidewalks and hills.[259] But make no mistake—the foam is anything but safe. The military has long known about its toxicity, but like DuPont, chose to expose its own people and the public at large.[260] As one 2016 investigation revealed, "Studies by the Air Force as far back as 1979 demonstrated the chemical was harmful to laboratory animals, causing liver damage, cellular damage and low birth weight of offspring."[261] These studies revealed damages to the animal subjects' "thymus, bone marrow, stomach, mesentery, [and] liver, and testes in the male rats."

Several years later, additional research demonstrated that female rats and their young were also harmed, with some off-spring suffering low birth weights and other pregnant females perishing before they could give birth. Throughout the 1990s, the Army Corps of Engineers, responsible for overseeing matters of environmental policy and regulation on behalf of the military, told the Air Force to stop using PFOS, warning it was "harm-ful to the environment." "Despite alarming findings," details one news report, "the service kept using it, leading it to seep into drinking water in Colorado and around the globe."[262] In 2001 fire-foam specialists, manufacturers, and the military acknowl-edged that PFOS was "persistent, bioaccumulating, and toxic."[263]

Thanks to the military's continuous usage of toxin-laden foam for a decade after it knew of its toxicity, water in many local areas has been contaminated. Beginning in 2014, twenty-two public supply wells and over 200 private drinking-water wells in the seventeen communities surrounding the military bases were shut down in the wake of contamination tests.[264] In Pennsylvania's Bucks and Montgomery Counties alone, more than 70,000 people have been exposed to the contaminant.[265] In some instances, drinking water in these areas registered as more polluted than the water supplies around DuPont's facility in West Virginia. Contamination rates near these military facil-ities show some of the highest PFC concentration rates in the nation. Areas around military bases in New Hampshire, Alaska, Nevada, and elsewhere have also exhibited dangerously high rates.[266] Public demand for clean water, groundwater cleanup, blood testing, and health studies continues to mount.

On October 18, 2016, Peterson Air Force Base, located outside Colorado Springs, revealed that it had accidentally released 150,000 gallons of PFC-laden water into nearby sewage systems (which themselves feed into community water supplies). Months before this catastrophe, the towns of Widefield, Fountain, and Security, all near Colorado Springs, already were shown to have alarmingly high rates of contamination, up to twenty times the EPA's maximum threshold for drinking water. After receiving notices of this contamination, and advisories that pregnant women and children stop drinking the water immediately, residents were understandably worried. Many installed expensive carbon filtration systems in their homes and purchased bottled water.[267]

Like many military members or those living near their bases, residents of Colorado Springs and environs have consumed this contaminated water their whole lives. They now must wait to see whether they will develop cancer or other illnesses linked to such exposure. Air Force base fire chief Steve Kjonaas was involved in many foam exercises during his nearly thirty-year career at the Peterson base in Colorado Springs. His career ended in 2007 when he developed prostate cancer. Speaking of the foam contamination, he said that he did "feel like a lab rat."[268] So did Bridgette Swaney, who moved to Widefield around 2010. Since the move, Swaney gave birth to her daughter and raised pet rats. Her rats have developed cancerous tumors, and Swaney herself has experienced thyroid troubles. She worries about her young daughter: what adverse consequences await her? Cory Gardner, a Republican senator from Colorado, is troubled by the American military's continued use of this chemical. "It is alarming that a substance was used that people knew then was a dangerous substance," he said. And just as was the case with fracking, the United States is an outlier when it comes to environmental and consumer protection laws. While Canada and the European Union have outlawed PFCs because of their toxicity, many US military bases continue to employ the substances in their fire-fighting materials.[269]

Innocent until Proven Guilty?

Cynics might expect that large corporations would put profits over people, but how could the US government expose its people to toxic chemicals for decades? For that matter, how can it continue to do so? Isn't the military's mission to *protect* the safety and security of the American people?

Given our country's troubling lack of environmental oversight, it isn't so surprising. In 2001, Rob Bilott pleaded for the US Environmental Protection Agency to outlaw PFOA and other PFCs. Despite compelling evidence that conclusively demonstrated these chemicals' toxicity, the EPA waited for decades before doing anything, even in the face of public fury and mounting water emergencies. It wasn't until 2015 that manufacturers agreed to phase out use of PFOA (but not other PFCs). In the intervening years, children frolicked in the magical foam, and Americans at large consumed infected fish, drank contaminated water, and served homemade dinner to their friends and loved ones using their sleek, PFOA-laden Teflon pans. Today PFOA is ubiquitous, found not merely in the continental United States, but "in the blood or vital organs of Atlantic salmon, swordfish, striped mullet, gray seals, common cormorants, Alaskan polar bears, brown pelicans, sea turtles, sea eagles, Midwestern bald eagles, California sea lions and Laysan albatrosses on Sand Island, a wildlife refuge on Midway Atoll, in the middle of the North Pacific Ocean, about halfway between North America and Asia."[270]

With water pollution, just like shale-gas fracking and natural-gas pipelines, our legislative protections have consistently failed us. Indeed, they have provided us with only the illusion of environmental protection. Captain Paul Eidman certainly can't rely on rules or regulations mandating a clean ocean. Allowing the unrestricted flow of untreated polluted water into the ocean isn't legal, but he still sees it happen every time it rains.[271] As a New Jersey resident, all Paul can do is hope for an environmentally friendly governor who might implement beneficial programs for anglers like him. When Christie Todd Whitman governed the state, Paul witnessed increased compliance with environmental codes. Helicopters routinely monitored pollution issuing from municipal pipes, power plants, and other industrial operations. "During her tenure," notes Paul, "there was less stuff floating in the water." The Chris Christie gubernatorial administration, however, has disappointed Paul and his fellow sportsmen, expressing little interest in ocean conservation unless it impacts the famed Jersey shore. And that's a problem. The health of our oceans shouldn't vary according to the whim of our elected officials.

And neither should the quality of our drinking water. But under current rules, the EPA must play regulatory defense, testing waterborne chemicals *only* if they have already demonstrated large-scale harm. "This arrangement," notes journalist Nathaniel Rich, "which largely allows chemical companies to regulate themselves, is the reason that the E.P.A. [sic] has restricted only five chemicals, out of tens of thousands on the market, in the last 40 years."[272] When environmental attorney Rob Bilott tried to initiate a class action lawsuit on behalf of individuals contaminated with PFOA, he was at a loss. How could he demonstrate that people were harmed by something that the federal government didn't even regulate?

Part of the problem is "regulatory capture," that is, when a government agency that is supposed to serve the public good instead sets about advancing the needs, goals, and desires of industry. This happened to the extreme in the DuPont case. As evidence of PFOA's toxicity mounted in the early 2000s, even the lead-footed EPA was prompted to act. In response, DuPont created a legal dream team comprised—you guessed it—of several prominent former EPA officials. William K. Reilly, leader of the EPA (1989–1993), was also a member of DuPont's corporate board.[273] Such corporate/regulatory overlap gave DuPont's legal team insights into the EPA's legal strategy they should not have had. DuPont knew the moves the EPA would make in advance and as a result could craft savvy public relations campaigns to manage its contamination scandal as it unfolded.

Because of regulatory capture, average people are at pains to address contamination problems even when they know something terrible is happening. When West Virginia residents received a notice in the mail that PFOA was in their water table, most did nothing. After all, the note attached to their water bills identified "low concentrations" of PFOA in drinking water sources. It also reassured people with the following: "DuPont reports that it has toxicological and epidemiological data to support confidence that exposure guidelines established by DuPont are protective of human health."[274] Still, local resident Darlene wasn't convinced. In fact, she was horrified. Her first husband had been an engineer at DuPont for most of his career. Like many, she had used her former husband's generous PFOA supplies to wash dishes and clean the car. Her ex-husband frequently contracted the so-called "Teflon flu," and she had suffered an array of health calamities.

Darlene's second husband, Joe, suffered from liver disease.

When he tried to seek help, it was not forthcoming. According to one account:

> Joe called the West Virginia Department of Natural Resources ("They treated me like I had the plague"), the Parkersburg office of the state's Department of Environmental Protection ("nothing to worry about"), the water division ("I got shut down"), the local health department ("just plain rude"), even DuPont ("I was fed the biggest line of [expletive] anybody could have been fed"), before a scientist in the regional E.P.A. office finally took his call.[275]

This experience is unfortunately typical. As we've seen so far in this book, many victims of environmental degradation face similarly insurmountable odds as they try to protect themselves or redress grievances after they've been wronged.

It wasn't supposed to be like this. The Safe Drinking Water Act (1974), passed at the height of the global environmental movement, provided the EPA with a strong mandate to proactively protect our country's drinking water.[276] The regulatory body went to work, identifying the various microbes, chemicals, and carcinogens hidden in our water. From 1986 to 1996, the EPA identified and monitored nearly one hundred chemicals. Water utilities, however, complained about the financial burdens and "red tape" that such oversight caused. In 1996, Congress curtailed the EPA's powers, making it difficult for the agency to regulate any emerging toxins. Since then, the EPA has gone from playing offense to defense, monitoring and regulating *only one* hazardous chemical—perchlorate, which is used to create explosives, and which infected the water of millions of Americans. The roughly one hundred industrial substances that the EPA has identified as toxins remain unregulated. We have no knowledge of when the next PFOA-style outbreak will surface, creating a public health nightmare and further degrading our environment.

The legislators who drafted the Clean Water Act, the Toxic Substances Control Act, and other environmental laws may have had the best of intentions. But over the years, industry has increasingly gained the upper hand. They simply have more money and thus more access to experts and lawyers willing to make their case. There are also more legislators working to weaken regulations under false claims of economic hardship, and more regulators willing to overlook enforcement needs or to simply give industry a slap on the wrist when major penalties or even criminal enforcement are warranted. Others, of course, deserve credit for stepping into the breach. Some individuals and government bodies have made heroic efforts to purge our water of contaminants. Under some administrations, the EPA has filed lawsuits; some states have worked for stricter and stronger standards; people like Rob Bilott and his firm have exposed major pollution stories to the world; and watchdog organizations like the Delaware Riverkeeper Network have notified the public and pressed for needed protection of water bodies. But these efforts aren't remotely sufficient. Our waterways remain contaminated, with more pollution being discharged legally and illegally every day.

To secure our health and the planet's future, we must turn to the Constitution. With a Green Amendment in place in New Jersey during the PFOA debacle, we could have brought a compelling claim to the courts, arguing that the government's failure to regulate PFOA amounted to a violation of its supreme mandate to ensure a healthy, clean environment. We would have had the authority to prevent a gubernatorial administration from disbanding the institute tasked with studying and recommending drinking-water standards that keep people safe. With a robust Green Amendment in place at the federal level, we can go from leaving emerging toxins unregulated to treating them like new pharmaceuticals. GlaxoSmithKline or Eli Lilly and Company can't simply manufacture a new drug and then advertise it to consumers. These pharmaceutical companies must perform rigorous and expensive scientific studies, proving their products safe before bringing them to market. As anyone who has encountered drug advertisements knows, pharmaceutical companies must also disclose any conceivable side effects their products might produce.

In other words, with the Constitution's help, we can mandate use of the precautionary principle (i.e., avoiding action unless all its potential environmental consequences are proven positive and safe), adding it to the government's mandate, rather than turning our communities into the industry's testing grounds. In Europe, new chemicals must first be proven safe before companies can bring them to market. In the United States, it's exactly the opposite. As journalist Sharon Lerner describes, "In America, killer chemicals are essentially innocent until proven guilty."[277] While this might be a compelling standard for criminal justice, it doesn't work for water quality. And as we'll explore in the next chapter, it doesn't work either as a general approach for deciding whether and how to develop our land resources. We rush to build and pave over our beautiful spaces, putting the burden on the public to establish a compelling reason why we shouldn't. As a result, we're paving over paradise to a frightening extent, despite the laws and regulations ostensibly in place to protect our enjoyment of nature. This needs to stop, and with Green Amendments in place, it increasingly will.

CHAPTER SIX

THE PAVING OF AMERICA

If you've ever gazed out the window while flying in an airplane over the American West, you might have noticed a checkerboard pattern in the landscape below, alternating parcels of land put to different economic purposes. Ever wonder where that comes from? It doesn't reflect natural features of the landscape. Rather, it's the result of an historical pattern of land ownership. During the nineteenth century, as railroad companies extended their operations westward, Congress and individual states passed a series of land grants (ca. 1850–1871) to help finance the companies' efforts and encourage modernization of the country's transportation system.[278] But the government didn't give the companies large, uninterrupted stretches of land. Rather, it allocated alternating parcels to railway companies and the American public.[279] Typically, one square mile of land went to a railroad company, subsidizing its work to construct one mile of reliable rail lines. An adjacent square-mile lot became public land. Hence the checkerboard patterns still visible today.

As the government anticipated, railway companies raised money by selling their lands to newly arrived settlers, ranchers, and logging companies. The logging companies initially sought to maximize their real estate investments by clear-cutting as much of the West's forested land as regulations would allow. Clear-cutting diminished somewhat during the late nineteenth and twentieth centuries as coal and steam technologies reduced demand for wood. By the end of the twentieth century, imported wood, plastic, and steel had sent America's timber and logging industries into precipitous decline.[280] Timber companies and other private ranchers increasingly sold their lands for development.

The presence of small, disconnected land parcels might not seem like much of a nuisance. Who cares if wild forest, resort communities, timber harvesting spaces, and housing subdivisions are packed right up close together? Actually, it's a big problem in the West. If you're a hiker traversing a checkered landscape near the Cascade or Sierra Nevada mountain ranges, you'll alternate between dense forested public lands and developed or logged lands every *twenty minutes* or so.[281] This can turn a pleasant recreational jaunt through nature into what ecologist Julie Morse describes as a "confusing quagmire."[282] It's far worse for animals. Grizzly bears, native to the region, have trouble navigating such subdivisions, as they require a five-hundred-mile roaming range. Other animals, like the endangered northern spotted owl, only like densely thicketed, old-growth forests. Land alternation forces such species into fragmented habitats, where their closest rivals are also packed, further decreasing these species' odds of survival.

Land alternation causes other environmental damage, like increased susceptibility to forest fires. In 2016, 5,762 wildfires ravaged 147,373 acres in California alone, devastating both the environment and the economy.[283] To prevent these deadly fires, the US Forest Service designated areas to preemptively burn (a precaution that helps forestall unplanned fires). But the Forest Service couldn't burn wild land interspersed with private residences. Constrained by patchwork land ownership patterns, forest managers cordoned off old-growth forest reserves, which could provide a haven for wildlife, and burned around them. "One of the unintended consequences of setting aside [old growth] reserves," Morse notes, "is that these often are the stands with the highest fuel levels and consequently the most likely to burn with high severity during a wildfire."[284] As a result, we've exacerbated the conditions that can lead to wildfires and haven't well protected old-growth forest ecosystems and the infinite richness they provide.

Checkerboard land ownership also makes areas of the Sierra Nevada mountain range more vulnerable to residential land development and its attendant ills. Perry Norris is executive director of the nonprofit Truckee Donner Land Trust, located in California's Sierra Nevada mountain range. As he has told me, the larger Truckee region has seen an influx of wealthy city or suburban dwellers from the nearby San Francisco Bay Area who purchase second homes or large empty plots on which to build. Their ranchettes and McMansions, as Norris calls them, eat into those relatively few parcels of wild land that existed despite patchwork land ownership.[285] Norris's land trust routinely tries to "de-checker" the land and prevent development, buying up larger wild parcels (e.g., 650 acres) and uniting them with adjacent land parcels to create a continuous ecosystem for wildlife and trees. Unfortunately, when the land trust seeks out 650-acre parcels, it often finds them already subdivided into 160- 100-, or 60-acre plots deeded to wealthy landowners for ranchette-style development. These ranchettes by themselves are not ecological disasters. But any time development and wild land interface with one another, you damage the land's delicate ecological balance, increasing the presence of invasive plant and animal species. The invasive pine bark beetle has killed millions of trees throughout the country, devastating the already beleaguered trees in the Sierra Nevada, which have been weakened by drought. Non-native cheatgrass has also invaded the West, destroying native ecosystems while greatly increasing the prevalence of forest fires.[286] Wealthy ranchers might enjoy a paradise away from urban and suburban sprawl, but the "rural sprawl" they're creating is harmful.

The Truckee Donner Land Trust also tries to coordinate with large commercial real estate developers, encouraging them to build in places that won't further checker and fragment the landscape.[287] Golf courses, resorts, and subdivisions began dotting the Sierra Nevada in the 1990s, and they have left the largest imprint in Placer and Nevada counties (where Truckee is located). At the turn of the twenty-first century, these two counties had developed more timberland into housing developments than any other area in the state of California. As Ed Walker, vice president of the logging company Robinson Enterprises, notes, the timber industry "is kind of drying up a little bit," and timber companies have turned to real estate development to stay solvent, a strategy that has "worked out well" for them.[288] Beginning in 2004, Robinson logged timberland to create the Jack Nicklaus and Coyote Moon golf courses, a cluster of luxurious homes called Old Greenwood, and the nearly five-hundred-home Eaglewood housing subdivision. Developers have more projects in sight, and government officials continue to render decisions supporting their efforts. But everyone must take heed:

the more land they take, the more the region loses its scenic and recreational value, destabilizing the natural environment and imperiling the ecotourism economy of which they are a part. This dynamic has already claimed its casualties. In the Truckee hardware store, where locals like to gather, Norris has heard fishing guides detail the demise of large trout populations in the Truckee River. The likely cause: development over the city's giant aquifer and along the banks of the river. Consequences of this development—erosion, nutrient runoff, and a warming of the waters—have made the river less hospitable to the fish. Meanwhile, resort building projects have destroyed the riparian habitats and tree cover over the river that are also necessary for the trout to thrive. Climate change has exacerbated these trends, bringing less frequent rains to recharge groundwater, which nourishes and cools the river. And trout populations aren't the only part of nature that is suffering in Truckee. The very character of the landscape is changing. As journalist David Bunker notes, "Once a land prized for its plentiful natural resources—timber, minerals and grasslands— the mountain range's forests that have long accommodated tourism and recreation are now being carved up for real estate development."[289]

The Theft of Nature's Crown

While the checkerboard land ownership pattern creates unique environmental challenges in the American West, few wild places on earth are truly safe from the ravages of development. Since the dawn of civilization, the number of trees in the world has decreased by nearly half, reflecting a commensurate decline in the number of forested acres.[290] The pace of destruction is only increasing. Beginning around 1990, we've destroyed, on average, a thousand forested football fields per hour. The loss roughly equals the surface area of South Africa![291]

The United States has the fourth largest number of forested acres in the world, trailing only Russia, Brazil, and Canada. Like these other countries, we've been poor stewards of our precious resources. When Europeans arrived in North America, relates Christopher Roddick, chief arborist at the Brooklyn Botanic Garden in New York, "it's said that squirrels could travel from tree to tree from the Northeast to the Mississippi without ever having to touch the ground."[292] At that time, old-growth forests were still intact on the East Coast, with chestnuts, hemlocks, and other New World staples soaring hundreds of feet into the sky, providing a protective canopy to sustain the rich biodiversity below. After Europeans arrived, massive deforestation occurred, which in turn created conditions for tree diseases and parasitic infestations to take hold. The trees that remain today are more vulnerable than ever.

Forested areas are hardly the only kinds of wild lands that are disappearing at alarming rates. Since the turn of the twentieth century, the world has lost 64 percent of its global wetlands.[293] The contiguous United States, between the 1780s and the 1980s, lost an average of sixty wetland acres per hour—a staggering 53 percent total loss.[294] People throughout the world tend to view wetlands as worthless and disposable—it doesn't matter, they think, if developers pave them over or if farmers clear them for agriculture. But nothing could be farther from the truth! Wetlands are vital to a healthy landscape, capturing carbon, supporting biodiversity, purifying and recharging water supplies, and constraining floodwaters. Because of massive wetland loss, according to international conservation group Ramsar and the Wetlands Extent Index, "access to fresh water is declining for one to two billion people worldwide."[295]

Of all our country's extraordinary wetland ecosystems, the Mississippi Delta ranks among the most environmentally rich.[296] Since the end of the last glacial period seven thousand years ago, the Mississippi River has deposited a rich assortment of silt in the area. Spring floods have distributed this silt, creating the landmass that is now southern Louisiana. In the eighteenth century, European settlers constructed levees to prevent annual flooding, halting the continual process of wetland creation. When the Army Corps of Engineers installed the industrial levees that exist today, the river could no longer access the delta that had been so integral to the natural river system. Then along came the energy industry. Prospectors discovered underground energy deposits, and oil and gas companies, unhindered by wetland protection laws, began harvesting energy and devastating the delta. As Bob Marshall, an expert on coastal land loss in Louisiana, documented in his study "Losing Ground," "Eventually 50,000 wells were permitted in the coastal zone. Over 10,000 miles of canals were dredged for oil and gas, 500 miles for shipping—and we basically eviscerated this incredible delta." The oil and gas industry destroyed as much as 60 percent of the existing natural habitat. With no natural protection against rising waters from climate change, we continue to lose more wetland area. Louisiana has the country's highest rates of sea-level rise, and those rates are among the highest globally as well. As Marshall documented, we lose about sixteen square miles of land every year in Louisiana—the equivalent of a football field every hour.

Whether it is forests and wetlands, or tundra, grasslands, and savannahs, all of the primary classes of wilderness in the world are fast disappearing. A 2016 report found that since the 1990s, we've destroyed 10 percent of our global wilderness, defined as environments largely untouched by human development.[297] This wholesale destruction, an area twice the size of Alaska, has left a mere 20 percent of the world's wild ecosystems intact. South America (with 30 percent declines) and Africa (with 14 percent declines) witnessed the most staggering losses, leaving the globe's remaining wilderness—an area a little over 30 million square kilometers—largely concentrated in Australia and the northern reaches of Asia, the Americas, and Africa. Study researchers were particularly alarmed to discover that remote and largely uninhabited areas like Siberia, the Sahara, or the Arctic tundra weren't self-sustaining wild areas, as many specialists had previously assumed, but were instead imperiled.[298] "The amount of wilderness loss in just two decades is staggering," noted forest scientist Oscar Venter, PhD, of the University of Northern British Columbia. "We need to recognize that wilderness areas, which we've foolishly considered to be de-facto protected due to their remoteness, [are] actually being dramatically lost around the world. Without proactive global interventions, we could lose the last jewels in nature's crown."

In the United States, we might debate the merits of converting our wild lands over to agriculture, livestock, and housing for an increasingly populated planet. After all, we need places to live, recreate, and grow our food. Businesses, shops, and roadways all require spots on the landscape to operate, as do the solar panels and wind turbines that will power our future. Despite these many development needs, there is no question that we have unnecessarily sacrificed many of these "last jewels in nature's crown," and deeply and irreparably harmed ourselves in the process. Dick Riseling owns the sustainable and energy independent Apple Pond Farm, located in the Catskill Mountains of New York.[299] During a recent presentation we gave together, he made a poignant observation: "Nature gives us life. It gives us special places to enjoy. Nature is beautiful. And we are giving nature a kick in the heart. We all came from nature. We need to start taking care of nature."[300]

You would expect kindred spirits like Dick and me to feel that way, but the extent of overdevelopment is becoming increasingly obvious to many others, including some in the real estate industry itself. Consider the problem of excessive mall space. From 1970 to 2015, malls multiplied at double the speed of the overall population.[301] According to Derek Thompson, an economics and labor markets specialist, "the U.S. has 40 percent more shopping space per capita than Canada, five times more than the U.K., and 10 times more than Germany."[302] After the Great Recession, cash-strapped Americans stopped frequenting these malls, shopping plazas, and retail complexes, converting what was previously thriving mall space into abandoned, boarded-up wastelands, with grass and weeds sprouting through the asphalt parking lots. As commercial real estate expert Ethan Rothstein relates, such overdevelopment means that "most of the United States is left with hundreds of millions of retail square footage that no one appears to want."[303] And yet even as these old malls sit vacant and acres of blighted land stand empty in cities like Detroit, developers still can't resist cutting down forests and filling in wetlands in order to build new retail spaces. It's crazy!

I've heard stories of such overdevelopment in towns across America. When George van Amelsfort moved to the Township of Hamilton in Mercer County, New Jersey, in the early 1990s, he encountered quaint neighborhoods with homes nestled amidst trees, wide-open spaces, and free-flowing creeks.[304] Local politicians affectionately dubbed Hamilton "America's favorite hometown." In recent decades, however, development has exploded. As George notes, rather than repurposing shuttered strip malls, city officials have green-lighted the construction of new ones. As of this book's writing, the town is approving construction of a new strip mall that requires the destruction of fourteen acres of mature oak woodlands. This stand of oaks is among the few remaining mature woodlands in this part of the community, and now it will be sacrificed for *yet another* strip mall. "Since I have moved to Hamilton, the loss of trees means a loss of nature to enjoy, a loss of shade as you walk down the sidewalk," George says. "I now hear the interstate, whereas years ago a mitigating natural buffer significantly dulled the noise."

In addition to the sprawling development that continues to engulf Hamilton, the town has also adopted poor stormwater management practices. Best practices dictate that municipalities require preservation of natural landscapes within and around development areas, and that they limit the development footprint as much as possible. The undeveloped lands absorb stormwater runoff that would otherwise cause flooding. They also filter out pollution like fertilizers, road salts, herbicides, and garbage that otherwise would surge into local creeks and water systems. Rather than benefit from nature's sponge and contaminant filter, Hamilton Township allows developers to oversize their projects. Adding insult to injury, to handle the problem of rainfall runoff their developments create, developers routinely bypass strategies that mimic nature and instead use engineering strategies that make problems worse, like building detention basins designed to capture the runoff and discharge it directly into local streams through a system of pipes. And to prevent erosion, developers armor stream banks with concrete or riprap. Unfortunately, such measures don't protect the environment, but rather push floodwaters and erosion farther downstream.

Because of the township's overdevelopment and irresponsible stormwater practices, Hamilton now experiences increasing floods during small, frequent storms, with large volumes of water flowing from town streets and lawns into local creeks. The creek that George once enjoyed has diminished in beauty and biodiversity. "Pond Run, the stream near my house, is dying a slow death," laments George. "Because of increased pollution and stormwater dumped into the stream rather than soaked into the landscape, there is more pollution, fewer fish, fewer amphibians, fewer birds, and an overall collapse of the ecosystem. At the same time as our community is losing its quality of life and its natural beauty, there is more frequent flooding." Because these stormwater systems are designed in a way that inhibits rainfall from soaking into the ground, they don't recharge groundwater supplies. This means that when it rains in Hamilton Township, there is often not enough water soaking into the ground to provide local streams with their base flows.

One day George noticed that Pond Run began drying up in the summer, leaving only small pockets of water where fish struggled to survive. George scrambled to rescue as many as possible, transporting buckets of stranded fish to where water was more plentiful. He has had to repeat this rescue mission in the following years. George can't rescue all the fish, and most of them die, their rotting carcasses serving as a sad (and odorous) reminder of the perils of environmental destruction, overdevelopment, and poor stormwater management. This is not the kind of scene you would expect in America's favorite hometown.

In 2004, the New Jersey state government had had enough of this environmental mayhem and implemented progressive stormwater regulations. These rules modestly restrained development practices, encouraging protection of natural buffer areas and the use of water infiltration strategies so that rain could seep naturally into the ground instead of surging off impervious surfaces. But much of the power to implement and enforce these new standards was entrusted to towns like Hamilton. So despite the state's environmental mandates, Hamilton continued to allow detention basins, armored stream banks, and ill-advised development projects—all in flagrant violation of its own stormwater mandates.

The state of New Jersey also failed to hold Hamilton and other similarly situated towns accountable. Sometimes the state claimed it didn't have the financial resources to enforce compliance. In truth, New Jersey's government officials didn't prioritize environmental protection. Year after year, George and his neighbors advocate for smarter development decisions and better stormwater management practices at their township meetings. Township officials consistently ignore them. Such regulatory oversight isn't, unfortunately, unique to the township of Hamilton. New Jersey's stormwater rules are frequently overlooked throughout the state. Hamilton and other townships approve project after project, increasing runoff and degrading the environment. And the state allows them to get away with it.

The Buried Toxins at Bishop Tube

Excessive commercial development saddles us with more than boarded-up strip malls and increased flooding. It also creates potentially toxic environments that are hard to remediate and that pose long-term threats to residents. East Whiteland Township in Pennsylvania's Chester County is home to the now-defunct Bishop Tube Company, a manufacturer of stainless-steel pipes. In 1972, government officials found elevated levels of fluoride in Little Valley Creek, which they later traced back to industrial discharges emanating from Bishop Tube's facility.[305] But that was only the first hint that the Bishop Tube site was spewing harmful contaminants from the plant into the environment and neighboring communities.

In the 1990s, the federal EPA began studying an industrial solvent called TCE, querying its possible effects on people. According to Ralph Vartabedian, who broke a two-part exposé on the chemical for the *Los Angeles Times*, EPA officials determined that "trichloroethylene, or TCE, was as much as 40 times more likely to cause cancer than the EPA had previously believed."[306] As the EPA planned to alert the public and control the substance, the Defense Department intervened. Apparently, over a thousand military bases were contaminated with TCE, and the EPA's actions would prove onerous from a financial and public relations standpoint. The EPA, under the stewardship of Bush administration officials supportive of the Defense Department, was powerless to continue its work. "As a result," notes Vartabedian, "any conclusion about whether millions of Americans were being contaminated by TCE was delayed indefinitely."[307]

But ignoring TCE didn't make it go away. According to TCE expert and Boston University epidemiologist David Ozonoff, it just meant more unexplained birth defects and cancer in the country. "It is a World Trade Center in slow motion," noted Ozonoff. "You would never notice it."[308] UC San Francisco environmental medicine expert and Natural Resources Defense Council scientist Dr. Gina Solomon concurred. "The evidence on TCE is overwhelming," she said. "We have 80 epidemiological studies and hundreds of toxicology studies. They are fairly consistent in finding cancer risks that cover a range of tumors."[309] The White House provided a large grant to the National Academy of Sciences to study the substance in 2004; in 2007, it linked the chemical to many human health diseases, and in 2011, the EPA belatedly classified TCE as a "human carcinogen."[310] Jonathan Harr helped introduce the perils of TCE to the public at large. His book, *A Civil Action* (1995), detailed a harrowing episode of TCE water contamination in Woburn, Massachusetts, and the child leukemia that resulted. This book, which also became a major motion picture featuring John Travolta and Robert Duvall, forms part of many law school curricula.

Although many residents of Chester County didn't realize it, Bishop Tube was using TCE all along—lots of it. During the manufacturing process, the company "pickled" its pipes, bathing the stainless steel in an acidic chemical bath laced with TCE. The toxin also figured prominently in the final part of the pipe preparation, known as degreasing, when the finished products also soaked in a giant vat of TCE.[311] Keith Hartman, a long-time company employee, describes TCE's ubiquity on company grounds, noting that people interfaced with the substance without covering their skin, utterly unaware of any danger. David Worst, a seventeen-year Bishop Tube veteran (1972 to 1989), likewise describes seeing open-waste pits, spills, and other "hot spots" of TCE contamination. He and his coworkers were shocked to learn that while the company was purchasing clean water for communities nearby to use (concerned that water in these communities had been contaminated), it failed to take similar protective steps for its own workers.

Other residents of East Whiteland Township interfaced with the site, too. Paula Warren has lived nearby since she was born in 1951, the same year that Bishop Tube began its operations.[312] She still vividly remembers the day in 1972 when she and her cousin Dale swam in Little Valley Creek, located approximately 10,000 feet from her home. As they wound their way down the stream, they gazed in disbelief at the fluorescent blue-green water issuing from a nearby culvert. They traced the water to its source—a place called Bishop Tube. They excitedly told their family about it, and no one even considered that it could be deadly. "If only," Paula says, shaking her head in regret.

In 1990, Paula received notice that her family's well water, which they had been innocently consuming since 1953, was contaminated with deadly levels of TCE and many other carcinogens. The Philadelphia Suburban Water Company told her family to thereafter "minimize consumption." Paula's small family of two parents and three children, which had no predisposition for cancer, developed five different types. Her brother and mother ultimately died of the disease. Twenty-seven years after Paula's initial contamination notice arrived, the groundwater still tests positive for high levels of TCE. Besides rendering her family's beautiful 1.1 acres totally worthless, the toxic groundwater has taken a physical toll. Memory loss, chronic vertigo, headaches, decreased mental function, brain fog, and liver failure—her family has experienced them all. These are precisely the kinds of illnesses that the scientific literature has associated with TCE exposure.[313] "Our house is trying to kill us," she notes.

Living approximately a hundred yards from the plant over the years of its operation, Kate and Larry Stauffer noticed intermittent chlorine-like smells around their property, but thought little of it.[314] "We were busy raising a family and didn't pay too much attention to what was going on," Larry remembers. The plant closed in 1999, when the couple's oldest son, Nicholas, was in high school. He often joined his friends to hang out in the facility's abandoned buildings. The couple's daughter, Liz, who was born in 1990, played in nearby Little Valley Creek—the same creek that was later found to be heavily contaminated from the site. All three Stauffer children collected rocks from the creek for a geology unit in their middle school science classes. On his daily walk with the dogs, Larry sometimes noticed overwhelming chemical smells coming from the buildings. He and his wife discouraged their children from playing in these areas, but as the couple later learned, people didn't have to enter the buildings to be exposed to toxins from Bishop Tube's operations.

Since 2006, Liz has been diagnosed with three brain tumors. Kate and Larry don't know whether to blame Bishop Tube for their daughter's cancer. Because of the many toxins and contaminants in the environment, medical and legal professionals often can't conclusively link individual toxins and specific health outcomes. The Stauffers nonetheless find it eerie that so many in nearby neighborhoods have suffered serious illnesses, including other children. Five neighborhood children received cancer diagnoses within a year of each other, including Liz's friend from down the road. After conducting their own research, the Stauffers found TCE exposure has been linked to central nervous system defects. Although Liz is thankfully in remission now, many others in the small community continue to suffer from life-threatening illnesses. David Worst, for example, now suffers from an incurable cancer, and many of his former coworkers have died from cancer or other neurological diseases. As Paula Warren notes, "Perhaps the ones who died of cancer are the lucky ones. They weren't around long enough to experience the long-term effects of TCE—the gift that keeps on giving."

What should become of the Bishop Tube site? In 2005, developer J. Brian O'Neill began surveying the property, hoping to entice another commercial operation to move in.[315] When that didn't materialize, he flirted with the idea of converting the site into an athletic complex.[316] O'Neill eventually discarded those plans, applying to rezone the facility as residential space, where his firm envisioned building over two hundred town homes. O'Neill has applied to the township for a variance that would allow him to carve out steep slopes on the site to accommodate his building plans. According to the proposed plan, O'Neill's firm would cut trees and excavate the natural areas that cover much of the site to accommodate homes, roads, driveways, and lawns. As contaminated as the land may be, Bishop Tube is the only open space available to this community. It's the only place residents can go to hear the birds, see the trees, and enjoy nature's serenity. Likewise, Little Valley Creek is part of a watershed that is officially designated as "exceptional value" and entitled to significant protection under Pennsylvania state law. O'Neill has reached out to Pennsylvania's DEP, seeking exceptions to a protected buffer requirement that the creek and community are entitled to under state law. The closer O'Neill can get to the creek, the more homes he can build, and the greater his return on investment in the property.

Residents weren't happy about losing their oasis of green space to a development project. But community members were positively alarmed to discover the inadequate cleanup measures that O'Neill's development company planned to undertake before breaking ground, and that the Pennsylvania DEP seemed to be accepting. TCE and the other heavy metal contamination persist on the site, with contamination extending down to the bedrock through saturated soils and infusing toxins into groundwater supplies. TCE compounds have been found at 50, 200, and even more than 300 feet below the ground's surface. O'Neill planned to remediate contamination from only a portion of the site, and these efforts would extend only to soils approximately 7 to 25 feet below the earth.[317] Contaminated groundwater, saturated soils, and the deeper areas of contamination would be left unaddressed. Contamination of Little Valley Creek would continue. To David Worst, these efforts were woefully inadequate. Having struggled for over a decade to have the site remediated before any new activity was allowed, he was "appalled" that O'Neill's plan would fail to clean up all the contamination in and under the entire property prior to development.[318] "Our objective was to have this cleaned up [completely]," Worst said. "And once it's cleaned up, then we talk about what to do with it."

At one community meeting, Larry asked O'Neill's lawyer if the company had tested the whole site for contaminants. As community members recall, the lawyer said the company was only testing what the state DEP required, which was not the entire site. O'Neill remained adamant that he would only address identified hotspots. There was also talk of vapor barriers to prevent potentially harmful fumes from entering the new town houses. But the actual plan remained unclear.

That response hardly assuaged local residents. It was clear to them that the site would remain dangerously contaminated, not fully cleaned up, as part of O'Neill's development plans. They also realized that no one could answer the question of when they might expect full remediation, or anything close to it. At subsequent community meetings, residents expressed fear that these inadequate remediation efforts would further expose the community, including its children, to toxins. What would happen when you had children playing in the backyard and a company started digging into the ground, releasing airborne contaminants? Would the kids be exposed to the toxins? Can you imagine raising *your* family in that kind of environment? And what about the new families buying homes built on a still-contaminated site, what about their health and their children?

Further questions arose about how O'Neill's development plan would impact future attempts to remediate groundwater, Little Valley Creek, or other contaminated areas associated with the site. When residents raised such issues, O'Neill and his spokespeople were defiant, telling the community that no one would be willing to do a better job than they would. But the community disagrees. It now fights for a full cleanup of the site and the preservation of its little patch of nature. As is so often the case, the developer and the state are using the site's contaminated condition as an excuse to try to force development rather than to protect and restore it.

Bishop Tube is among some 450,000 contaminated sites dotting this country. Known as "brownfields," these sites often result from unbridled, environmentally irresponsible activities.[319] Such sites that may endanger public health or the environment and that the EPA has identified as candidates for federal investment and intervention to secure remediation join the Superfund program. In March 2017, the US had 1,337 such Superfund sites, with New Jersey claiming the most (114) and California coming in second (with 98).[320] Mathy Stanislaus, who oversaw the EPA's Superfund program during the Obama administration, notes that about one in six citizens, totaling 53 million people, lives only miles from such a site.[321]

Federal and state Superfund sites are often inadequately

remediated. Saturated with dangerous levels of toxins, they endanger new developments as well as nearby residents who are unlucky enough to live close by. Consider Niagara Falls's Love Canal neighborhood.[322] Unbeknownst to the local inhabitants, Hooker Chemical Company discharged over 21,000 tons of toxins into the canal during the 1940s and 1950s. Developers sealed the contaminants, constructing schools and homes atop the waste site. All was fine until 1977, when the region experienced unusually high volumes of precipitation. Contaminants leached into the town's groundwater and surged into local homes and yards. After Love Canal's residents reported increased rates of cancer, miscarriage, and children's disabilities, the Carter administration evacuated the area and compensated hundreds of families. Congress enacted the Superfund program to help ensure that such a tragedy would never befall another community.

Love Canal, which the Associated Press referred to as "a symbol of environmental catastrophe," was subsequently remediated. Or at least that was the plan. "Although complete streets were permanently bulldozed around Love Canal," notes the Associated Press, "those immediately north and west of the landfill were refurbished following a $230 million cleanup that involved capping the canal with clay, a plastic liner and topsoil." During the 1990s, developers attracted new residents with lower real estate prices and assurances that all chemicals were long gone. But once residents repopulated the town, the same mysterious ailments began reemerging. Lois Gibbs was a Love Canal housewife who spread awareness about the contamination in the 1970s and urged people against reoccupying the remediated community. Describing her return to the community in 2013, she said, "It was so weird to go back and stand next to someone who was crying and saying the exact same thing I said 35 years ago."

Too often, real estate developments near the myriad toxic sites dotting America's landscape are not safe. The University of Missouri's School of Medicine and the University of Florida recently collaborated on a study linking Superfund sites and cancer spikes in Florida.[323] Florida ranks sixth in the country for contaminated land, with seventy-seven Superfund sites in total. Researchers looked for cancer clusters proximate to these sites, focusing on adult cancers that are less likely attributable to genetics. What they found was alarming, according to Emily Leary, PhD, assistant professor at Missouri's School of Medicine and co-author of the study:

> We reviewed adult cancer rates in Florida from 1986 to 2010. . . . Our goal was to determine if there were differences or associations regarding cancer incidence in counties that contain Superfund sites compared to counties that do not. We found the rate of cancer incidence increased by more than 6 percent in counties with Superfund sites.[324]

While this information is useful for public health professionals and city planners, it provides yet more data to support a truism we've observed multiple times throughout this book: environmental toxins are deadly for our landscapes and our bodies.

When the residents of East Whiteland contacted me about the contamination and proposed development of the Bishop Tube site, they felt besieged. It's hard to understand the state and federal laws that deal with toxic contaminated sites—even environmental advocates and attorneys like me who work 24/7 on environmental protection issues have difficulty. The community had little experience organizing itself, and it couldn't secure the expensive scientific and legal expertise it needed to pursue its interest in a healthy environment. Further, residents felt as if government officials charged with serving the community either weren't listening or weren't prioritizing the community's best interests. Residents certainly didn't realize that those same officials had an obligation under Pennsylvania's constitution to protect them. Meanwhile, the developer, township, and Pennsylvania DEP all had their advocates and experts arguing for their points of view. For residents, the fight seemed intractable.

East Whiteland residents called the Delaware Riverkeeper Network for help, and we brought the community the resources it needed. We secured expert reviews and legal advice from experienced attorneys, helping the community identify and pursue actions that would finally allow it to be heard. Among the most important insights we brought was confirmation that residents' concerns were justified, and that town and state officials had a *constitutional obligation* to protect their environmental rights—to protect the water and air that flowed through their towns, and to protect the scenic, aesthetic, and natural values of their environment that residents treasured. "I don't think people realize that a clean environment is a constitutional right," says Kate. But now that she knows, she and her neighbors have a renewed determination to fight hard for what is theirs. They understand that they are defending an entitlement that rivals, and arguably even surpasses, any property rights that the owners of the Bishop Tube site might claim.

Reining in Real Estate

Such stories of inappropriate or excessive land development will appeal to many people's sense of fairness or justice, but they hit me especially hard. When I was growing up, my town of Villanova in the Philadelphia suburbs formed part of a swath of communities known affectionately as the Main Line. While most people on our street lived in single-family homes, my family inhabited a duplex that was also the last house on our street. Through the walls on one side of our house, we could hear our neighbors. Through the walls on the other side, nothing but nature's music filtered through. Our house sat next to an enchanting patch of forest, and I spent countless hours as a child having adventures in those woods. My friends and I found special places, navigated massive rocks, and marveled at the large trees whose mangled roots jutted up like knots above the moist dirt floor. The forest canopy covered a small waterway called Ithan Creek, where we played, fashioning moon pies out of wet soil. At a bend in the creek, a sediment bar served as a little beach, the perfect place for us to build muddy sand castles, draw pictures with sticks, and wriggle our feet into the soft, wet sand.

On warm spring or summer days, my best friend, Cecily Liversidge, and I reveled in nature's beauty, searching for animals and little gnomes we were convinced lived in the forest. With my friend looking on, I tested my agility, trying to balance on rocks without toppling into the water, or using fallen trees as balance beams. Sometimes my mother joined in the fun as we wandered the twists and turns of the well-worn forest paths we had created over years of use. She was just as excited about seeing an orange mushroom or Indian pipe popping up from the forest floor as she was to catch a rare glimpse of a deer, fox, or other wildlife. And sometimes my adventures were solitary.

When I was sad, angry, or just puzzled by life, I ran down to the creek and nestled into the folds of the large, sprawling, radiating tree roots to sit, cry, ponder, and heal.

What I didn't realize as a child was that a new six-lane highway was being built, and the plans called for it to run straight through my enchanted playground. The community fought the new highway as best it could, just like the Stauffers fought the Bishop Tube project. But like so many development projects, this one was approved. Years later, when I was in college, I returned to my childhood home and was shocked to find the massive highway under construction. The trees were gone, the soil was bare, and heavy construction equipment and debris blocked all access to the creek. A few years later, the construction was finished, and the area was blasted night and day with noise and air pollution from the continuous traffic. I still feel devastated at the loss of my once beautiful forest. And I still recall my mother's sadness and anger. She had heard the buzz saws cutting the trees and had watched the bulldozers scraping the soil. For her, the sudden absence of the birds and wildlife she had so enjoyed was devastating. For many years thereafter, she would work to restore a little patch of nature for her own benefit and that of the area's suddenly homeless creatures. Within eight years, she created a small natural habitat bountiful with color and life, which was a treat for the eye. But this small stand of nature could never drown out the noise of the highway behind.

With the highway came still more development, an influx of homes and shopping malls, and a dramatic reduction in open space. I'm not opposed to development per se. But in places like Radnor, where Villanova is located, and nearby Hamilton, the fever to build was so great that it proceeded without proper care for the environment. Rather than gently nestle homes into the forest, preserving as many trees as possible, developers (with the government's blessing) clear-cut forests and moonscaped the land, creating massive homes with lots of lawn, oversized driveways, and thick roads to accommodate increased traffic. Rather than building away from the creeks and wetlands, volunteering a buffer of vegetation that would protect both the natural habitat and the community from flooding, erosion, and pollution, developers built as close to the water's edge as possible. The rainfall that once soaked into the soil now had nowhere to go. Rather than see this rainfall-turned-stormwater as the resource that supported the wetlands and creeks, and rather than developing in ways that would soak the water back into the ground as nature had intended, developers in Radnor and Hamilton constructed vast detention basins that collected and delivered water directly into local creeks. The predictable result was endemic flooding, erosion, and pollution problems across the region.

As of this writing, these development practices persist in Radnor, Hamilton, and most communities across the country. They are common development and stormwater strategies. That's why more communities are joining forces with people like George in Hamilton, rising up to oppose unwise development. In the community of Eastwick, Pennsylvania, located near the John Heinz National Wildlife Refuge, the Philadelphia airport, and Darby Creek, Fred Stine spends much of his time working with community members to protect the environment and to educate communities located upstream about the harms they inflict on their downstream neighbors. As citizen action coordinator for the Delaware Riverkeeper Network, Fred finds it commonplace and unfair that a wealthier upstream community like Radnor would fail to fully consider the harms its development strategies are inflicting not just on its own residents but on downstream

Eastwick, which is poorer and inhabited by communities of color that already face disproportionate environmental harms. "Even though these communities are twelve miles apart as the crow flies, the unnecessary level of impervious cover associated with development in Radnor, as well as other upstream communities, along with the practice of dumping their runoff into local creeks, contributes to the chronic, catastrophic flooding and pollution problems which the residents of Eastwick must face every day," Fred says.[325]

Radnor is not the sole cause of Eastwick's environmental problems. Eastwick was built on top of a 6,000-acre tidal marsh, of which only 285 acres remain, rendering the community far more vulnerable to flooding. The situation is so bad that many Eastwick residents must store rows of sandbags so that they're ready when a storm passes through. In 1999, the community's Pepper George Middle School was forced to close when floodwaters from Hurricane Floyd sent nine feet of water surging into the school, leaving the campus a mold-covered mess when waters receded. The city of Philadelphia and Eastwick's government didn't have the money to refurbish the school. Although Radnor has enjoyed many benefits from development, Eastwick has been left to bear its environmental costs.

But Eastwick residents are no longer sitting still in the face of this injustice. In 2012, they faced yet another ill-advised development: the construction of 722 rental units, a massive parking lot, and an airport expansion on a 128-acre land parcel that the Federal Emergency Management Agency (FEMA) designated as a special flood hazard area. This project was sure to exacerbate flooding. A handful of residents organized as the Eastwick Friends and Neighbors Coalition and reached out to environmental organizations like the Delaware Riverkeeper Network, obtaining access to legal counsel and expertise on flooding and land use. With these resources at their disposal and thanks to their own tenacity and grit, residents have extracted many concessions from government officials, including the withdrawal of the zoning proposal that would have green-lighted the project and the hiring of a highly competent community-planning group that will work on environmental and economic improvements in Eastwick.

Eastwick residents also took their message upstream—to Radnor. In 2015, I hosted a forum at which Terry Williams and other members of the Eastwick Friends and Neighbors Coalition explained to their Darby Creek neighbors upstream in Radnor how flooding impacted the downstream community of Eastwick. While most people worry about whether they left a window open in their house during a rainstorm, Eastwick residents wonder if they'll need to leave work to stack sandbags before the Darby Creek overflows its banks. Hearing these concerns, Radnor residents reacted positively—they really seemed to care. It remains to be seen, however, if that compassion and sense of responsibility to their downstream neighbors will translate into real change. As of this writing, the Delaware Riverkeeper Network continues to struggle to get Radnor to appreciate the value of good development decisions and stormwater strategies, and to recognize the need to put in place ordinances that mandate best practices.

The real tragedy of situations like Eastwick's is that they don't need to happen. In this country we know how to develop communities in ways that don't inflict so much harm. All too often, we simply don't do it. Under the current system of legislative environmentalism, real estate developers nearly always have carte blanche to undertake projects, with little concern for the effects on nature. Municipal officials approve development projects on a piecemeal basis and fail to put in place legal mandates that ensure best practices. While some development projects require initial community planning, developers inevitably argue that exceptions to environmental prohibitions should be made for their projects. Think of O'Neill's insistence on "relief" from protecting steep slopes, trees, and the exceptional watersource buffer so that he could maximize profit on his investment. Because approval processes tend to be piecemeal, any regulator or government official can accept a developer's rationale and grant relief while still claiming to comply overall with regulatory standards and zoning ordinances. Although a single development project—like Bishop Tube, a Sierra Nevada ski resort, a Hamilton Township strip mall, or another Radnor McMansion—may seem to contribute relatively little to water pollution, flooding, or land despoliation, cumulatively these projects have devastated our environments and endangered our communities.

A constitutional provision would bring about meaningful improvements in US real estate regulation by compelling government agencies to change the way they think about development. Imagine what Truckee, Love Canal, or Hamilton Township would look like if regulators weren't just constrained by local ordinances that are too easy to circumvent on a case-by-case basis, but were instead held to a higher, constitutional standard. Instead of quibbling about code and variances, the courts would be asking a whole different set of questions: Would subdividing this parcel for ranchettes in the Sierra Nevada allow for a healthy environment for all California? Or would it imperil wildlife and cause forest fires? Would sealing the Love Canal and building a community on top of it ensure that the environment was healthy and protected? Or would this be unacceptably perilous, given the site and local conditions? Would the next strip mall in Hamilton Township impact the rights of locals to a healthy environment? Or must developers consider stormwater, flooding, and drought precautions, as well as the right to healthy creeks with healthy fish? With a constitutional provision in place, decision-makers would be forced to look beyond short-term economic benefits and instead consider the cumulative impacts of all the projects they approve.

Most who would object to a constitutional approach to real estate development invariably raise the specter of money. "Times are hard," developers constantly say in the face of community opposition to their projects. "We need to build in order to increase our tax base, pump money into the local economy, and create jobs." Developers rely heavily on this argument when attempting to secure approval for any industrial, commercial, or residential activity: "Protecting the environment sounds nice, but it hurts people. If we want jobs around here, if we want a thriving economy, industry needs to be able to invest and build as it sees fit." As we'll explore in the next chapter, such logic is deeply flawed. Not only is environmental protection economically feasible, it actually provides enduring financial benefits to our community, state, regional, and national economies. Opponents of Green Amendments might protest that our society simply can't afford it. The truth is the opposite: we can't afford *not* to put strong, constitutional safeguards in place to protect the environment for ourselves and our posterity.

CHAPTER SEVEN

CAN WE AFFORD A GREEN AMENDMENT?

In the summer of 2015, my family rented a cabin near Toman-nex State Forest, located along the East Branch of the Delaware River in upstate New York. It was both a sad and exciting time for us. I had recently entrusted my mother's Columbia County forest to its original owner, who promised to safeguard it against fracking, and my family was in search of our new piece of paradise. My ten-year-old son Wim had developed an interest in fishing, and when he asked during our vacation if he could cast a line into the river, I told him that we hadn't brought our fishing equipment from home. Imagine my surprise when Wim approached my husband Dave and me as we enjoyed a morning cup of coffee on the deck, clutching a mass of knotted-up fishing line and a broken stick. Dave, a veteran angler, sprang into action. He looked everywhere for a barbless hook for Wim, finally finding one that had been shoved into an old cork dart board. Within an hour, Wim had a fishing rod.

Although the East Branch of the Delaware River is renowned for its fly-fishing, we didn't anticipate a catch that day. Wim had no experience, and our makeshift rod didn't allow the line to go out very far. But Wim stood on the riverbank the entire afternoon as Dave waded again and again through the water to unhook Wim's casts from the trees so that he could try again. I found a nice place to sit and listen to the water rush and the leaves rustle, marveling as a bald eagle soared overhead and a kingfisher surveyed the landscape for food from his perch on a branch. As evening came and it began to cool off, I ventured down the riverbank to tell the fellows it was time to go. I found them transfixed as Wim's fishing line became taut. After some effort, Wim and Dave reeled in a big, beautiful rainbow trout. Unbelievable!

Wim spent a few moments marveling at the trout's size and beauty. Then we gently released the fish back into the river's flowing waters. On our walk back to the cabin, Wim was flush with excitement. He couldn't believe that with his primitive pole he had caught something so magnificent, and neither could Dave. "This could never have happened at home!" Dave said, smiling in triumph.

My son then looked up at me, puzzled and confused. "We live near the Delaware River, too, mum," he said, "Why can't we catch fish like this at home?"

"The upper Delaware, where we are now, is a very special place," I explained to Wim. "It's one of the most special in our country." I then told him the story.

The reason this river has such bountiful, healthy fish is because the water is pure. New York City residents rely on this part of the watershed for their faucet water, referring to it as "the champagne of tap water."[326] As I related to Wim, much of the city's water originates in the rugged and rural Catskill mountain range, whose towering peaks capture rainfall from coastal storm systems and winter snow. Gravity then transports the water via a system of reservoirs and aqueducts to the metropolis below. The water tastes good because the Catskills' unique geology makes the water crisper and more crystalline than filtered alternatives.[327] Gourmands praise the water's ideal balance of magnesium and calcium, which some credit for the city's world-famous pizza crust and "crispy-on-the-outside, chewy-on-the-inside" bagels.[328] City officials and planners love the water system because it is gravity-fed, allowing residents in one of the world's largest cities to proudly drink unfiltered water from the tap, while keeping costs extremely low.

Yet the ongoing provision of pure water did not come without some struggle. During the 1980s, small farms dotting the Catskills fell on hard times and began selling their land to larger outfits or industrializing their operations. As water expert Daniel Moss and former DEP commissioner Albert Appleton relate, "Nutrient use increased, erosion accelerated, and pathogen contamination began to grow. Farmers also began selling off the forested portions of their land for environmentally damaging exurban development."[329] These trends intensified as the decade wore on, forcing the city to either yield to the pressures of industrial pollution and install expensive water-filtration systems or protect the watershed and its historically pristine waterways.

Recognizing that agriculture was polluting the watershed and its streams, the city devised a plan to help farmers reduce their pollution inputs while also supporting the efficiency of their farms. Working closely with individual Catskill farmers, city officials funded customized plans for each farm to achieve economic growth while responsibly stewarding the environment. Though the program wasn't mandatory, 93 percent of farmers volunteered to join.[330] Coupled with upgrades to wastewater treatment systems, the program reduced the amount of phosphorus flowing into one of the system's most imperiled reservoirs, the Cannonsville Reservoir, by more than 95 percent! While Cannonsville once turned neon green on account of the high nutrient content, it didn't anymore.[331]

City officials became convinced that with some extra investment, they could maintain and even improve the city's water supply without mechanical filtration. In the early 1990s the city applied to the federal EPA for a water filtration waiver, based on the purity of the water it provided to residents and a suite of programs designed to protect the watershed long into the future. Such a waiver was necessary because all surface water supplies in the United States must be filtered unless the supplier can demonstrate excellent water-cleanliness standards. New York was now up for the challenge!

In January 1993, the EPA granted New York City its first filtration waiver. Since that time, New York City has invested $1.7 billion in stream restoration projects, stormwater and wastewater management, land acquisition, forest and wetland programs, protective regulations, and economic stimulus initiatives.[332] Because of these unique and successful programs, state and federal regulators have renewed water filtration waivers for New York City ever since. According to David Warne, assistant commissioner of New York City's Watershed Protection Program, this investment in protecting drinking-water quality at its source has saved the city *billions*. A mechanical filtration system would cost approximately $10 billion in upfront construction costs and anywhere from $30 million to $100 million a year to operate.

In addition to allowing New York City to avoid the costs of filtration, the Watershed Protection Program has added economic value throughout the region in myriad ways. Watershed farmers consistently tell assistant commissioner Warne, for example, that safeguarding water quality also supports the economic viability of their businesses. For example, a typical plan involves testing crop fields for soil quality to ensure that farmers are not spreading more fertilizer and manure than necessary. This protects water quality by limiting the phosphorus load that could infiltrate tributaries. But it also saves farmers money. The soil tests often reveal that farmers can buy less fertilizer and still produce the same crop growth in their fields. Covered barnyards or manure sheds have also helped farmers manage their herds within controlled structures, rather than on muddy hillsides. Such infrastructure has improved the health of young animals like calves, which are prone to infections or disease if their rearing areas are not kept clean during the first few months of their lives.

Outbreaks of *Cryptosporidium* (also known as Crypto), a contagious parasite that causes illness in small calves, can spread from their fecal matter into water supplies meant for human consumption. Crypto outbreaks occur with unfortunate frequency throughout the country, going undetected through water filtration systems and causing extreme diarrhea and other problems for those infected. In 1993, a Crypto outbreak in Milwaukee's municipal water supplies afflicted half of the city. Outbreaks in Ohio, Nebraska, Utah, and elsewhere have caused public health scares and prompted class action lawsuits.[333] When outbreaks occur, the reputation of farmers in the local area often comes into question. Through investment in infrastructure, planning, and collaboration with local farmers, New York City's Watershed Protection Program simultaneously protects water quality and livestock health, and provides public support for local farms.

The New York City Watershed Protection Program also provides reimbursements for home repairs, benefitting residents, the economy, and the environment alike. Failing septic systems, for example, can pose a threat to water quality if they do not properly collect wastewater. Approximately 70,000 people live in the Catskill Mountains, a part of the watershed that surrounds New York City's unfiltered water supply. Septic systems service most of these homes. Fixing an ailing system can cost homeowners between $15,000 and $20,000. But if you live in the Catskill Delaware watershed and your septic system fails at your home or business, New York City provides funding to repair, rehabilitate, or replace it. Full-time residents receive 100 percent funding, while second-home owners and part-time residents receive a smaller but substantial subsidy. In 2016, the program celebrated its 5,000th replacement/repair. When a septic system fails, furthermore, the program employs local businesses to fix it. The entire watershed program employs nearly five hundred people in the Catskills and hires local contractors and engineers to fix septic systems or perform other vital tasks like stormwater retrofits and stream restoration projects. These employees and contractors pump their salaries back into the local economy, creating an economic ripple.

For conservationists like me, one of the watershed's most exciting initiatives is the land acquisition program, designed to prevent adverse impacts to water quality associated with development. The protection program surveys lands with high ecological value, proximity to a water feature, or development potential in the watershed. If identified lands fit the criteria and have willing sellers, the program purchases the property or preserves it through a conservation easement. The program also acquires easements on farmlands, helping farmers to keep their lands agriculturally productive while preventing them from being subdivided or developed when farmers retire. A similar program purchases streamside properties ravaged by flooding, simultaneously allowing homeowners to secure market value for their lands and enabling the city to protect and/or restore floodplains, which benefits water quality and provides downstream flood protection. At the same time, people who have suffered the damages and heartache of flooding can move to higher, safer ground. Since 1997, the land acquisition program has secured more than 140,000 acres of land. When you combine that acreage with the 210,000 acres of state-owned land in the area, the entire watershed that feeds New York City's drinking water reservoirs is now approximately 38 percent protected!

It gets better: the Watershed Protection Program also features an economic development initiative called the Catskill Fund for the Future, which helps to stimulate the local economy. Since 1997, this development fund has provided local businesses with $60 million in loans and grants—a big deal in a local area that has struggled economically. This money has helped create a thriving ecotourism industry in the region. People from around the nation and the world now descend on the area to enjoy trout fishing, boating, kayaking, and the many other recreational amenities that a healthy watershed provides. Such tourism boosts local businesses and real estate prices, since visitors often purchase second homes near great fishing and paddling. This tourism couldn't exist—let alone thrive—without clean waters.

No other public water system in the world has come close to rivaling New York's watershed-management program. As Paul Rush, the deputy commissioner who manages New York

City's water supply, noted, "I'm not aware of any other program in the United States or around the globe that is using all of the techniques we're using, on the scale that we're using them." If New York City had installed a filtration system for its water, a large percentage of the tens of millions in annual filtration costs would have gone to purchase the energy and chemicals necessary to treat contaminated water. Instead of lacing the water with these expensive decontaminants, this progressive program has invested $1.7 billion in *protecting the environment*, preventing contaminants from getting into the water in the first place.[334] New York's program also has regulations in place to ensure that future development and activities on privately owned land won't threaten water quality. The regulations make clear the city's expectations for all present and future landowners so they can use their land in a way that does not harm others. But the incentives and financial support are carefully crafted to motivate participation and compliance as much as possible. Overall, the New York City Watershed Protection Program is focused, to the greatest possible extent, on mobilizing the power of economic incentive and partnership to benefit the environment, individual householders, small businesses, and the regional economy.

The program's popularity and efficacy has inspired others throughout the country and the world. Government officials from Columbia, Chile, Singapore, Korea, Ireland, and other countries have visited the watershed to learn how New York handles nutrient-rich runoff coming from dairy farms. In 2017, officials from India also visited New York, seeking help to protect some of their water quality through forestry, agricultural programs, and similar practices. As others learn more about what New York has done, we can hope that one day soon many more cities around the world will be boosting their economies while serving champagne-quality tap water to their residents. Wim thinks this is a good idea, too!

The Costs—and Benefits—of Environmental Constitutionalism

In making the case for Green Amendments across the nation, I would be remiss if I didn't consider a predictable counterargument: it's economically unsustainable. Public policy analysts routinely suggest that we must choose between a healthy environment and a thriving economy. Ill advised political leaders similarly pit job creation and economic growth against environmental regulations. Impose too much "green tape," they say, and the cost of business becomes too burdensome. They paint nightmarish scenarios, predicting that factories and stores will close their doors and relocate abroad, where standards are less stringent. Jobs will be lost, they warn, and families will go hungry and lose their homes. The lights will go out from lack of energy as power plants find themselves unable to operate under the burden of regulation. Both national political parties routinely peddle such misinformation. Former President Barack Obama abandoned many of his environmental initiatives, like heightened ozone restrictions, under pressure from politicians and business groups who said they were simply too expensive.[335] His successor, Donald Trump, promised to abandon "unnecessary" environmental regulations and defund environmental protection agencies so that he could get America working again. He and his conservative allies pursued these goals with reckless abandon.[336]

To be fair, complying with existing regulations—environmental or otherwise—can be expensive. In 2012, the most expensive regulatory year on record, businesses and individual taxpayers did contend with new environmental regulations as well as extra red tape associated with the Affordable Care Act and Dodd-Frank legislation.[337] According to the American Action Forum, a conservative think tank, 2012 cost Americans a grand total of $216 billion in compliance fees and 87 million hours of paperwork. Compliance with new fuel emissions standards and restrictions on mercury emissions from coal- and oil-fired power plants accounted for three-quarters of these costs. That sounds like a lot of money. And it surely is, when you consider only this one side of the balance sheet.

As DC-based economic policy correspondent Jim Tankersley notes, the American Action Forum study only considers the up-front and annualized costs of regulatory compliance. It fails to consider the *economic benefits* that such regulations provide. That's like complaining about all the money you sink into paying for a college education without considering how tremendously an education *pays you back* over time through higher salaries, more career opportunities, and a richer, well-rounded life. If you consider both the costs and the benefits, for most people a higher education makes a great deal of sense, despite high student debt. That's because the economic benefits of a four-year college degree are tremendous.[338]

Likewise, if you think about the benefits of environmental regulation, the overall picture looks entirely different. According to the EPA, 2012's mercury standards cost an annual $10 billion in compliance and implementation. But they delivered between $37 and $90 billion in public health savings! Automobile energy compliance costs $150 billion—just a fraction of the $475 billion that consumers are projected to save on gasoline costs alone. Someone also had to build and install all the new technology required to meet the new standards. These new standards not only saved lives but supported jobs.

An analogous cost-benefit pattern emerges when we consider discrete pieces of legislation, like the Clean Air Act.[339] In its first twenty years of existence (i.e., 1970–1990), the Clean Air Act helped reduce fine particulate matter and ozone and resulted in "a 40 percent reduction in sulfur dioxide, a 30 percent reduction in oxides of nitrogen, a 50 percent reduction in carbon monoxide, and a 45 percent reduction in total suspended particles." Such reductions came at a price—an estimated half a trillion dollars. But consider this: over these twenty years, the Clean Air Act saved 184,000 people from pollution-related death. These cumulative health benefits represented between *$5 to $50 trillion in economic value.* Overall, the Clean Air Act injected between $5.1 and $48.9 trillion dollars in direct benefits into our economy. Many more people, moreover, are living longer, healthier, and more active lives as a result. As neurologist Dr. Alan H. Lockwood, who wrote *The Silent Epidemic,* a book on the topic, asked, "Who among us has an investment that has performed this well?"

If we project forward to 2020, the Clean Air Act's benefits and cost savings become even more impressive. As the law continues to cull deadly fine particulate matter and earth-warming ozone from the air, it will prolong the lives of 230,000 people and prevent 280 infant deaths annually. In addition, the reduction in pollution-borne diseases will save Medicare, Medicaid, the US military, employer-based health insurance plans, and private individuals some $2 trillion.

Other environmental regulations give rise to similar analyses. In 1978, when the United States began regulating ozone-depleting chlorofluorocarbons (CFCs), polluting industries expressed alarm. The adoption of more environmentally friendly CFC alternatives, however, saved the American economy $1.25 billion (spanning the years 1974–1983).[340] And how about clean water? While complying with the Clean Water Act poses short-term costs to pipeline, chemical, and large agricultural industries, most American small-business owners favor stringent regulation.[341] In 2014, the American Sustainable Business Council conducted a scientific poll of small-business owners across the political spectrum. The poll found that approximately 91 percent of Democratic-affiliated business owners and 78 percent of business owners identifying as Republican favored expanding water safety regulations. Sixty-two percent of all respondents polled believed water regulations were good for business, and 67 percent expressed anxiety that their businesses could be harmed by water pollution.[342]

We can ask how environmental regulations might impact the economy, but we should also consider what happens when we invert the question and pose it from the environment's point of view. What do industry, mining, energy, and rampant development cost our natural environment? Such natural capital costs, like the pollution of water and the destruction of carbon-capture landscapes like forests, usually go unpriced in our economies. But that's quite ridiculous when you think about it: in truth, clean air, pure water, and healthy wilderness are finite and priceless resources. Further, when natural capital is exploited by business and industry, the cost of their loss or their cleanup is externalized, meaning that it is thrust onto others, like local communities and governments. We pay for these costs through our tax dollars, increased health-care costs, and the impacts of extreme weather events, like flooding and wildfires.

A 2013 TEEB for Business Coalition study set out to determine the natural capital costs of global business, and their results were startling. Global businesses cost the natural environment an astounding $4.7 trillion a year![343] This extraordinary sum was roughly equivalent to 13 percent of all global production in 2009.[344] In certain global sectors, natural capital costs exceed the revenues generated by business. This is especially true for coal-based power generators in East Asia, where natural capital costs exceed annual revenues by nearly $10 billion.[345] Cattle ranching, along with wheat and rice production, also scored very high in natural capital costs. Absent environmental regulations and other market-based mechanisms that lower the harmful impacts of pollution-based activities, individuals, communities, and governments must shoulder these costs.[346] Politicians and business leaders who complain about the costs of regulatory red tape rarely acknowledge natural capital costs like floods, illness, lost recreation, and drinking-water purification, which are externalized to their constituencies.

At the local, regional, national, and global levels, environmental degradation acts as a drain on the economy. When heavy industry conglomerates like DuPont pollute our rivers, commercial fisheries and anglers suffer. This pollution, furthermore, imperils a whole host of ecologically based economies that depend on healthy rivers. When the federal government bows to political pressure and chooses to lessen emission standards because they are "too expensive," the economy is immediately impacted. To take just a couple of examples, immuno-compromised individuals suffering from asthma are at higher risk for premature death, exacting a price on the economy (not to mention the human cost). Also, real estate markets near industrial sites lose value, impacting all services and business in the area and decreasing the region's tax base. Requiring industrial operations to curtail pollution will certainly impact the bottom line of certain sectors like the automotive, natural gas, and other fossil-fuel-based industries, which must pay the up-front costs of regulatory compliance. But those up-front costs pale in comparison with the *trillions of extra dollars* their pollutants would inflict on the country's health-care system.

If you still doubt the economic harms that result from environmental degradation, despite all of this evidence, consider once again the example of municipal water systems. New York City protected its water, whereas Philadelphia historically did not, and it has paid the price ever since. As Chari Towne documented in her book *A River Again*, the Schuylkill River circa 1799 was, if not the "champagne of water," then a river of "uncommon purity," according to contemporary accounts.[347] But then the Industrial Revolution intruded, powered by the rise of coal mining. The Schuylkill became contaminated with a witches' brew of waste. Paper mills, sawmills, chemical and gas works, breweries, bleaching and printing operations, textile manufacturers and dye plants, iron furnaces, tanneries, and slaughterhouses all dumped pollution into the river.[348] Sewage waste and cesspool discharges also contaminated the river. By 1885, the Schuylkill was so polluted that Philadelphia began to look elsewhere for its water supply.[349] The city continued to use the Schuylkill for drinking water, although not as its primary source. By the 1930s, some considered the Schuylkill the nation's dirtiest river.[350] Eventually authorities worked to purify the river, restoring it as a reliable source of drinking water. But that process was extremely time-consuming and costly. Despite the vast funds spent on remediation, the Schuylkill's water would never again have the "uncommon purity" that would allow Philadelphia residents to consume it without filtration.

Whether you consider the costs of regulation or the costs of degrading the environment, the outcome is the same. It's not a question of whether we can afford laws that protect our environment. It's whether we can afford *not* to have them. Recognizing that environmental protection is good for the economy as well as the health and vitality of our communities, we simply can't afford *not* to pass Green Amendments at the state and federal levels.

The Value of a River

If we look more closely at the local economic impact of natural resources, the case for enhanced environmental protections becomes even more compelling. Let's consider my Delaware River.[351] From the late sixteenth to the mid-twentieth centuries of human settlement in the watershed, residences and industries dumped untold amounts of pollution and waste into the river. Those who lived in cities like Philadelphia were subjected to cholera and yellow fever outbreaks as well as sickening smells and unsightly pollution floating on the water. Philadelphia is located hundreds of miles downstream from the Catskills, where New York drew its drinking water. By the time the Delaware arrived in Philadelphia, development and industry of all kinds had taken their toll.

Weary of living next to a sewer system, nineteenth-century residents began fleeing the area. Those who could afford it retreated to country estates and vacation spots elsewhere during the summers, when waterborne illness was at its worst, and returned to their homes in the city during the winter months only. City dwellers in places like Philadelphia and Camden (located just across the river from one another) founded summer retreat communities upriver in present-day Washington Crossing, Pennsylvania, and Riverton, New Jersey. In time, after extensive cleanup efforts, communities have returned to enjoy life along the river year-round.

In recent years, improving water quality along the Delaware River has benefitted the real estate market, boosting property values an estimated 8 percent. This yields property value increases of $256 million in just the lower third of the river, the portion known as the Delaware Estuary. Because of the Delaware's high-quality water and scenic beauty, recreation and ecotourism are now vital parts of communities up and down the river, not just in the New York City Watershed Protection Program area. This is hardly surprising: the economic improvement and enhanced quality of life along the river's length mirror what communities nationally and even internationally experience when they sustain healthy ecosystems.

Ecotourism is on the rise throughout the world. A 2015 *PLOS Biology* study estimated that protected areas, which encompass one-eighth of the world's surface area, receive eight billion visits per year.[352] The study's authors termed this figure "strikingly large," as it represents more than the entire number of people on earth.[353] These visits yield an annual $600 billion in direct spending and $250 billion in additional spending. (By comparison, the world's people and institutions invest only an estimated $10 billion to protect these natural landscapes.) Averaging about 3.3 billion of these yearly visits, North America generates significant ecotourism revenues each year. It's hard to quantify these overall profits because the ecotourism industry encompasses myriad small businesses and activities as diverse as safaris in the Florida Everglades, interaction with bison in Montana, extreme river rafting in Alaska, and scenic bike tours throughout the Hawaiian island chain.[354] But the calculations that we can make reveal the creation of astounding economic value.

In 2016, for example, 331 million people visited one of America's 417 national park areas, spending $18.4 billion on lodging, gas, food, and other local expenses. According to the National Park Service, the combined visitor spending in 2016 "supported a total of 318,000 jobs, $12.0 billion in labor income, $19.9 billion in value added, and $34.9 billion in economic output in the national economy."[355] More than twice the number of visitors enjoying our state and national parks—more than two billion annually—flock to America's beaches, among the country's most attractive and economically beneficial tourism destinations. James Houston of the US Army Engineer Research and Development Center estimated that beach tourism generates $225 billion every year, contributing $25 billion to tax revenues.[356]

A healthy Delaware River represents a small but vital part of this national ecotourism-based economy, helping to keep rural river towns and bustling cities economically vibrant. Now that it's clean, visitors flock to the Delaware to enjoy fishing, boating, hiking, bird watching, biking, tubing, swimming, jogging, camping, and wildlife viewing. Pennsylvania's Bucks County has distinguished itself as an ecotourism destination, with Delaware River access points attracting visitors to local town wineries, breweries, nature parks, coffeehouses, museums, and charming bed-and-breakfasts. Fishing, hunting, birding, and wildlife viewing in the Delaware River watershed supports nearly 45,000 jobs and $1.5 billion in wages each year. Paddling in the Delaware River watershed supports another 4,200 jobs and generates nearly $400 million in sales. River recreation in the upper portions of the watershed, where Wim and Dave caught their prized rainbow trout, is responsible for $10 billion annually in economic value.[357]

Dozens of state parks flanking the watershed also add millions in revenue and thousands of jobs. New Jersey parks and forests alone attract 14 million visitors a year and support 7,000 jobs. These Garden State lands generate $347 million in direct sales and an additional $1.2 billion in indirect revenues. Approximately 5 million people visit the Delaware Water Gap National Recreation Area every year, making it an important economic driver for four counties in the middle portion of the Delaware River system. Visitor spending, on the order of $168 million, supports 1,750 local jobs, while park service employment provides $1.9 million in wages. Local governments benefit as well, securing an additional $2.5 million in tax revenue a year. For every $1 the government invests in the park, the economy reaps $24 in sales at local businesses.

Beyond the exciting recreational and educational opportunities it has created, protecting the Delaware's biodiversity has benefitted many other industries, including pharmaceuticals, commercial fishing, agriculture, and craft brewing. In the 1960s, biomedical researchers determined that the horseshoe crab's blood contained special properties that can help us test vaccines and medical devices to ensure that they are free of bacteria and safe to use. This test, dependent on the special substance in horseshoe crab blood known as Limulus Amebocyte Lysate (LAL), is now standard among pharmaceutical companies, making the Delaware River's horseshoe crab population indispensable to the biomedical industry. "Every drug certified by the FDA must be tested using LAL, as [are] surgical implants such as pacemakers and prosthetic devices," notes the PBS documentary "Crash: A Tale of Two Species—The Benefits of Blue

Blood, from the *Nature* series."[358] As of 2015, LAL industry revenues totaled $50 million, with one gallon of blood alone worth $60,000.[359] In each of the regions in which the industry operates, including the Delaware, the production of LAL creates 150 to 200 jobs and contributes upward of $100 million to local economies. Once scientists collect the horseshoe crabs' lifesaving blood, they return them to the water *alive*. Harvesting blood does result in some horseshoe crab mortality, and scientists are working to improve their methods, recognizing that these special creatures are more precious alive than dead, both in ecologic and economic terms.

At every opportunity, Tim Dillingham, executive director of the American Littoral Society and my longtime ally fighting to protect the horseshoe crabs of the Delaware Bay, is quick to point out the critical importance of horseshoe crabs. They comprise the primary food source for shorebirds like red knots, which stop over every spring at the Delaware en route from their wintering grounds in South America to their breeding grounds in the Arctic. Thousands of wildlife watchers descend on the Delaware Bay each year to view the spectacle of red knots and other migratory shorebirds feasting on billions of tiny, energy-rich eggs that the horseshoe crabs lay on the bay's beaches. These visitors spend money on equipment, food, accommodations, and more in New Jersey and Delaware each year. The horseshoe crab and migratory bird phenomenon provides upward of $32 million in annual economic benefits to the region.[360] This makes horseshoe crabs a linchpin in the regional ecotourism industry as well as the pharmaceutical industries.

Horseshoe crabs are hardly the only commercially valuable species to come out of the Delaware. Since the mid-twentieth century, when the river was so polluted that it contained a twenty-mile oxygen-dead zone, the Delaware has rebounded. It now supports local fisheries up and down the Eastern Seaboard, with the river serving as a spawning ground for fish species later harvested elsewhere. There are at least two hundred species of fish known to rely on portions of the river spanning the salty waters of the estuary and bay to the fresh waters of the upper river reaches.[361] New Jersey's Department of Fish and Wildlife credits remediation with creating the best trout fishery New Jersey has ever had. Thanks to a clean river, the Delaware Bay supports shad and striped bass fishing, as well as more select populations like alewife, Atlantic croaker, blueback herring, white perch, and blue crab. The estimated annual economic benefit of recreational fishing in the Delaware Estuary is approximately $52 million a year.[362] After suffering debilitating parasitic diseases, which nearly decimated the entire population, shellfish have also become lucrative again. In the period spanning 2008–2011, the cumulative value of Delaware Bay oysters was an estimated $3.8 million, creating an additional $23 million in the regional economy.[363] Local businesses throughout the watershed sell bait and tackle to anglers and charter sightseeing tours to interested outsiders—they, too, create economic value thanks to a clean Delaware River.

Clean water throughout the river system also sustains the rich soils and irrigation required for basin-based farming. Agriculture has a long history in the Delaware River watershed: Pennsylvania has become famous for its dairy; New Jersey for its peaches, blueberries, and cranberries; New York for its maple syrup and eggs; and Delaware for its vegetables and strawberries. Thousands of basin farms furnish local restaurants and markets with produce and sustainably raised livestock products. Bucks County, Pennsylvania, has nearly 1,000 farms today, producing $60 million in agricultural products. Locally based agriculture provides a range of other benefits as well. Local shoppers save on transportation costs for food, while decreased food importation in the watershed ultimately reduces the region's carbon footprint.

Clean water from the Delaware River and its tributaries doesn't just provide food and water, but what for many people is another kind of sustenance: craft beer. About a dozen craft beer makers operate within the city limits of Philadelphia alone. Victory Brewing Company touts the great taste and quality of its beer made from the clean water of Brandywine Creek, a major tributary in the Delaware River watershed. Saint Benjamin Brewing Company also boasts of great taste, and its brewing process uses water from Philadelphia's water system (which comes from the Delaware River). Yards Brewing Company, another Philadelphia brewer, gets double value from the Delaware River, using river water for its brewing and its waterfront location as a means of enticing customers to enjoy its beers.

And then there is the river's historical and cultural value. The Delaware River is the ancestral homeland of the Lenape people, who used the river for transportation, food, and water. Later, the Delaware River figured prominently in the founding of the United States. On December 25, 1776, George Washington crossed the river to surprise his adversaries, scoring an important symbolic victory in the Revolutionary War. Each Christmas, visitors descend on the site in Washington Crossing, Pennsylvania, one of the watershed's most popular tourist destinations. Meanwhile, archaeological remains of Lenape settlements dot the landscape near the Delaware and major tributaries like the Neshaminy Creek. The Lenape nation remains an important part of our watershed community, contributing their rich culture and river connections.

We should not ignore the significant industrial activity that clean Delaware River water supports—this, too, adds economic value. Beginning in the eighteenth century, lumber mills, paper mills, tanneries, stone quarries, cement makers, iron and rubber manufacturers, and later the coal industry set up shop on the Delaware's banks, using the river for transportation and power generation. As I've related, these industries damaged the river so much that many people turned their backs on the Delaware. Today, companies are much more appreciative of the values of clean water, and many recognize their obligation to help protect it. Electricity companies are the largest industrial consumer of Delaware River water, using three times more water than all other businesses combined. Uncontaminated water is just as vital for these industries as it is for agriculture, ecotourism, and biomedicine. Polluted water causes electrical power plants to operate less efficiently, increasing corrosion in pipes and other problems. The Delaware River's freshwater port locations at Philadelphia and Camden are among the world's busiest, employing over 4,000 workers and generating $326 million in annual revenues. While in the past dockworkers could become deathly ill as a result of their contact with the water, today they can appreciate the river's beauty as they work on its banks.

As this brief overview suggests, the protection of the Delaware River tracks well with the cost-benefit analysis of environmental regulations like the national Clean Water Act and Clean Air Act. The notion that environmental regulations weigh heavily on business doesn't survive scrutiny in the Delaware River watershed. Besides its immeasurable intrinsic value, the river is an indispensable part of the economy across many sectors. In the past, increasing the water's purity and cleanliness has added substantial economic value. Supporting and advancing environmental protection will continue to enable such value creation going forward.

Is Environmental Constitutionalism Undemocratic?

Beyond objections to Green Amendments on economic grounds, skeptics might point out the drawbacks of an approach to activism that relies on the court system rather than the legislative branches of state and federal governments. Using the courts to challenge environmentally harmful action on constitutional grounds is fundamentally undemocratic, they might contend.[364] After all, in a free and democratic society like the United States, we elect legislators to enact our collective will. When we appeal to constitutions for our rights, we empower the (largely unelected) judiciary to interpret the constitutionality of individual policies and pieces of legislation (e.g., a local development project, or Act 13), a process known as judicial review. Why should we create vast new opportunities for a handful of unelected judges to invalidate legislation created by the representatives of millions of voters?

In the United States, judicial review has exercised a tremendous influence on national policy. Courts have decriminalized abortion, legalized gay marriage, and instituted affirmative action policies. Perhaps the most famous and far-reaching instance of judicial review occurred in the foundational civil rights case *Brown v. Board of Education of Topeka* (1954). With the stroke of a pen, nine federal judges invalidated, on constitutional grounds, over a century of state and national legislation that provided for the segregation of black and white Americans. As the court argued, segregationist policies promulgated under the doctrine of "separate but equal" violated the equal protection clause of the Constitution's Fourteenth Amendment. As a result of this decision, the entire country was desegregated over a period of years. While both liberals and conservatives would certainly applaud the outcome of the *Brown* decision and other decisions like it, we might still question—and many conservatives have—whether the practice is good in principle as a means of driving such momentous societal change.

I support judicial review and judicial empowerment because, in general, the courts have a strong record of upholding democratic rights. (Though they sometimes get it wrong, eventually the courts get it right.) As we noted in the introduction, the 1970s marked the full flowering of global environmentalism and the broader rights-based revolution that would sweep the world. At this time, most of the world's constitutions came into existence or were significantly modified, granting rights to previously overlooked groups of people, like indigenous communities, and previously overlooked entities, like the environment. Critically, it was the *combination* of constitutional empowerment backed by court enforcement that ultimately granted these rights. The mere existence of a constitution doesn't guarantee that people can exercise their rights. If the judiciary lacks the power of review, then the people are left without remedy. Cass Sunstein, professor of jurisprudence at the University of Chicago, put it well: "Without judicial review, constitutions tend to be worth little more than the paper on which they are written. They become mere words, or public relations documents, rather than instruments which confer genuine rights."[365] While it has taken time, the courts have played critical roles in securing recognition of many of our constitutional rights. Without judicial review, the courts wouldn't have struck down segregation, and the civil rights and environmental movements would be significantly worse off today. In Pennsylvania, where the state supreme court justices are in fact elected, we never would have gotten our Act 13 decision, and our environment would be even more degraded, even more the plaything of powerful industrial interests.

As we've observed throughout this book, furthermore, large business interests like shale gas and chemical conglomerates exercise disproportionate influence in our democratic institutions. In 2014, researchers at Princeton and Northwestern universities released a well-known study comparing all the laws passed between 1981 and 2002 and voter preferences on each policy decision. As researchers found, the policies overwhelmingly *didn't* reflect the will of the people, but rather the preferences of special interest groups. Policies, note the study, "tend to tilt towards the wishes of corporations and business and professional associations," and especially diverge from the will of non-elite Americans.[366]

This finding holds especially true in relation to the environment. Despite current legislative and executive threats to environmental regulation and policy, Americans want enhanced protection. In 2016, nearly 75 percent of Americans responding to a Pew Research Center poll said that the US "should do whatever it takes to protect the environment."[367] And recall the poll we discussed earlier about small-business owners who overwhelmingly support increased environmental protections for water.

Clearly our legislatures today are not doing whatever it takes to keep our environment healthy—not even close. On the contrary, they quite often seem to be doing whatever it takes to further industry objectives at the expense of the environment.

We can no longer rely on legislatures and regulatory agencies, all too often beholden to special interests, to protect the environment. Given these circumstances, turning to the courts as a final arbiter—as our forebears have so often and legitimately done—can help to reinforce, actualize, and reinvigorate the will of the people. Of course, whatever your view of the courts, constitutional provisions securing our environmental rights are, in the first instance, a result of the will of the people carried out through a democratic process. In this sense, environmental constitutionalism is quite firmly in accord with our democratic traditions.

Answering the Critics

Economic and political objections to environmental constitutionalism are misguided. As we've seen, safeguarding our natural resources is an excellent economic investment. New York City's water supply system demonstrates how such farsighted, environmentally responsible stewardship of natural resources saves billions in dollars while stimulating the regional economy. My Delaware River also testifies to the manifold benefits that conservation and protection confer. We all deserve to drink pristine "champagne" tap water and enjoy the many economic amenities that natural resources like the Delaware River provide. As citizens of or residents in a democracy, we also all deserve to have our voices heard. Rather than obscuring or thwarting the will of the people, environmental constitutionalism actually allows for its clear expression. With Green Amendments in place, the majority who care about the environment will finally be able to make themselves heard, overwhelming the powerful industrial interests who have in recent decades shaped and distorted environmental public policy. Democracy will reign, our natural environments will be protected, and our economies will grow and prosper.

But what about you and your community? You might have a whole other objection to raise. Although the notion of a Green Amendment may sound good, you might worry that you live in a town or state where environmental constitutionalism seems hopelessly unrealistic. With industry so powerful and officials so eager to do their bidding, do we really stand a chance to get our right to a healthy environment recognized in the courts? How can that possibly happen?

It is possible. And furthermore, merely campaigning for a Green Amendment brings significant benefits. When people come to demand their rights to pure water, clean air, and a healthy environment, they change the way they think about the environment, their rights, and whether those they are electing to office will help them achieve those rights or thwart them. On the flip side, we surely know that a Green Amendment will never happen if we don't try. The key is to get started and work our way up.

As we'll explore in the next chapter, we can begin to claim our constitutional rights to a healthy environment at the grassroots level, reaping the many benefits—economic and otherwise—that such protection entails. If we start at the local level, organizing meetings with others and demanding protection of our inalienable rights to a healthy environment, including by recognizing those rights in our state constitution, we can take meaningful and much-needed steps towards saving our natural world.

CHAPTER EIGHT

FIGHTING FOR A
GREEN AMENDMENT

As good as New York City water now is, not long ago it actually ceded the mantle of water excellence to a small village called Hoosick Falls.[368] Located thirty miles north of Albany in upstate New York, Hoosick Falls won the 1987 New York State Fair's competition for the state's best-tasting drinking water. That year, the village emblazoned the competition results on a sign welcoming people into the town: "Village of Hoosick Falls, Home of New York State's Best Drinking Water, 1987."

Gazing at a picture of that sign, Hoosick Falls resident Michele Baker could only manage a sardonic laugh. Unbeknownst to the state fair competition's participants or to her fellow residents, two multinational conglomerates—the plastics manufacturer Saint-Gobain, and the consumer and aerospace systems firm Honeywell—had been contaminating Hoosick Falls's water for decades. In the course of their operations, these companies had leached perfluorooctanoic acid (PFOA) contaminants into municipal water systems and had pumped it into the air through industrial smokestack emissions. As of 2017, most Hoosick Falls residents contained thirty to fifty times the national average of PFOA concentrations in their bloodstreams. They also suffered from increased illnesses, cancer rates, and premature death. Hoosick Falls may have been a small village, but it had big problems.

The Baker family could attest to that. In 1998, Michele purchased a home in Hoosick Falls. Within a few short years, she welcomed her recently widowed mother, Maryann, into the area, and gave birth to her daughter, Mikayla. As of 2017, Michele, Maryann, and Mikayla all had elevated levels of PFOA coursing through their veins. "My child and mother have PFOA in their blood because two of the largest companies on this planet decided to pollute our little town," Michele explains.

When Mikayla was born, she arrived prematurely—a potential side effect of PFOA. Maryann, whose blood had triple-digit parts-per-trillion PFOA concentrations, suffered a stroke—yet another potential result of PFOA exposure the family laments. During a harrowing eight-day ordeal, Maryann was shuttled away in a helicopter and struggled for her life in intensive care. Since these episodes, any time Michele's daughter developed an infection or her mother started to cough, Michele wondered if they had sprouted a PFOA-related illness. "Every day you go home and you hate looking at your house because you know [about the contamination]," she notes wistfully.

Following Rob Bilott's exposé of PFOA's toxicity in 2005 (see chapter 5), many manufacturers made an agreement with the EPA to phase out the chemical, ending its use in 2015. Saint-Gobain continued to buy and use PFOA-containing materials in some of its Hoosick Falls operations until some time in 2014.

That same year, news of PFOA contamination in the small village made national headlines, thanks to insurance underwriter Michael Hickey, who was shocked and brokenhearted when his vigorous, healthy father died of kidney cancer. There was nothing in his family's genetic background that predisposed his father to such an illness, so Michael began investigating on the Internet. "All I typed in was Teflon and cancer, because that's what was in the [Saint-Gobain] factory that was in Hoosick Falls where my father worked," said Michael.[369] He was convinced that PFOA took his dad's life, and he also believed the contaminant was responsible for a whole series of strange illnesses and premature deaths afflicting his small village.[370]

When Michael discovered the water's toxicity in 2014, he immediately notified Hoosick Falls's government leaders. Yet they did nothing about it. In fact, the state health department issued a statement in January 2015 alleging that the water test "does not constitute an immediate health hazard," and that "health effects are not expected to occur from normal use of the water."[371] In November 2015, however, Judith Enck, a regional administrator for the EPA, sent a letter to Hoosick Falls's mayor, criticizing the village leadership for not protecting its residents from waterborne toxins. The letter recommended that the village provide an alternative source of drinking water for residents, and that they not use the town's water for cooking, not even for steaming vegetables.[372] In a public statement issued on December 17, 2015, the EPA formally warned residents not to drink the water.[373] The following January, Enck held an informational session at a high school and, before a standing-room-only crowd, apologized for the town's situation and reiterated EPA's message, urging everyone to stop drinking the water *immediately*.[374]

In addition to the health problems they experienced,

residents like Michele have taken a severe economic hit from the contamination of their water. By 2015, Hoosick Falls had been experiencing a renaissance, with new bike paths, arts and culture centers, and small artisanal businesses sprouting up. As the *Albany Times Union* related, Hoosick Falls was "the kind of place that seems primed to attract families looking for a great place to raise children."[375] So imagine Michele's shock that same year upon learning that her bank wouldn't issue her a new mortgage on her property (she was divorcing and needed to refinance), citing non-potable drinking water in her home. "I have a private well three miles away," she explained to the bank. "I don't rely on village water."

To appease the bank, Michele asked the Department of Health to test her private well. "You'll be fine," the officials told her. "You're three miles away from Saint-Gobain, nothing to worry about here." Two weeks later, however, she got a call from a health department official informing her that her well water was tainted with PFOA. After that, she surveyed the real estate market, wondering if she could sell her home. She found that most village homes, including her own, had experienced staggering reductions in property value. Almost overnight, they were worth half of their original, pre–water scandal values. When I spoke to Michele in 2017, she seemed sadly understanding of her predicament. After all, her previously quaint home now contained an eight-foot-high, Frankenstein-looking chemical purification system in its basement that expelled menacing gurgles. What prospective home buyer would want to deal with *that*—a constant reminder of the home's polluted water?

The travails foisted on Michele and her neighbors have transformed many of them into "accidental activists." After news of the contamination broke, a group of concerned mothers formed a community advocacy group to raise awareness and protect the community. In addition to balancing homemaking, caring for their children, and employment, these moms now talk to government officials and other advocacy groups, attend environmental events and government hearings, and organize meetings at local coffee shops. On January 30, 2016, these concerned residents attended a public meeting in the neighboring town of Bennington, Vermont, after the town of Hoosick Falls refused to rent local space to organizers. At this heated event, angry and fearful residents discussed their plight with the press and weighed legal options with a local law firm. Well-known environmental activist Erin Brockovich flew into town for the occasion, expressing solidarity with the community members and pledging to help them take on Saint-Gobain, just as she had taken on PG&E decades earlier in Hinkley, California.[376] A month later, the law firm filed a class-action federal lawsuit against Saint-Gobain and Honeywell, seeking relief for all residents suffering from the negligence, liability, health problems, and plummeting property values that the PFOA-industrial users had inflicted on them. Michele served as the lead plaintiff.

And then Hoosick Falls's children became involved. One Friday afternoon in February 2016, they convened a press conference at Hoosick Falls High School, expressing their fear and frustration, and taking the governor to task for failing them. "How dare you let us drink this water and do nothing about it?" they asked indignantly. "You owe us a safe water source!" While adults in Hoosick Falls hadn't gotten Governor Andrew Cuomo's attention despite their indefatigable efforts, their angry and visibly scared children sure did. That very Sunday, Governor Cuomo flew into town and promised to allocate money from the state's Superfund program to filter water for the residents. David

Borge, the mayor of Hoosick Falls, praised the children for their
work, saying, "Our local students brought this issue to everyone's
attention today. I commend each student who participated in
today's forum. Their poignant comments demonstrated the toll
this crisis has taken on each and every one of us."[377]

Meanwhile, Michele's community advocacy group, which
in the spring of 2017 formally became the New York Water
Project, was embarking on their crowning achievement thus
far: extending the statute of limitations in environmental tort
cases. Under existing laws, victims of environmental contamination could only file lawsuits within three years of *when an
injury occurred* or when it was *likely to have occurred*. But how
could that standard possibly apply to Hoosick Falls's victims,
who without knowing it had been poisoned and "injured" over
decades?[378] Michele's group of concerned residents championed a new bill that extended the statute of limitations to three
years *after* a toxic site entered the Superfund program. Michele
and her fellow accidental activists fought tirelessly to shepherd
this bill through the legislature, hosting press conferences with
assembly members and state senators and spreading grassroots
awareness at local events and on social media. After a protracted
battle, their hard work finally paid off. In July 2016, Governor
Cuomo signed the new statute of limitations bill into law.[379]

New York declared Saint-Gobain Performance Plastics a
state Superfund site in 2016, soon after the general assembly
amended the statute of limitations in environmental tort cases,
extending it to three years from the date on which a facility is
made a Superfund site. This meant that Hooksick Falls's contamination victims, previously deprived of a legal remedy, could
now hold companies accountable for the damages they inflicted.
Jerry Williams, an environmental and personal injury attorney,

has filed a class-action suit on behalf of residents, seeking relief from property damage and medical monitoring needs. As of this book's writing, Jerry and his colleagues are also preparing to file individual suits for clients who suffer from ulcerative colitis, thyroid disease, as well as kidney and testicular cancer, all diseases that the toxicological and epidemiological records suggest are typical following PFOA exposure. Michele hung a framed copy of the new law in her living room—this was her contribution to her fellow New Yorkers, one that would potentially protect millions of victims suffering chemical exposure–related illnesses. While Michele still worries every day about her own family, she is happy that future parents might worry less, thanks to her and her fellow moms' efforts.

It often "takes a village" to redress environmental wrongs. In the case of Hoosick Falls, that was literally true: the entire village played a defining role. It took a whistle-blower like Michael Hickey to stand up for what he knew was right. It also took a group of strong-minded, tireless mothers dedicated to protecting their own children and preventing toxins from wreaking havoc on others. And it took the village's children, whose touching articulation of their plight helped spur the state's governor into action. And the people of Hoosick Falls weren't stopping there. As of this writing, they were part of a growing effort to secure a strong environmental rights provision in New York's constitution.

Mikayla Baker (Michele's daughter) and Ashlynn Sagendorf are two Hoosick Falls children on the forefront of this constitutional struggle.[380] Ten-year-old Ashlynn had watched her neighbors flee Hoosick Falls following the contamination scandal. For her, the toxins in the water had taken some of the fun out of being a kid in Hoosick Falls, and she believes, as she states in her video on the matter, that all kids (and "even all adults") should have the right to clean drinking water. Mikayla believes similarly: "I think one of the highest priorities of New York State should be to have a healthy environment," she says. "It's ridiculous that we should even have to ask for the right of clean water and clean air." Bill Samuels, founder of EffectiveNY, reflects on the power of these kids in the movement to secure constitutional protections for the environment. "Nobody," he says, "makes a more eloquent case for the obvious need for New Yorkers to have a constitutional right to clean drinking water, fresh air, and a healthful environment than these two bright children who are suffering the consequences of our state not currently [having] these essential rights enshrined in our Constitution."

Hoosick Falls, in effect, was the Flint, Michigan of New York State. As Jerry Williams noted, lead filtered into Flint, Michigan's water supply for the same reason that PFOA leached into Hoosick Falls's: both were due to a fundamental "shortcoming of government." Yet, despite the great damage and distress that PFOA caused in Hoosick Falls, a phoenix was rising from the ashes. With the help of environmental leaders like Peter Iwanowicz at Environmental Advocates of New York, Hoosick Falls was helping to galvanize the state of New York into action. Together, they were catalyzing the movement for an environmental amendment to the state constitution. And that's what it will take, not just in New York, but everywhere. It will take local people rising up, neighborhood by neighborhood, town by town, until all Americans coast to coast have constitutionally protected rights to a clean, healthy, and safe environment. It will take the energy, passion, and commitment of people like you, as well as your family, friends, and neighbors.

Toward a Provision

This book has highlighted a number of local environmental stories that haven't received great play in the media, but that are harrowing and outrageous nonetheless. Whether its fracking gas companies setting up shop on your local cattle farm, a compressor station ruining your town, developers cutting forests and causing flooding, pollution (legal as well as illegal) contaminating rivers, or chemical spills and industrial contaminants damaging your children's health, these stories are scary—and they are *real*. Every day, local, state, and federal agencies grant industries permission to pollute, deforest, denigrate, and despoil our natural environment. I know, because I spend my days meeting personally with victims of this degradation, helping them to try and restore the sanctity to their homes and to reclaim their rights to a healthy environment.

You might be facing similar problems in your community. Perhaps local officials are advertising a new compressor station, industrial plant, or damaging development project. Or perhaps the facilities are already built and are causing contamination, but local officials don't want to speak out against the harm, prevent future contamination, or hold despoilers of the environment accountable. Even if you're not aware of these problems in your community, you might simply have become alarmed about what you've read in this book or are seeing in the media and as a result feel anxious about our planet's future (after all, every one of these stories is related, in some way, to the global threat of climate change). Whatever the case, don't despair, and don't feel powerless against Big Industry and its political allies. You *can* help to protect our environment, now and for future generations. It's time to *fight* for the passage of a Green Amendment in your state, in every state, and eventually at the federal level.

Before you can begin your struggle, you must consult geography, because individual states have different procedures for amending their constitutions.[381] Eighteen states permit constitutional modification through grassroots, direct democracy. If you live in Arizona, Arkansas, California, Colorado, Florida, Illinois, Massachusetts, Michigan, Mississippi, Missouri, Montana, Nebraska, Nevada, North Dakota, Ohio, Oklahoma, Oregon, or South Dakota, you have the most democratic system on offer in the United States.[382] People in your state can circulate a petition calling for a right to a healthy environment. If enough registered voters sign on, the initiative will appear on the following election cycle's ballot. If a majority of voters elect to pass the measure on Election Day (or a supermajority of 60 percent in certain states like Florida),[383] then the constitution is amended. In states beyond these eighteen, the legislature must first decide to change the constitution, and then, after legislators have voted (sometimes more than once), residents can vote on proposed modifications during statewide elections.[384]

Understanding the process of constitutional change in your state will help you craft a strategic path forward. And if your state already has environmental language in its constitution, this, too, will impact your strategy. Fifteen states in the union have no environmental provision in their constitutions whatsoever. If you live in Connecticut, Delaware, Indiana, Iowa, Kansas, Maine, Maryland, Mississippi, Missouri, Nevada, New Hampshire, New Jersey, Oregon, South Dakota, or West Virginia, this applies to you. Within these states, there is no history of environmental constitutional protection, which means you'll need to start from scratch in pursuing a Green Amendment. This blank slate can prove advantageous, enabling you to make a clear statement that no environmental rights are recognized in your state and that you need them. In New Jersey, for example, the Delaware Riverkeeper Network is working with New Jersey Clean Water Action's David Pringle, New Jersey Sierra Club's Jeff Tittel, and Environment New Jersey's Doug O'Malley, three of the state's staunchest environmental leaders, demonstrating how widespread environmental degradation is and how urgently a constitutional provision is needed.

The thirty-five remaining US states (including Montana and Pennsylvania) possess environmental provisions of varying strength and rigor. Those last few words—"varying strength and rigor"—are key. Many of these states, for example, have language in their provisions that artificially curtails environmental liberties, protecting fishing, hunting, and navigation instead of all shared natural resources, and/or limiting the provision to simply a statement of policy. If you inhabit a state with a preexisting but inadequate provision, you are likely at a slight disadvantage, as you must convince the public that while environmental language exists in your constitution, it does not rise to the necessary level of protection, and a change is needed.

Environmental advocates in New York are working hard as of this writing to make such an argument. In 1894, New York's constitutional convention adopted the "forever wild" provision, guaranteeing that the Adirondack and Catskill mountain ranges remain free of development (article 7, section 7). This was the only constitutional amendment to pass unanimously (122–0) at the entire convention (or at any New York constitutional convention preceding it!). It became a popularly cherished freedom thereafter as judges ruled against timbering legislation (1896) and other development interests for infringing on the provision.[385] During the years that followed the "forever wild" provision's installation, the state added additional wild lands to the protected areas, with voters passing bond measures and legislators allocating necessary funds to further enhance these prized natural resources.[386] Concerned residents and environmental groups, like Environmental Advocates of New York and the Delaware Riverkeeper Network, were arguing as of this writing that while the popular "forever wild" provision is wonderful, it alone doesn't suffice to protect the state's environmental rights. After referring to the proud history of conservation that the provision inspired, the New York People's Convention argued that "as the pollution of drinking water in areas of the state like Hoosick Falls has vividly demonstrated of late, New York must still do much more to protect our environment."[387]

No matter where you reside, it's no use going to the trouble of passing an amendment if it lacks the vigor, optimal positioning, and language that will enable courts to successfully implement it. An environmental rights provision must exist in the state constitution's bill of rights or "declaration of rights," as it is called in some states. This position reflects the primacy of the liberty, elevating it to the highest levels of protection, alongside the fundamental freedoms of speech, association, religion, and due process. The amendment must furthermore contain an affirmative statement of environmental rights as well as the duty of the state to protect those rights. Specifically, the constitution must articulate an individual's right to "clean air, clean water, and a healthy environment." This broad wording suggests that the amendment applies to all natural resources, and not simply public lands, state parks, hunting areas, or revenue-generating landscapes. You may also consider adding language linking your right to a stable climate and other issues of concern to your community and state.

Crucially, the stipulated rights must accrue to *individuals*. Florida's constitution says, "It shall be the policy of the state to conserve and protect its natural resources and scenic beauty" (article 2, section 7). By employing such wording, Florida has relegated environmental protection to a policy statement, instead of making it a definitive right that individuals possess and can contest in court. Environmental amendments should include language that designates the state as a trustee of all natural resources, which the government has a duty to protect and maintain for the benefit of all the people, including future generations. As Jordan Yeager, the distinguished environmental attorney who spearheaded the constitutional environmental argument against Pennsylvania's Act 13, notes, having the state described as a "trustee" is ideal because such language invokes the rigorous duties that trustees shoulder in other legal contexts. Article 1, section 27 of Pennsylvania's constitution does just that: "As trustee of these [natural] resources, the Commonwealth shall conserve and maintain them for the benefit of all the people." Pennsylvania's responsibilities as the designated trustee of these resources extend to both present and future generations, setting a high bar of environmental protection. Other states should also emulate this explicit declaration of intergenerational obligation to a healthy environment.

Prime positioning of these individually defined liberties within bills of rights, furthermore, helps ensure that environmental amendments are "self-executing." One of the ways that courts have historically restricted and undermined fundamental liberties like environmental protections is to insist that people can't enforce them directly. Instead, courts need a legislature to define the scope of these liberties. But if environmental rights are strategically situated and worded within a constitution, we can help ensure that they are self-executing, which means that we can directly appeal to them in court if they are infringed. One of the reasons the environmental provision enshrined in

Pennsylvania's constitution languished for decades was because judges and legal experts insisted they weren't self-executing. But jurists like Ronald D. Castille, Pennsylvania's supreme court justice who wrote the court's Act 13 plurality opinion, have dramatically altered that undemocratic interpretation. Castille acknowledged that any plain and fair reading of Pennsylvania's environmental amendment revealed that it didn't simply enunciate a policy, principle, or set of goals. Pennsylvania's constitution explicitly confers individual environmental rights alongside other long-cherished freedoms. As such, Justice Castille acknowledged them to be self-executing liberties that thereafter didn't require legislative interference to claim and contest in court.

All of these legal technicalities and geographical considerations are admittedly complex and daunting. This is precisely why I drew upon the legal expertise of Jordan Yeager and others to help me create the "For the Generations" initiative at the Delaware Riverkeeper Network. For the Generations is dedicated to inspiring, supporting, and advancing constitutional rights throughout the United States. Following our victory over Act 13, I also designed For the Generations to become a clearinghouse for grassroots organizing around state amendments.

If you are interested in beginning the process in your state, please look to our website for tools we have created to help. Contact us at any time (ForTheGenerations@delawareriverkeeper .org), and we'll happily offer guidance in how to find allies in your area, how to frame the conversation, and strategies for interfacing with the media, local nongovernmental organizations (NGOs), and sympathetic legislators. We'll also help you draft an ideal amendment to your constitution. For the Generations has transformed the daunting process of altering a state constitution into something achievable. Let's begin mobilizing for a Green Amendment in your state. You can make this happen. It just involves a little organizing on your part.

Generating the Groundswell

For those of you who haven't attempted grassroots organizing before, let me take you through some of the basics. To galvanize your community around a Green Amendment, start small. Simply organize a local meeting. Anyone can do that, right? Where you decide to hold this meeting is important, so please give it some thought. The ideal location might be your living room, a public library's meeting space, or a community space in a local coffee shop or church. Once you've decided on a meeting place, be sure to get the word out. Create an announcement that can be emailed, tacked onto community bulletin boards, and shared via social media. Make sure the announcement offers information about when, where, and what. For example:

In *Pennsylvania* the Right to Pure Water, Clean Air and a Healthy Environment Is Constitutionally Protected!

NOT IN OUR STATE. IT'S TIME TO CHANGE THAT.

Please Join us
April 22, 2017
6:30 p.m.
At the community room of the
Lorax Coffee Shop,
422 Truffula Tree Drive in Seusstown

to learn how we too can get constitutional protection
for our environmental rights.

To accompany your flyer, organize a Facebook event page that can be shared via other social media networks like Twitter and Instagram so that everyone—especially young people—gets the message. Consider creating a meme, with an image that captures something essential about the movement. This powerful message can be disseminated to thousands of people in a single tweet. You don't have to be the savviest social-media user or content creator. Do what you can to attract people, and after your first meeting you'll likely find others with skills in digital communication and messaging. But no matter how tech-savvy you are (or are not), never forget the more traditional, low-tech means of communication. There is nothing like taking the time to go door to door and invite neighbors personally, or printing up flyers that you can slip into doorways, place on car windshields, or post on community boards for people to peruse while waiting for their coffee or laundry.

At the meeting, you'll need an opening attraction to break the ice and spark enthusiasm. Perhaps you know a member of a local environmental organization who might be willing to speak about the state of environmental protection in your area. It is no problem, however, if you don't know a speaker. Look online for environmental organizations working in and around your town and ask if a representative would be willing to speak. If they ask for an honorarium (a fancy word for a donation), politely inform them that you are just getting started and don't have the resources to pay. Many organizations request honoraria to help defray the costs of travel, the time required to craft a talk specifically for your audience, and printing materials to hand out. Still, most will waive the honoraria for a good cause and a chance to connect with members of the community. As an environmental leader in my region, I am often asked to speak. And while my organization does request an honorarium from those who can pay it, my river and mission are far more important to me. A donation in support of a talk is appreciated, but I am quick to waive it if I can help a community launch a new campaign or embark on an important environmental cause. If your outreach takes you to an organization unwilling to speak without a donation, then thank them for their time and call another.

Live speakers are not the only attraction useful for kicking off a meeting. You might consider screening an environmental film highlighting a specific issue, ecosystem, or threat. Many films out there can energize people and provide the initial catalyst for community change. In 2010, filmmaker Josh Fox produced *Gasland*, an influential, Oscar-nominated documentary showcasing the effects of shale gas fracking on our aquifers, landscapes, and people. The image of local inhabitants setting their tap water on fire has moved many audiences, but even more important, the documentary has helped organize people against shale gas extraction and fracking. According to Iowa University professor Ion "Bodi" Vasi, who authored a study analyzing the film's impact, "Local screenings of *Gasland* contributed to anti-fracking mobilizations, which, in turn, affected the passage of local fracking moratoria."[388] If your community is affected by fracking, *Gasland* could be especially helpful in energizing your group.

Other films can spark awareness and action as well. Perhaps your town or community especially values local wildlife. In that case, you might screen *Sacred Cod*, which documents the precipitous decline of cod populations along the East Coast; *The Cove*, which depicts dolphin harpooning practices in Japan; or *A Plastic Ocean*, a documentary detailing the ravages of plastic pollution.[389] For those worried about climate change, Al Gore's *An Inconvenient Truth* (2006) made a huge impact, helping to elevate climate change from a partisan issue to a deeply held, scientific truism for a large segment of the population. There are also more recent films focused on climate change to pick from, such as Al Gore's *An Inconvenient Sequel* (2017). Select the one that strikes you as most compelling. As long as the message isn't that climate change is a hoax, your choice is likely to be great. Films like these have the virtue of bringing environmental harms alive, allowing people to visualize what might otherwise seem abstract or distant. These productions also frequently prompt outrage, alerting audiences to the failures of legislative environmental approaches to effect change and protect the environment. Follow your movie screening with a panel discussion to answer questions, provide action alerts, and translate indignation into positive and defined action.

In some cases, a movie screening may not be the best means of raising awareness in your local community. Maybe your town wants to focus on a specific environmental peril or concern facing the region—a development or industrial project, water quality concerns, or the expansion of fossil fuel infrastructure. Sometimes focusing on the big picture makes the prospect of action seem overwhelming and daunting. Oxford University economic and public policy scholar Eric Beinhocker believes that an emphasis on big topics like global trade, the automation of the world workforce, and international carbon emissions cause people to lose sight of an important fact: "Most of the progress on the issues they care about—environment, education, economic opportunity and work-force skills—has happened at the local level. Because that is where the trust lives."[390] Beinhocker advocates an approach to change called the new progressive localism, which proceeds from the same axiom that has long motivated environmentalists: think global, act local.

I can attest to the merits of a local approach. In my experience, people are much more open to learning about environmental issues when they become involved in a local action that concerns them directly. Who wants to learn about stormwater runoff for fun? But someone facing a new development project that will destroy a favorite woodland or wetland, or someone personally suffering from flooding every time it rains, has a much different perspective. Such a person is typically curious about all the scientific details and will help brainstorm environmentally protective solutions. Like Michele Baker, such an individual can transform into an accidental activist, doing whatever she can to champion and preserve the local environment.

If your community faces an environmental threat garnering attention in your town, all you need to do is arm yourself with information and invite folks to come over and discuss it. To get the facts you might attend town meetings in which the issue is discussed or visit your town's administration building or website to consult files about the case. (As a member of the public you have a right to public information and just need to learn the particular rules your state, town, or agency has governing access.) Or maybe you don't have time to do a lot of research but are still concerned. In that case, organize your meeting. Once you gather folks together to talk about the issue, you'll be amazed at how quickly the details come together. When using a local issue as your draw, just be sure, at some point in the discussion, to introduce the idea of a constitutional environmental right.

It's one thing to hold a meeting at your house and energize a group of people, but it's quite another to actually alter your constitution. While this journey will begin with meetings to get folks informed and engaged, the ultimate path you take toward a constitutional provision will be unique and dictated by the needs of your community. That's precisely why I created For the Generations. At ForTheGenerations.org you'll find a tool kit, brochure, and fact sheet to help guide your journey (and we'll add more materials as the movement grows). You can also join our Facebook page and partake in an active conversation about developments related to this issue nationwide. Let's work together, under the umbrella of For the Generations, to create awareness and build a national Green Amendment movement in the United States. And let's start with naming our efforts. When we organize a group of people in a state committed to this cause, let's name it For the Generations XX (with "XX" representing your state's initials). For instance, in New Jersey the effort might be named For the Generations NJ; in California, For the Generations CA; and so on.

Within our states, let's broadcast the fact that a healthy environment is an inherent, indefeasible right that needs to be recognized and protected at the constitutional level. Consider me a resource in this effort. Once you assemble at least fifty people with interest in the cause, please contact me at the Delaware Riverkeeper Network (ForTheGenerations@delawareriverkeeper .org). If it's possible for me to come speak to your group, I'll be happy to do so. Let's work together, using the For the Generations framework, to generate grassroots momentum for state-level Green Amendments, as well as the eventual passage of a federal amendment to the Constitution. Let's launch the Green Amendment movement together.

The Power of Constitutional Environmentalism

Creating a groundswell for environmental constitutionalism may not prove as hard as it seems. That's because we've reached a moment of environmental reckoning. As Pennsylvania Representative Franklin L. Kury said in 1970 when he was first advancing the language that ultimately became article 1, section 27, ". . . population and technology have run amok through our environment and natural resources. If we are to save our natural environment we must therefore give it the same Constitutional protection we give to our political environment."[391] This statement is as true today for our nation as it was in 1971 for Pennsylvania.

As detailed in chapter 2, we are engulfed in an environmental catastrophe. World leaders have recognized this fact and are working together, as they did at the 2015 United Nations Climate Change Conference in Paris. Although President Donald Trump announced the withdrawal of the United States from the agreement, other major powers promised drastic action to save the planet. And so, too, did states and local governments in the United States. For as local environmental harms have escalated, so have resistance efforts in the increasingly panicked and dispirited communities that are most affected. As environmental advocate Naomi Klein has observed, people of all walks of life and in all regions of the earth are increasingly joining grassroots networks, risking their lives and livelihoods to stop pollution in their communities. Klein terms this phenomenon Blockadia. "Blockadia," she notes, "is not a specific location on a map but rather a roving transnational conflict zone that is cropping up with increasing frequency and intensity wherever extractive projects are attempting to dig and drill, whether for open-pit mines, or gas fracking, or tar sands oil pipelines."[392] As Klein suggests, and as I have observed throughout the United States, people are dissatisfied with the despoliation of their rivers, aquifers, wild lands, air quality, and health. And they are refusing to remain silent. I believe that by harnessing the power of constitutional environmentalism, we can form a productive part of this larger grassroots movement. Indeed, we stand to become the most successful part, stemming the environmental crisis currently under way and safeguarding our planet for future generations.

To achieve its goals, the Green Amendment movement must draw support from many quarters. Environmental leaders, for example, are pivotal. My colleagues and I at the Delaware Riverkeeper Network join many organizations across the country, exercising environmental leadership in a professional capacity. But sometimes leaders aren't born, they're made. Throughout this book, we've witnessed how environmental catastrophes have inspired newcomers to assume the mantle of leadership. Farmer and artist Asha Canalos helped lead her community after it was faced with a devastating compressor station. Kate Stauffer, Trisha Sheehan, Michele Baker, and other moms at the New York Water Project went from being full-time parents to being accidental activists following water contamination in their communities. Inspired by the threat of fracking and other environmental concerns, Jill Wiener joined with her community to form Catskill Citizens for Safe Energy.

Such leaders can help galvanize millions of diverse individuals behind the Green Amendment movement. We need insurance underwriters like Michael Hickey, who refused to accept his father's premature death as an accident and who tested Hoosick Falls's municipal water supplies at his own expense. We need people like Rob Bilott, who courageously risked his livelihood and reputation to take on the DuPont corporation and expose the dangers of PFOA to the world. Once PFOA was exposed in New Jersey and Hoosick Falls, we needed individuals working behind the scenes to help spread awareness, disseminate flyers, organize events, make infographics exposing environmental harms, and write letters to the editor. Such logistical behind-the-scenes work is critical for environmental victory. Whether whistle-blower or workaday, everyone is vital.

This movement will also depend on the experience and resources of nonprofit organizations and the skill and expertise of lawyers and lawmakers. As we've observed throughout this book, it takes a well-funded organization to take on the shale fracking, pipeline, and mining industries. The Delaware Riverkeeper Network took the lead against shale fracking in Pennsylvania and the Delaware River watershed, while the Montana Environmental Information Center (MEIC) did the same to defeat the Seven-Up Pete mining venture in Montana (see chapter 2). Environmental organizations like ours in turn must mobilize the knowledge and ingenuity of legal experts. We need pipeline experts like Aaron Stemplewicz to take on agencies like FERC, lawyers like Jordan Yeager who spearheaded the ingenious and well-executed legal strategies that defeated Act 13, and public servants like Brian Coppola and Dave Ball, who helped rally governmental support against fracking.

Artists, too, will play an important role in the Green Amendment movement, just as they increasingly do in the environmental movement generally. Artists possess an incredible talent for capturing and communicating the essence of an environmental message in a painting, performance, poem, or song. Kim Fraczek, the director of the Sane Energy Project, uses art to help generate awareness about the perils of shale gas extraction (including fracking and pipeline infrastructure) and to spark enthusiasm for renewable energies. Prior to an environmental rally or public hearing over a compressor station or power plant, Kim routinely facilitates art projects during which people paint banners, build models of clean-energy windmills, or practice the march songs that will lead an effort to come. Such activities build camaraderie, generate positive energy, and develop relationships necessary to sustain the advocacy effort.[393] This kind of environmental messaging can be used as well to inspire a call for constitutional protection of our environmental rights. Social media, flyers, fact sheets, and meetings are important for organizing and communicating our message. Engaging artists creates exciting new pathways of communication that can energize people and galvanize them to participate.

I distinctly recall sensing the power of art during an environmental hearing that the Delaware River Basin Commission (DRBC) held over fracking. Expert after expert delivered three-minute speeches at the podium about the importance of protecting clean water and instituting a fracking ban. These people were armed with powerful facts, figures, and citations from scientific journals, and they even delivered gripping personal stories of how a fracking operation or pipeline cut through their property and personally harmed them. All of this data was vitally important, but you could see the DRBC commissioners in the front of the room biding their time, completely unengaged. But then a young woman approached the microphone and, in a nervous and shaky voice, began to sing. She sang about the earth, about the beauty of the environment, about the important role the environment plays in all our lives, and about how important it is to protect the environment from fracking. Everyone was enthralled, and after she finished, the auditorium fell into a stunned silence. Such is the power of art.

Because this movement of advancing and securing constitutional recognition and protection for our environmental rights must be generational, our children and youth will play instrumental roles. Children are already becoming advocates and leaders, speaking out against Hoosick Falls's water contamination and advocating environmental protection in New York State's constitution. The children active in those struggles aren't alone. As of this book's writing, twenty-one youth across the country have partnered with a nonprofit organization called Our Children's Trust, suing the President of the United States for his role in climate destabilization. Just as with our battle against Act 13, these children are using the Constitution, claiming their indefeasible rights to a clean and healthy environment, based on the public trust doctrine.

A legal principle dating back to Roman antiquity, the public trust doctrine suggests that some natural resources are so critical for a nation's survival and well-being that the government must protect them from impairment, for the sake of both present and future generations. In this country, federal public trust litigation began in the late nineteenth century, when the court declared that a railroad company couldn't purchase a swath of Lake Michigan for its commercial uses (that shoreline and the water were deemed part of the public trust).[394] With the assistance of Our Children's Trust, these bold and determined youth are expanding the public trust doctrine to encompass the atmosphere. Such a concept nicely dovetails with constitutional environmentalism, as it uses the courts and relies on every person's right (stated or not) to a clean and healthy environment.

A few years ago, my then–fifteen-year-old daughter Anneke, a budding environmental leader, struck a similar chord as these youth, speaking about the burdens her generation will bear due to the environmental catastrophe engulfing this world. In July 2012, the Delaware Riverkeeper Network joined other organizations for a rally and lobbying effort on Capitol Hill. We had come to meet with legislators and inform them about fracking's harms. A dozen or so teams of five or six people fanned out, each morning of the two-day effort, to meet with legislators and their staff. We discussed fracking and its impacts on communities and the environment, and we asked our elected representatives to take legislative action to rein in the devastating industry. During one such meeting, when it was her turn to speak, Anneke said simply, directly, and eloquently:

> My generation is the one that will suffer the consequences of the decisions you are making today. We are going to have to clean up the mess you are creating for us all. We are going to have to suffer the devastating environmental harm. We are the ones that are going to miss out on the benefits and beauty of healthy nature. So I am here to ask you to change, and to make decisions that protect our earth for the benefit of us all.

Anneke's statement speaks to the fundamental injustice facing contemporary youth. They've done the least to contribute to the environmental harms now under way, but they will pay the highest price as inheritors of despoiled lands, toxic water supplies, and a destabilized climate system. That's why young adults like Anneke, teens like Mikayla, and young children like

Ashlynn are taking part in grassroots environmental movements, partnering with nonprofit organizations, and taking their struggles to the courts. They will play an indispensable role in the Green Amendment movement.

Ultimately, we must mobilize *everyone* behind the movement. We need talented advocates like Tracy Carluccio, Karen Feridun, and Wes Gillingham; budding advocates like Anneke, Wim, and Bridget Brady now working with me at Delaware Riverkeeper Network to become the next generation of environmental leaders; social media–savvy experts like Tim White; environmental leaders like Peter Iwanowicz and David Pringle willing to walk the legislative halls; generous benefactors and organizations like the Woodtiger Fund, which financed our legal battle against Act 13 without reservation; inspirational and well-spoken attorneys like Jordan Yeager, Jerry Williams, Bradley Campbell, and Aaron Stemplewicz; distinguished and environmentally conscious scientists like Tony Ingraffea and Bob Howarth; talented videographers like Ed Rodgers; accidental activists like Kate and Larry Stauffer, Michele Baker, and David Worst; artists like Kim Fraczek; and equally important, colleagues who are willing to stay behind to pay the bills and assure that advocacy organizations like ours are running smoothly (Delaware Riverkeeper Network's Claire Biehl does this supremely well).

And we also need you. Perhaps you are inspired by this book and want to enlist your state in the Green Amendment movement. You can rally others to the cause. As this book has demonstrated, whether a person's ultimate concern is the environment, jobs, education, the economy, family values, recreation, property rights, health, or public safety, it matters little—a clean environment is in everyone's interest. A constitutional obligation to a healthy environment will best ensure that everyone's particular interest will prevail.

When I'm not advocating on behalf of the river or helping a community mobilize, I go with my family to our special New York forest. I try to take these trips as often as I can, and I know that Dave, Wim, and Anneke enjoy them, too. We walk amidst the trees, kayak the nearby Delaware River, and sit and enjoy the peace and silence. At our New York home, just as with our house in Radnor, we have invested in solar panels and geothermal technology to provide ourselves with clean energy. In both homes, we use well water for drinking, and our wastewater seeps back into the soil through a septic system, where it can be cleansed and used to recharge nature. Both homes feature natural landscapes filled with native trees, shrubs, and flowering plants. We work hard to do our part to restore and protect nature, while also enjoying its many bounties. But as much as we love to immerse ourselves in these natural places, I feel the constant threat of intrusion from development, industry, and pollution. I know that our rights to a healthy environment are not well protected. It is time to change that. We *must* change that—for our own sake, and to protect the generations still to come.

Let's get organized and rise up in our states. Let's make everyone aware that each person on this earth has the inalienable and indefeasible right to a clean and healthy environment. Let's secure Green Amendments for ourselves, our children, and future generations. The time for action is *now*.

ABOUT THE AUTHOR

Maya K. van Rossum is a veteran environmentalist who joined the Delaware Riverkeeper Network in 1994 as executive director and since 1996 has served as the Delaware Riverkeeper, championing the rights of over 17 million people to a free-flowing, clean, and healthy Delaware River and its tributary streams.

In 2013, van Rossum was one of the original petitioners in the landmark *Robinson Township v. Commonwealth of Pennsylvania* case. That case led to a watershed legal victory that strengthened the state's Environmental Rights Amendment, protecting people's right to pure water, clean air, and a healthy environment.

She is a licensed attorney in three states: Pennsylvania, New Jersey, and the District of Columbia. Since 2002, she has served as an adjunct professor and director of the Environmental Law Clinic at Temple's Beasley School of Law, which she founded.

van Rossum grew up in the Delaware River watershed and lives there today with her family.

MayavanRossum.green | delawareriverkeeper.org

NOTES

Introduction: We Need a Green Amendment

1   Christopher Bateman, "A Colossal Fracking Mess," *Vanity Fair*, June 2010, http://www.vanityfair.com/news/2010/06/fracking-in-pennsylvania-201006.

2   If a ban is not pursued correctly or successfully, moreover, municipalities are at risk. As a result, the ability of a Pennsylvania town to ban still hangs in the balance with communities seeking other options until their right to enact a ban is legally vetted and decided. (Jordan Yaeger, communication with author, June 20, 2017).

Chapter 1: Living in the Sacrifice Zone

3   "Harris J R EI," *USA Today* (Special Report: The Smokestack Effect), http://content.usatoday.com/news/nation/environment/smokestack/school/86422; Lynne Peeples, "Keystone XL Risks Harm to Houston Community: 'This Is Obviously Environmental Racism,'" *Huffington Post*, updated May 1, 2013, http://www.huffingtonpost.com/2013/03/27/keystone-xl-pipeline-houston-air-pollution_n_2964853.html.

4   Javier Sierra, "A Toxic Bone," Sierra Club, http://vault.sierraclub.org/ecocentro/ingles/bone.asp.

5   Sierra, ibid

6   Sierra, ibid

7   For example, Roy Scranton, assistant professor of English at the University of Notre Dame and author of the environmental bestseller *Learning to Die in the Anthropocene* (2015) calls Manchester "one of the most polluted neighborhoods in the United States" ("When the Next Hurricane Hits Texas," *New York Times*, October 7, 2016, http://www.nytimes.com/2016/10/09/opinion/sunday/when-the-hurricane-hits-texas.html?_r=0).

8   According to a University of Texas School of Public Health study that widely shocked the country. See the summary "Disease Clusters in Texas," National Disease Clusters Alliance/National Resource Defense Council, March 2011,

https://www.nrdc.org/sites/default/files/texas_diseaseclusters.pdf; Cindy Horswell, "Study: Children Living Near Houston Ship Channel Have Greater Cancer Risk," *Houston Chronicle*, January 18, 2007, http://www.chron.com/news/houston-texas/article/Study-Children-living-near-Houston-Ship-Channel-1544789.php; and the study's executive summary, "Preliminary Epidemiologic Investigation of the Relationship Between the Presence of Ambient Hazardous Air Pollutants (HAPs) and Cancer Incidence in Harris County," City of Houston official website, Health and Human Services, http://www.houstontx.gov/health/UT-executive.html.

9   Dave Mann, "Separate but Toxic," *Texas Observer*, March 23, 2007, https://www.texasobserver.org/2451-separate-but-toxic-the-houston-environmental-magnet-school-thats-an-environmental-catastrophe/.

10   Mann, ibid See also Eric Kayne, "Fighting for Clean Air in the Shadow of Oil Refineries," Earth Justice, http://earthjustice.org/slideshow/fighting-for-clean-air-in-the-shadow-of-oil-refineries. Resident Yudith Nieto, for example, developed stomach pains after eating contaminated fruit.

11   Dianna Wray, "Benzene Leaks from Pipelines Have Been Quietly Adding to the Ship Channel Toxic Mix," *Houston Press*, May 10, 2016, http://www.houstonpress.com/news/benzene-leaks-from-pipelines-have-been-quietly-adding-to-the-ship-channel-toxic-mix-8389333.

12   Jessica Roake, "Think Globally, Act Locally: Steve Lerner, 'Sacrifice Zones,' at Politics and Prose," *Washington Post*, September 22, 2010, https://www.washingtonpost.com/express/wp/2010/09/23/steve-lerner-book-sacrifice-zones/.

13   Dave Pruett, "We're All in the Sacrifice Zone Now," *Huffington Post*, May 3, 2016, http://www.huffingtonpost.com/dave-pruett/were-all-in-the-sacrifice-zone-now_b_9823482.html.

14   "Deepwater Horizon–BP Gulf of Mexico Oil Spill," epa.gov, https://www.epa.gov/enforcement/deepwater-horizon-bp-gulf-mexico-oil-spill.

15   Merlin Hearn, "Water Benefits Health: 20 Water Pollution Facts for the US and throughout the World," waterbenefitshealth.com, http://www.waterbenefitshealth.com/water-pollution-facts.html.

16   Jonathan Kaiman, "China Says More Than Half of Its Groundwater Is Polluted," *Guardian*, April 23, 2014, https://www.theguardian.com/environment/2014/apr/23/china-half-groundwater-polluted.

17   Up to half of Bangladesh's 150 million people have been exposed through drinking water to arsenic, which, even at very low levels, is linked with cancer, organ diseases, and other ailments. Margie Mason, "Arsenic Water Killing 1 in 5 in Bangladesh," NBC News, June 27, 2010, http://www.nbcnews.com/id/37958050/ns/health-health_care/t/arsenic-water-killing-bangladesh/#.WUfZGmjyvIU.

18   "International Decade for Action 'Water for Life' 2005–2015," United Nations Department of Economic and Social Affairs (UNDESA), http://www.un.org/waterforlifedecade/scarcity.shtml.

19   Hearn, "Water Benefits Health."

20   David Andrews and Bill Walker, "'Erin Brockovich' Carcinogen in Tap Water of
      More Than 200 million Americans," September 20, 2016, http://www.ewg.org/
      research/chromium-six-found-in-us-tap-water.

21   Merrit Kennedy, "300 Million Children Are Breathing 'Extremely Toxic,' Air,
      UNICEF Says," National Public Radio, October 31, 2016, http://www.npr.
      org/sections/thetwo-way/2016/10/31/500048135/300-million-children-are-
      breathing-extremely-toxic-air-unicef-says.

22   Kennedy, "300 Million Children."

23   "State of the Air 2016," American Lung Association, http://www.lung.org/
      assets/documents/healthy-air/state-of-the-air/sota-2016-full.pdf.

24   Jie Jenny Zou, "State Cutbacks, Recalcitrance Hinder Clean Air Act
      Enforcement," Center for Public Integrity, updated October 11, 2016, https://
      www.publicintegrity.org/2016/10/11/20303/state-cutbacks-recalcitrance-hinder-
      clean-air-act-enforcement.

25   Emily Underwood, "The Polluted Brain," *Science* magazine, January 26, 2017,
      http://www.sciencemag.org/news/2017/01/brain-pollution-evidence-builds-
      dirty-air-causes-alzheimer-s-dementia.

26   World Health Organization's International Agency for Research on Cancer,
      "IARC: Outdoor air pollution a leading environmental cause of cancer deaths,"
      press release number 221, October 17, 2013, https://www.iarc.fr/en/media-
      centre/iarcnews/pdf/pr221_E.pdf.

27   "Air pollution 'kills 7 million people a year,'" *Guardian*, March 25, 2016, https://
      www.theguardian.com/environment/2014/mar/25/air-pollution-kills-7m-
      people-a-year. _

28   "International Decade for Action 'Water for Life 2005–2015," United Nations
      Department of Economic and Social Affairs (UNDESA), http://www.un.org/
      waterforlifedecade/quality.shtml.

29   Underwood, "The Polluted Brain."

30   "U of T researchers part of study linking dementia to living near major traffic,"
      University of Toronto News, January 6, 2017, https://www.utoronto.ca/news/u-t-
      researchers-part-study-linking-dementia-living-near-major-traffic.

31   Underwood, "The Polluted Brain."

32   "Toxic Substances Portal, Arsenic," Agency for Toxic Substances &
      Disease Registry, August 2007, http://www.atsdr.cdc.gov/toxfaqs/
      tf.asp?id=19&tid=3#bookmark06.

33   "Lead," Columbia Center for Children's Environmental Health, http://ccceh.
      org/our-research/research-studies/lead.

34   "Mercury Emissions," United States Environmental Protection Agency,
      https://cfpub.epa.gov/roe/indicator.cfm?i=14; "Mercury and health," World
      Health Organization, updated March 2017, http://www.who.int/mediacentre/
      factsheets/fs361/en/.

35   Alycia Halladay, PhD, "Pesticide Exposure and Risk of Autism," Autism Speaks,

https://www.autismspeaks.org/blog/2012/07/27/pesticide-exposure-and-risk-autism.

36   Halladay, ibid

37   "Key Findings: Trends in the Prevalence of Developmental Disabilities in U.S. Children, 1997–2008," Centers for Disease Control and Prevention, https://www.cdc.gov/ncbddd/developmentaldisabilities/features/birthdefects-dd-keyfindings.html.

38   Currently, the Centers for Disease Control and Prevention suggests 1 in every 68 American children have autism, with many more boys than girls diagnosed. The reasons for the increase are, of course, complex. "Autism Spectrum Disorder: Data & Statistics," Centers for Disease Control and Prevention, http://www.cdc.gov/ncbddd/autism/data.html; Jessica Wright, "The Real Reasons Autism Rates Are Up in the U.S.," *Scientific American*, March 3, 2017, https://www.scientificamerican.com/article/the-real-reasons-autism-rates-are-up-in-the-u-s/.

39   "Attention-Deficit/Hyperactivity Disorder (ADHD): Data & Statistics," Centers for Disease Control and Prevention, http://www.cdc.gov/ncbddd/adhd/data.html; Lisa Rapaport, "More than one in 10 U.S. kids have ADHD as diagnosis rates surge," Reuters, December 8, 2015, http://www.reuters.com/article/us-health-adhd-diagnosis-surge-idUSKBN0TR2SJ20151208.

40   This number is constantly in flux. "America's Children and the Environment (ACE): Key Findings of the ACE3 Report," United States Environmental Protection Agency, https://www.epa.gov/ace/key-findings-ace3-report.

41   "Deeper Understanding of Link between Chemical Pollutants and Autism," Autism Speaks, https://www.autismspeaks.org/science/science-news/top-ten-lists/2012/deeper-understanding-link-chemical-pollutants-and-autism.

42   "About ADHD," CHADD, The National Resource on ADHD, http://www.chadd.org/Understanding-ADHD/About-ADHD.aspx.

43   Molini M. Patel and Rachel L. Miller, "Air pollution and childhood asthma: recent advances and future directions," National Institutes of Health, https://www.ncbi.nlm.nih.gov/pmc/articles/PMC2740858/pdf/nihms121748.pdf.

44   "Cancer Statistics," National Cancer Institute, https://www.cancer.gov/about-cancer/understanding/statistics.

45   "Health: Childhood Cancer," United States Environmental Protection Agency, "America's Children and the Environment (Third Edition)," https://www.epa.gov/sites/production/files/2015-06/documents/health-childhood-cancer.pdf: p. 229.

46   Lisa W. Foderaro, "Group Petitions to Save a Prehistoric Fish from Modern Construction," *New York Times*, July 21, 2015, http://www.nytimes.com/2015/07/22/nyregion/group-petitions-to-save-a-prehistoric-fish-from-modern-construction.html?_r=0.

47   Dewayne Fox (associate professor at Delaware State University), conversation with author, June 29, 2017.

48   For a scientific explanation for this behavior see K. J. Sulak, R. E. Edwards, G.

W. Hill, and M. T. Randall, "Why Do Sturgeons Jump? Insights from Acoustic Investigations of the Gulf Sturgeon in the Suwannee River, Florida, USA," *Applied Ichthyology* 18 (2002): pp. 617-620.

49   Daniel Kelly, "Universities Team Up to Track Atlantic Sturgeon and Prevent Accidental Bycatch," *Environmental Monitor*, May 22, 2013, http://www. fondriest.com/news/track-atlantic-sturgeon-and-prevent-accidental-bycatch. htm.

50   "NOAA lists five Atlantic sturgeon populations under Endangered Species Act," National Oceanic and Atmospheric Administration Fisheries, January 31, 2012, http://www.nmfs.noaa.gov/stories/2012/01/31_atlantic_sturgeon.html.

51   Atlantic sturgeon were nearly the exclusive source of caviar in the Delaware. John Nathan Cobb, *The Sturgeon Fishery of Delaware River and Bay* (Washington: Government Printing Office, 1900); John A. Ryder, *The Sturgeons and Sturgeon Industries of the Eastern Coast of the United States with an Account of Experiments Bearing upon Sturgeon Culture* (Washington: Government Printing Office, 1890).

52   Juliet Eilperin, "Atlantic Sturgeon Listed as Endangered Species," *Washington Post*, February 1, 2012, https://www.washingtonpost.com/national/health-science/atlantic-sturgeon-listed-as-endangered-species/2012/02/01/ gIQARbAmiQ_story.html.

53   Erik Silldorff (aquatic ecologist), conversation with author, May 2, 2017.

54   Ted Williams, "Atlantic Sturgeon: An Ancient Fish Struggles against the Flow," February 12, 2015, http://e360.yale.edu/features/atlantic_sturgeon_an_ancient_ fish_struggles_against_the_flow.

55   Williams, ibid When it comes to nuclear energy, I agree with Naomi Klein's assessment: "About 12 percent of the world's power is currently supplied by nuclear energy, much of it coming from reactors that are old and obsolete." Governments, she suggests, should impose moratoria on existing construction, retire unsafe facilities, and phase them out as renewable energies improve. *This Changes Everything: Capitalism vs. The Climate* (New York: Simon & Shuster, 2014), pp. 137-138.

56   Silldorff, conversation with author, May 2, 2017.

57   Foderaro, "Group Petitions to Save a Prehistoric Fish."

58   Foderaro, ibid

59   "NOAA lists five Atlantic sturgeon populations"; J. J. Brown and G. W. Murphy, "Atlantic Sturgeon Vessel-Strike Mortalities in the Delaware Estuary," *Fisheries* 35 (2010): 72–83.

60   International Union for Conservation of Nature, "Sturgeon More Critically Endangered Than Any Other Group of Species," March 18, 2010, https://www. iucn.org/content/sturgeon-more-critically-endangered-any-other-group-species.

61   Dewayne Fox (associate professor at Delaware State University), communication with author, June 30, 2017.

62   "Forest Habitat Overview," World Wildlife Fund, https://www.worldwildlife.
     org/habitats/forest-habitat.

63   "Deforestation," *National Geographic*, http://www.nationalgeographic.com/
     environment/global-warming/deforestation/.

64   "Land Cover," United States Environmental Protection Agency, https://cfpub.
     epa.gov/roe/indicator.cfm?i=49#3 (see exhibit 3).

65   "Deforestation," *National Geographic*; Emily Adams, "Eco-Economy Indicators:
     Forest Cover," Earth Policy Institute, August 31, 2012, http://www.earth-policy.
     org/indicators/C56/forests_2012.

66   "Forest Habitat Overview," World Wildlife Fund.

67   Craig Cox, "Going, Going, Gone!" Environmental Working Group, July 23,
     2013, http://www.ewg.org/research/going-going-gone.

68   "Land Cover," United States Environmental Protection Agency, https://cfpub.
     epa.gov/roe/indicator.cfm?i=49#3 (see exhibit 2).

69   "What Are Wetland Functions?" United States Environmental Protection
     Agency, https://www.epa.gov/wetlands/what-are-wetland-functions.

70   "Living Planet Report 2016: Risk and resilience in a new era," World
     Wildlife Federation, http://www.wwf.org.uk/sites/default/files/2016-10/
     LPR_2016_full%20report_spread%20low%20res.pdf?_ga=1.23797562.1875
     175102.1477576193; Joshua Keating, "The Earth Has Lost More than Half
     Its Animals Since 1970," *Slate*, October 27, 2016, http://www.slate.com/blogs/
     the_slatest/2016/10/27/the_earth_has_lost_more_than_half_its_animals_
     since_1970.html.

71   Rob Jordan, "Stanford Researcher Declares That the Sixth Mass Extinction Is
     Here," *Stanford News*, June 19, 2015, http://news.stanford.edu/2015/06/19/
     mass-extinction-ehrlich-061915/.

72   The idea was popularized by Scranton's *Learning to Die in the Anthropocene*.

73   Jordan, "Stanford Researcher Declares That the Sixth Mass Extinction."

74   For background on this story, I rely on Janine Bauer (Tri-State Transportation
     Campaign), personal communication with author, June 11, 2017.

75   "Trucking," New Jersey Department of Transportation, http://www.state.nj.us/
     transportation/freight/trucking/faq.shtm.

76   "Urbanization," United Nations Population Fund, http://www.unfpa.org/
     urbanization.

77   "Burden of disease from environmental noise: quantification of healthy life
     years lost in Europe," World Health Organization, 2011, http://www.who.int/
     quantifying_ehimpacts/publications/e94888.pdf?ua=1; Ron Chepesiuk, "Missing
     the Dark: Health Effects of Light Pollution," *Environmental Health Perspectives*
     117 (January 2009).

78   A. Huss, A. Spoerri, M. Egger, and M. Röösli, "Aircraft Noise, Air Pollution, and
     Mortality from Myocardial Infarction," *Epidemiology* 21 (2010): pp. 829-36.

79   "Sleep and Disease Risk," Division of Sleep Medicine at Harvard Medical
      School, http://healthysleep.med.harvard.edu/healthy/matters/consequences/
      sleep-and-disease-risk.

80   Richard Louv interview, National Public Radio.

81   Richard Louv, ibid

82   John Abraham, "Global warming continues; 2016 will be the hottest year
      ever recorded," *Guardian*, October 21, 2016, https://www.theguardian.com/
      environment/climate-consensus-97-per-cent/2016/oct/21/global-warming-
      continues-2016-will-be-the-hottest-year-ever-recorded.

83   Naomi Klein, *This Changes Everything*, p. 1.

84   George Monbiot, "If children lose contact with nature they won't fight
      for it," *Guardian*, November 19, 2012, https://www.theguardian.com/
      commentisfree/2012/nov/19/children-lose-contact-with-nature.

85   Monbiot, ibid

86   Monbiot, ibid

87   For reference to this literature, see Richard Louv's *Last Child in the Woods* (New
      York: Workman Publishing Group 2005).

88   Monbiot, "If children lose contact with nature."

89   Susan Carroll, "Texas High Court Rejects City Air Pollution Rules,"
      Houston Chronicle, April 29, 2016, http://www.houstonchronicle.com/news/
      houston-texas/houston/article/Texas-high-court-rejects-city-air-pollution-
      rules-7384795.php.

90   Juan A. Lozano, "Texas Court Blocks Houston From Using Tougher Clean-
      Air Laws," *Associated Press*, April 30, 2016, http://bigstory.ap.org/article/
      b6caf6fe274045a68cb74b0962d7e84a/texas-court-blocks-houston-using-
      tougher-clean-air-laws.

91   Lozano, ibid

Chapter 2: The Right to a Healthy Environment

92   David James Duncan, "The War for Norman's River," *Sierra Magazine*, May/June
      1998, https://vault.sierraclub.org/sierra/199805/blackfoot.asp.

93   Duncan, ibid

94   David James Duncan, *My Story as Told by Water: Confessions, Druidic Rants,
      Reflections, Bird-Watchings, Fish-Stalkings, Visions, Songs and Prayers Refracting
      Light, from Living Rivers, in the Age of the Industrial Dark* (San Francisco: Sierra
      Club Books, 2001), p. 137.

95   Duncan, ibid, pp. 137-138.

96   Duncan, "The War for Norman's River"; Duncan, *My Story as Told by Water*, 138.

97   Duncan, ibid, p. 138.

98   Duncan, ibid, p. 139.

99   Duncan, "The War for Norman's River,"

100 Duncan, *My Story as Told by Water*, pp. 145–147.

101 Duncan, ibid, pp. 145–146.

102 Montana Environmental Information Center, "Montana's Right to a Clean & Healthful Environment," http://meic.org/issues/constitution-of-montana-and-mepa/clean-healthful-environment/.

103 Montana Environmental Information Center, ibid

104 "America's Sewage System and the Price of Optimism," *Time* magazine, August 1, 1969, http://content.time.com/time/magazine/article/0,9171,901182,00.html.

105 Barton H. Thompson Jr. "Constitutionalizing the Environment: The History and Future of Montana's Environmental Provisions," *Montana Law Review* 64 (2003): p. 160.

106 Thompson, ibid, pp. 157–158.

107 See, e.g., S. Morgaine McKibbena et al., "Climatic Regulation of the Neurotoxin Domoic Acid," *Proceedings of the National Academy of Sciences of the United States of America* 114 (2016): pp. 239–244.

108 Jack R. Tuholske, "U.S. State Constitutions and Environmental Protection: Diamonds in the Rough," *Widener Law Review* 21 (2015): pp. 240–245.

109 *City of Elgin v. County of Cook*, 660 NE 2d 875 - Ill (PA Supreme Court 1995).

110 *Commonwealth v. Nat'l Gettysburg Battlefield Tower*, 454 Pa. 193; 311 A.2d 588 (PA Supreme Court, Oct 3, 1973).

111 *Commonwealth v. Nat'l Gettysburg Battlefield Tower*, ibid

112 *Commonwealth v. Nat'l Gettysburg Battlefield Tower*, ibid

113 Thompson, "Constitutionalizing the Environment," pp. 171-172. See also, *Cape-France Enterprises v. Estate of Peed*.

114 Thompson, "Constitutionalizing the Environment," p. 172.

115 David R. Boyd, *The Environmental Rights Revolution* (Vancouver: University of British Columbia Press, 2012), p. 68.

116 According to Portugal's Article 52 (Right to petition and right to popular action), "Everyone shall be granted the right of *actio popularis*, to include the right to apply for the appropriate compensation for an aggrieved party or parties, in such cases and under such terms as the law may determine, either personally or via associations that purport to defend the interests in question. The said right shall particularly be exercised to: a) Promote the prevention, cessation, or judicial prosecution of offenses against public health, consumer rights, the quality of life or the preservation of the environment and the cultural heritage" (Boyd, *Environmental Rights Revolution*, p. 71).

117 Boyd, *Environmental Rights Revolution*, p. 70.

118 James R. May and Erin Daly, *Global Environmental Constitutionalism* (New York: Cambridge University Press, 2015), p. 102.

119 This was true as of August 1, 2011 (Boyd, *The Environmental Rights Revolution*, pp. 47, 76). There are geographical trends noticeable across the globe. Nearly all countries in Africa, Latin America, and Europe contain these provisions, while

nations in North America, the Caribbean, and Oceania lag behind. Indeed, it is the Western, English–speaking powerhouses—the United States, Canada, the United Kingdom, and Australia—that conspicuously lack federal environmental provisions. This discrepancy seems largely due to a peculiarity in global legal traditions. Most countries in the globe adhere to either common or civil law systems. Common law, which arose in medieval England and spread throughout the British Empire, is premised on legal precedent established through the courts. Civil law countries, by contrast, are more focused on describing and preserving law through meticulous legal codes. While a large majority of the globe's civil law countries readily enshrined environmental protections in their constitutions, common law countries remain hesitant to do so. While common law countries tend to grant sweeping political and civil rights, other cultural freedoms remain outside the traditional ambit of constitutional protection (Boyd, *The Environmental Rights Revolution*, p. 92).

120   Boyd, *Environmental Rights Revolution*, 76. Compare the right to health stipulated in seventy-four constitutions and the right to food in twenty-one constitutions.

121   May and Daly, *Global Environmental Constitutionalism*, p. 110.

122   May and Daly, ibid, pp. 110–111.

123   May and Daly, ibid, pp. 13, 116–117; Boyd, *Environmental Rights Revolution*, 129–130, 136, 167–168, 177, 179, 196, 218.

124   Mark Buckley and Austin Rempel, "Economic Benefits of Installing a Closed-Cycle Cooling System at Salem Nuclear Generating Station," *ECONorthwest*, September 2015, http://www.delawareriverkeeper.org/sites/default/files/DRN%20Expert%20EcoNW%20Final%20Report%20re%20Salem%20NGS%2009%2017%2015.pdf.

125   Jordan Yeager (environmental attorney), interview with author, October 4, 2016.

126   Mike Goens, "Other States Show How, and How Not, to Reform Constitution," *New York Times Regional Newspapers*, November 19, 2001, http://www.constitutionalreform.org/archive/news/reformnews_flor111801.html.

127   Jordan Yeager (environmental attorney), interview with author, October 4, 2016.

Chapter 3: Fracking Away Our Future

128   "Terry Greenwood: Pennsylvania Farmer; Location: Daisytown, Washington County, PA," *ShaleField Stories: A Project of Friends of the Harmed*, http://www.shalefieldstories.org/terry-greenwood.html.

129   Briget Shields (founder of Friends of the Harmed), interview with author, January 18, 2017.

130   Greenwood concluded, "When the gas company put the fence up, and the horse got hurt, got all tangled up, it was because they didn't put ribbons on it [the fence] . . . They hooked their temporary fence into the electric fence and the horse had skin taken off his legs, it hurt him, it scared him. I had to have the vet come right out . . . The horse is ok now but it took a while. The gas company

doesn't care what they do, they don't have respect." Iris Marie Bloom, "Gas drilling impacts: PA farmer Terry Greenwood's cows gave birth to zero calves this year, after ten dead calves in 2008," Protecting Our Waters, November 4, 2011, https://protectingourwaters.wordpress.com/2011/11/04/gas-drilling-impacts-pa-farmer-terry-greenwoods-cows-gave-birth-to-zero-calves-this-year-after-ten-dead-calves-in-2008/; "Terry Greenwood: Pennsylvania Farmer."

131   "Terry Greenwood: Pennsylvania Farmer."

132   Kirsi Jansa, "A Cattle Farmer," Gas Rush Stories Documentary, https://vimeo.com/74660630.

133   Bloom, "Gas Drilling Impacts."

134   Bloom, ibid

135   Jansa, "A Cattle Farmer."

136   Jansa, ibid

137   Their remarks had no impact on Pennsylvania's DEP, whose very mission statement is "to protect Pennsylvania's air, land, and water from pollution and to provide for the health and safety of its citizens through a cleaner environment": "Mission Statement," Pennsylvania's Department of Environmental Protection, http://www.dep.pa.gov/About/Pages/default.aspx.

138   Bloom, "Gas Drilling Impacts."

139   "Marcellus Shale Gas Fracking Destroys Farm Family's Water," video filmed in Daisytown, Pennsylvania, October 2009, https://youtu.be/DI_81WwSLbM.

140   Bloom, "Gas Drilling Impacts."

141   Jansa, "A Cattle Farmer"; "Terry Greenwood: Pennsylvania Farmer."

142   Bloom, "Gas Drilling Impacts."

143   The first instance of multi-stage slickwater fracturing of horizontal wells was in 2002, and the first time this occurred in the Marcellus Shale was 2003. The technologies making this possible, however, were "perfected" in the late 1990s. Dr. Anthony Ingraffea elaborates on this timeline and other features of slickwater hydraulic fracturing in his Scott Cannnon Lecture, "The Facts of Fracking," delivered March 23, 2011, and published on YouTube on June 15, 2011, https://www.youtube.com/watch?v=mSWmXpEkEPg&t=3372s. See 21.29 ff. for this timeline.

144   For a schematic overview of the process, see "Fracking: Is Exploration a Danger to Earth or Much-Needed Boost to Energy?" CNN, updated August 16, 2013, http://www.cnn.com/2013/08/16/business/fracking-shale-gas-process-infographic/index.html.

145   Steven Habicht, Lars Hanson, and Paul Faeth, "The Potential Environmental Impact from Fracking in the Delaware River Basin," CNA Analysis & Solutions, August 2015, iv, https://www.cna.org/CNA_files/PDF/IRM-2015-U-011300-Final.pdf.

146   Jake Hays, Seth B. C. Shonkoff, "Toward an Understanding of the Environmental and Public Health Impacts of Unconventional Natural Gas

Development: A Categorical Assessment of the Peer-Reviewed Scientific
Literature, 2009–2015," PLOS One, updated April 20, 2016, http://journals.
plos.org/plosone/article?id=10.1371/journal.pone.0154164 .

147 Alan Neuhauser, "Respiratory, Skin Problems Soar Near Gas Wells, Study Says,"
US News and World Report, September 10, 2014, http://www.usnews.com/news/
articles/2014/09/10/respiratory-skin-problems-soar-near-gas-wells-study-says.

148 Alan Neuhauser, ibid

149 Neuhauser, "Toxic Chemicals."

150 Concerned Health Professionals of New York and Physicians for Social
Responsibility, "Compendium of Scientific, Medical, and Media Findings
Demonstrating Risks and Harms of Fracking (Unconventional Gas
and Oil Extraction)," fourth ed., November 17, 2016: p. 22 ff., http://
concernedhealthny.org/wp-content/uploads/2016/12/COMPENDIUM-4.0_
FINAL_11_16_16Corrected.pdf.

151 Concerned Health Professionals, "Compendium," p. 23.

152 Joe Romm, "Methane Leaks Erase Climate Benefits of Fracked Gas, Countless
Studies Find," Think Progress, February 17, 2016, https://thinkprogress.org/
methane-leaks-erase-climate-benefit-of-fracked-gas-countless-studies-find-
8b060b2b395d#.ijt2yr683.

153 Elizabeth Ridlington and John Rumpler, "Fracking by the Numbers, Key
Impacts of Dirty Drilling at the State and National Level," Environment
American Research & Policy Center, October 2013: p. 5, http://www.
environmentamerica.org/sites/environment/files/reports/EA_FrackingNumbers_
scrn.pdf.

154 Concerned Health Professionals, "Compendium," p. 37 ff.

155 Concerned Health Professionals, ibid, pp. 74-75.

156 Marvin Resnikoff, "Review of Pennsylvania Department of Environmental
Protection Technologically Enhanced Naturally Occurring Radioactivity
Materials (TENORM) Study Report," Radioactive Waste Management
Associates, December 2015.

157 Rick Jervis, "Oklahoma Earthquake Reignites Concerns That Fracking Wells
May Be the Cause," USA Today, November 7, 2016, https://www.usatoday.com/
story/news/2016/11/07/oklahoma-earthquake-fracking-well/93447830/.

158 Andrew Dewson, "A disaster waiting to happen in Oklahoma? The link between
fracking and earthquakes is causing alarm in an oil-rich town," Independent,
April 6, 2015, http://www.independent.co.uk/news/world/americas/a-disaster-
waiting-to-happen-in-oklahoma-the-link-between-fracking-and-earthquakes-
is-causing-alarm-10158524.html; "Exploring the Link Between Earthquakes
and Oil and Gas Disposal Wells," National Public Radio (State Impact), https://
stateimpact.npr.org/oklahoma/tag/earthquakes/. Oklahoma leads the forty-eight
contiguous United States in earthquakes. As William Ellsworth, professor of
geophysics at Stanford, notes, Alaska registers the most tremors overall (Jervis,
"Oklahoma Earthquake Reignites Concerns").

159 Henry Fountain, "In Canada, a Direct Link between Fracking and Earthquakes,"
     New York Times, November 17, 2016, https://www.nytimes.com/2016/11/18/
     science/fracking-earthquakes-alberta-canada.html?_r=0. Elsewhere, in regions
     like Ohio and western Pennsylvania, increased seismicity is due to fracking itself
     (Michael Rubinkam, "DEP ties fracking to western Pa. earthquakes" *Times
     Leader*, February 17, 2017, http://timesleader.com/news/635744/dep-ties-
     fracking-to-western-pa-earthquakes).

160 Jervis, "Oklahoma Earthquake Reignites Concerns."

161 Dewson, "A Disaster Waiting to Happen."

162 Dewson, ibid

163 Concerned Health Professionals, "Compendium," p. 131.

164 Concerned Health Professionals, ibid, p. 92–93.

165 Concerned Health Professionals, ibid, p. 18.

166 Karen Feridun (founder of Berks Gas Truth), interview with author, October 25,
     2016.

167 Concerned Health Professionals, "Compendium," p. 6.

168 Concerned Health Professionals, ibid, p. 209.

169 Neuhauser, "Toxic Chemicals."

170 CNN wire staff, "Vermont First State to Ban Fracking," CNN, May 17, 2012,
     http://www.cnn.com/2012/05/17/us/vermont-fracking/index.html.

171 Jon Hurdle, "With Governor's Signature, Maryland Becomes Third State to
     Ban Fracking," National Public Radio (State Impact), April 4, 2017, https://
     stateimpact.npr.org/pennsylvania/2017/04/04/with-governors-signature-
     maryland-becomes-third-state-to-ban-fracking/.

172 Concerned Health Professionals, "Compendium," pp. 4–5.

173 Jeff McMahon, "Six Reasons Fracking Has Flopped Overseas," *Forbes*, April
     7, 2013, http://www.forbes.com/sites/jeffmcmahon/2013/04/07/six-reasons-
     fracking-has-flopped-overseas/#340ff7a02bd5.

174 Aleem Maqbool, "The Texas Town That Banned Fracking (and Lost)," BBC
     News, June 16, 2015, http://www.bbc.com/news/world-us-canada-33140732.

175 Maqbool, ibid

176 Bruce Finley, "Colorado Supreme Court Rules State Law Trumps Local Bans
     on Fracking," *Denver Post*, updated June 23, 2016, http://www.denverpost.
     com/2016/05/02/colorado-supreme-court-rules-state-law-trumps-local-bans-
     on-fracking/.

177 Concerned Health Professionals, "Compendium," p. 6.

178 Brian Coppola, interview by author, October 4, 2016.

179 Dave Ball, interview by author, October 25, 2016.

180 Coppola, interview by author, October 4, 2016.

181 John Finnerty, "Drillers' Donations Continue to Flow, Despite Slowdown,"
     Community Newspaper Holdings, Inc., October 6, 2016, http://www.cnhi.

com/featured_stories/drillers-donations-continue-to-flow-despite-slowdown/
article_fb794a74-8c0c-11e6-9ab9-f725d6d792ab.html; Tom Barnes, "Energy
Companies Make Big Donations to Scarnati," *Pittsburgh Post-Gazette*, October
20, 2010, http://www.post-gazette.com/news/state/2010/10/20/Energy-
companies-make-big-donations-to-Scarnati/stories/201010200191; Susan
Phillips, "Republicans Win Big with Gas Industry Donations," National
Public Radio (State Impact), November 12, 2014, https://stateimpact.npr.org/
pennsylvania/2014/11/13/republicans-win-big-with-gas-industry-donations/;
Lauren Townsend, "Marcellus Money: Natural Gas Industry Has Spent $49
Million to Influence PA Elected Officials since 2007," Conservation Voters of
Pennsylvania, November 13, 2014, http://www.conservationpa.org/marcellus-
money-natural-gas-industry-has-spent-49-million-to-influence-pa-elected-
officials-since-2007/.

182   "Oil & Gas Activity in Pennsylvania," Fracktracker Alliance, https://www.
fractracker.org/map/us/pennsylvania/.

183   Habicht, Hanson, and Faeth, "The Potential Environmental Impact." Tony
Ingraffea commented on the significance of this report in "Big Oil and Gas have
Big Impacts to Health, Air, Water and Climate," Earthworks, August 14, 2015,
https://www.earthworksaction.org/earthblog/detail/big_oil_and_gas_have_big_
impacts_to_health_air_water_and_climate#.WUrWKGjyu00.

184   For this section, I rely on Tony Ingraffea, interview with author, February 27,
2017.

185   R. W. Howarth, R. Santoro, and A. Ingraffea, "Methane and the Greenhouse-
Gas Footprint of Natural Gas from Shale Formations," *Climatic Change* 106:679
(2011); Stacey Shackford, "Natural Gas from Fracking Could Be 'Dirtier' than
Coal, Cornell Professors Find," *Cornell Chronicle*, April 11, 2011, http://www.
news.cornell.edu/stories/2011/04/fracking-leaks-may-make-gas-dirtier-coal.

186   Dan Gearino, "Obama's Former Energy Secretary Says Fracking Can Be Done
Safely," *Columbus Dispatch*, updated September 18, 2013, http://www.dispatch.
com/content/stories/business/2013/09/17/chu-natural-gas-energy-conference.
html.

187   Blaine Friedlander, "Howarth Alerts White House of Growing Methane
Danger," *Cornell Chronicle*, June 2, 2016, http://news.cornell.edu/
stories/2016/06/howarth-alerts-white-house-growing-methane-danger.

188   "OBIT: Daisytown Farmer Terry Greenwood, Whose Well Water Was Polluted
by Dominion Energy, Dead at 66," *Marcellus Monitor: Investigative journalism
from the shale fields of Pennsylvania*, June 10, 2014, https://marcellusmonitor.
wordpress.com/2014/06/10/obit-daisytown-farmer-terry-greenwood-whose-
well-water-was-polluted-by-dominion-energy-dead-at-66/.

189   List of the Harmed, Pennsylvania Alliance for Clean Water and Air, updated
May 24, 2017, https://pennsylvaniaallianceforcleanwaterandair.wordpress.com/
the-list/.

Chapter 4: The Perils of Pipelines

190   All information about Minisink and the battle to prevent the compressor station taken from Asha Canalos, interview with author, January 18, 2017.

191   Mireya Navarro, "Yoko Ono and Sean Lennon Organize Artists against Fracking," *New York Times*, August 29, 2012, https://green.blogs.nytimes.com/2012/08/29/yoko-ono-and-sean-lennon-organize-artists-against-fracking/?_r=2; Phil Radford and Mark Ruffalo, "Don't Let America Get 'Fracked,'" CNN, updated April 25, 2013, http://www.cnn.com/2013/04/25/opinion/radford-ruffalo-natural-gas-fracking/index.html?iref=allsearch.

192   Mireya Navarro, "N.Y. Assembly Approves Fracking Moratorium," *New York Times*, November 30, 2010, https://green.blogs.nytimes.com/2010/11/30/n-y-assembly-approves-fracking-moratorium/?scp=1&sq=approves%20fracking%20moratorium&st=Search&_r=0.

193   For a detailed description see Thomas Kaplan, "Citing Health Risks, Cuomo Bans Fracking in New York State," *New York Times*, December 17, 2014, https://www.nytimes.com/2014/12/18/nyregion/cuomo-to-ban-fracking-in-new-york-state-citing-health-risks.html.

194   Ellen Cantarow, "Rural New York Township Fights FERC-Approved Gas Compressor," *Truthout*, September 22, 2013, http://www.truth-out.org/news/item/18636-rural-new-jersey-township-fights-ferc-approved-gas-compressor.

195   Cantarow, ibid

196   Southwest Pennsylvania Environmental Health Project, Summary on Compressor Stations and Health Impacts," February 24, 2015, http://www.environmentalhealthproject.org/files/Summary%20Compressor-station-emissions-and-health-impacts-02.24.2015.pdf.

197   Jon Bowermaster, "Knock, Knock: Your New Neighbor Might Be a Neurotoxin," *Take Part*, March 7, 2013, https://dev.takepart.com/article/2013/03/01/can-compressor-station-be-good-neighbor/index.html

198   Mary Esch, "NY Town of 9/11 Workers Wages Gas Pipeline Fight," *San Diego Union Tribune*, February 14, 2013, http://www.sandiegouniontribune.com/sdut-ny-town-of-911-workers-wages-gas-pipeline-fight-2013feb14-story.html.

199   Bowermaster, "Knock, Knock."

200   See, e.g., Wilma Subra, "Human Health Impacts Associated with Chemicals and Pathways of Exposure from the Development of Shale Gas Plays," Earthworks Oil and Gas Accountability Project, https://www.earthworksaction.org/files/publications/SUBRA_3_Shale_Gas_Plays-Health_Impacts_sm.pdf.

201   *Minisink Residents for Environmental Preservation and Safety, et al. v. Federal Energy Regulatory Commission (Respondent) and Millennium Pipeline Company, L.L.C.* (Intervenor), 12-1481 (DC 2014).

202   Esch, "NY Town of 9/11 Workers."

203   James Hansen, "Game Over for the Climate," *New York Times*, May 9, 2012, http://www.nytimes.com/2012/05/10/opinion/game-over-for-the-climate.html; Damian Carrington, "Tar sands exploitation would mean game over for climate,

warns leading scientist," *Guardian*, May 19, 2013, https://www.theguardian.com/environment/2013/may/19/tar-sands-exploitation-climate-scientist.

204   Eli Watkins and Joyce Tseng, "Trump's Policies and How They'll Change America—in Charts," CNN, updated March 15, 2017, http://www.cnn.com/2017/03/14/politics/donald-trump-policy-numbers-impact/; Morgan Winsor, Connor Burton, Phillip Mena, James Hill, and Julia Jacobo, "Dakota Access Pipeline Protest Site Cleared After Police in Riot Gear Enter Main Camp," ABC News, February 23, 2017, http://abcnews.go.com/US/police-riot-gear-enter-main-protest-camp-dakota/story?id=45684166.

205   Jon O'Connell, "Tennessee Gas Pipeline Co. To Pay $800,000 Following Numerous Sediment Violations," *Times-Tribune*, December, 23, 2014, http://thetimes-tribune.com/news/tennesse-gas-pipeline-co-to-pay-800-000-following-numerous-sediment-violations-1.1807060.

206   Please see the following study that the Delaware Riverkeeper commissioned: Spencer Phillips, PhD, Sonia Wang, and Cara Bottorff, "Economic Costs of the PennEast Pipeline: Effects on Ecosystem Services, Property Value, and the Social Cost of Carbon in Pennsylvania and New Jersey," Key-Log Economics, LLC, January 2017, p. 24–31, http://www.delawareriverkeeper.org/sites/default/files/EconomicCostsOfThePennEast_TechnicalReport_FINAL.pdf.

207   Spencer Phillips, Sonia Wang, and Cara Bottorff, ibid

208   Karen Feridun (founder of Berks Gas Truth), interview with author, October 25, 2016.

209   Helen Baker (mother of James Baker), interview with William Huston, June 5, 2016, https://archive.org/details/HelenBakerInterview.

210   Feridun, interview with author, October 25, 2016.

211   Anya Litvak, "Corrosion Discovered Four Years Before Westmoreland County Pipe Blast: Investigation Finds Gas Pipeline Had Coating Problems in 2012," *Pittsburgh Post-Gazette*, September 13, 2016, http://powersource.post-gazette.com/powersource/companies/2016/09/13/Pipe-that-burst-showed-defect-four-years-ago-Spectra-investigation-found/stories/201609130202.

212   Litvak, ibid

213   Using tape is now against industry standards, as it has proven to exacerbate rather than help corrosion. It tends to rip apart from the pipe, further compromising its structural integrity. For a more in-depth explanation of this process see Litvak, "Corrosion Discovered Four Years Before Westmoreland County Pipe Blast."

214   Litvak, "Corrosion Discovered Four Years Before Westmoreland County Pipe Blast."

215   Litvak, ibid

216   Litvak, ibid

217   For up-to-data data about pipeline incidence, see the Pipeline and Hazardous Materials Safety Administration's website, phmsa.dot.gov. These figures are taken from "Significant Incidents," phmsa.dot.gov, https://hip.phmsa.dot.gov

/analyticsSOAP/saw.dll?Portalpages&NQUser=PDM_WEB_USER&NQ_
Password=Public_Web_User1&PortalPath=%2Fshared%2FPDM%20Public%
20Website%2F_portal%2FSC%20Incident%20Trend&Page=Significant&
Action=Navigate&col1=%22PHP%20-%20Geo%20Location%22.%22State%20
Name%22&val1=%22%22.

218   See, e.g., "Are Old Pipelines Really More Dangerous?" *Pipeline Safety Trust
(pstrust.org)*, Spring 2015, http://pstrust.org/wp-content/uploads/2013/03/
Incidents-by-age-of-pipes-PST-spring2015-newsletter-excerpt.pdf.; Jon
Hurdle, "New York State Denies Permit to Constitution Pipeline, Halting
Construction," *National Public Radio* (state impact), April 22, 2016, https://
stateimpact.npr.org/pennsylvania/2016/04/22/new-york-state-denies-permit-to-
constitution-pipeline-halting-construction/.

219   For this section I rely on Megan Holleran, interview with author, January 20,
2017.

220   Jon Hurdle, "New York State denies permit to Constitution Pipeline, halting
construction," *National Public Radio* (state impact), April 22, 2016, https://
stateimpact.npr.org/pennsylvania/2016/04/22/new-york-state-denies-permit-to-
constitution-pipeline-halting-construction/.

221   Sharon Kelly, "Proposed Marcellus Gas Pipeline Sparks Protest at Prized Maple
Farm," *Desmog*, February 25, 2016, https://www.desmogblog.com/2016/02/25/
protest-against-constitution-pipeline-dimock.

222   For the legal considerations around pipelines, I rely on Aaron Stemplewicz
(environmental and pipeline attorney), interview with author, April 7, 2017.

223   For a more detailed and nuanced exploration of this topic, please see "People's
Dossier: FERC's Abuses of Power and Law," *Delaware Riverkeeper Network*,
http://www.delawareriverkeeper.org/sites/default/files/FERC%20Dossier%20
Stripping%20People%27s%20Rights%20pdf%20w%20attach.pdf.

224   Itai Vardi, "Former FERC Official Hired By Company with $1.8 Million Stake
in Spectra Energy Pipeline Project He Had Reviewed," *Desmog*, June 6, 2016,
https://www.desmogblog.com/2016/06/05/former-ferc-official-hired-company-
1-8-million-stake-spectra-energy-pipeline-project-he-had-reviewed.

225   Itai Vardi, "Exposed: Husband of FERC Official Responsible for Reviewing
New Spectra Energy Pipelines Consults On Related Spectra Project," *Desmog*,
November 1, 2016, https://www.desmogblog.com/2016/11/1/exposed-husband-
ferc-official-responsible-reviewing-new-spectra-energy-pipelines-consults-
spectra-related-project.

226   Itai Vardi, "Revealed: Contractors Hired by FERC to Review a New Spectra
Energy Pipeline Work for Spectra on a Related Project," *Desmog*, May 26, 2016,
https://www.desmogblog.com/2016/05/26/revealed-contractors-hired-ferc-
review-new-spectra-energy-pipeline-work-spectra-related-project.

227   See Federal Energy Regulatory Commission fees and annual charges, 42 U.S.
Code § 7178(a)(1).

228   Jon Blistein, "Trump Reverses Obama Orders on Keystone XL, Dakota Access

Pipeline," *Rolling Stone*, January 24, 2017, http://www.rollingstone.com/politics/
news/trump-advances-keystone-xl-dakota-access-pipelines-w462723.

229   Bowermaster, "Knock, Knock."

Chapter 5: Wasted

230   For background on PFOA and DuPont, I rely on Nathaniel Rich, "The Lawyer
Who Became DuPont's Worst Nightmare," *New York Times Magazine*, January
6, 2016, https://www.nytimes.com/2016/01/10/magazine/the-lawyer-who-
became-duponts-worst-nightmare.html?_r=0, and Sharon Lerner's The Teflon
Toxins series, especially "The Teflon Toxin, Part 1," *Intercept*, August 11, 2015,
https://theintercept.com/2015/08/11/dupont-chemistry-deception/.

231   Lerner, "The Teflon Toxin, Part 1."

232   "C8 Science Panel Final Quarterly Newsletter," C8 Science Panel, November
2012, http://www.c8sciencepanel.org/newsletter10.html; Paula I. Johnson et
al., "The Navigation Guide—Evidence-Based Medicine Meets Environmental
Health: Systematic Review of Human Evidence for PFOA Effects on Fetal
Growth," *Environmental Health Perspectives* 122 (2014).

233   Rich, "The Lawyer Who Became DuPont's Worst Nightmare."

234   Please see, "Fact Sheet: 2010/2015 PFOA Stewardship Program," *Environmental
Protection Agency*, https://www.epa.gov/assessing-and-managing-chemicals-
under-tsca/fact-sheet-20102015-pfoa-stewardship-program.

235   Lerner, "The Teflon Toxin, Part 1."

236   For PFOA's infiltration into the Delaware River basin, along with other general
studies and facts in this section, I rely on Tracy Carluccio (deputy director of the
Delaware Riverkeeper Network), interview with author, January 17, 2017.

237   "Highlights from the Clean Air Act 40th Anniversary," United States
Environmental Protection Agency, accessed March 30, 2017, https://www.epa.
gov/clean-air-act-overview/highlights-clean-air-act-40th-anniversary.

238   "Highlights from the Clean Air Act." Some of these figures are projections, as
the precise data are yet to be confirmed.

239   "State of the Air 2016," American Lung Association.

240   "National Water Quality Inventory: Report to Congress," United States
Environmental Protection Agency, January 2009, https://www.epa.gov/sites
/production/files/2015-09/documents/2009_01_22_305b_2004report_2004
_305breport.pdf.

241   "Commonwealth of Pennsylvania Public Health Advisory: 2017 Fish
Consumption," Pennsylvania Fish and Boat Commission, http://pfbc.pa.gov/
fishpub/summaryad/sumconsumption.pdf.

242   http://www.nj.gov/dep/dsr/fishadvisories/2016-fish-advisories.pdf.

243   Ann Faulds et al., "Patterns of Sport-fish Consumption at Six Pennsylvania Sites
Along the Tidal Portion of the Delaware River with Special Emphasis on Shore
Anglers," Pennsylvania Coastal Zone Management Program Technical Report,

March 31, 2004, p. 4–5; "Revised Human Health Water Quality Criteria for Total PCBs for the Protection of Human Health from Carcinogenic Effects," *Delaware River Basin Commission*, July 2013.

244   Faulds et al., "Patterns of Sport-fish Consumption," "Revised Human Health."

245   The information about the Donna Reservoir and lake provided by Alexa Ura, "State, Feds Know Valley Residents Have Eaten Toxic Fish for Decades," *Texas Tribune*, April 23, 2016, https://www.texastribune.org/2016/04/23/south-texas-toxic-lake-raises-environmental-justic/.

246   "Fish Tissue Data Collected by EPA," United States Environmental Protection Agency, https://www.epa.gov/fish-tech/fish-tissue-data-collected-epa.

247   Captain Paul Eidman (professional fisherman/angler and marine conservationist), interview with author, May 15, 2017.

248   For the Paulsboro vinyl chloride spill I rely on Trisha Sheehan (Holistic Moms Network), interview with author, January 6, 2017, and Mark Cuker (environmental attorney), interview with author, March 22, 2017.

249   Kristen D. Jackson et al., "Trends in Allergic Conditions among Children: United States, 1997–2011," *National Center for Health Statistics Data Brief*, No. 121, May 2013, https://www.cdc.gov/nchs/data/databriefs/db121.pdf.

250   "Vinyl Chloride," National Cancer Institute, accessed July 13, 2017, https://www.cancer.gov/about-cancer/causes-prevention/risk/substances/vinyl-chloride.

251   "Railroad Accident Report: Conrail Freight Train Derailment with Vinyl Chloride Release: Abstract," National Transportation Safety Board, https://www.ntsb.gov/news/events/Pages/2014_Paulsboro_NJ_BMG-Abstract.aspx.

252   David Matthau, "Fighting to Prevent NJ Chemical Disaster," New Jersey 101.5, February 28, 2014, http://nj1015.com/fighting-to-prevent-nj-chemical-disasters-audio/.

253   Tara Nurin, "First Responders Share Blame for Problems at Paulsboro Toxic Spill, NTSB Says," *New Jersey Spotlight*, July 30, 2014, http://www.njspotlight.com/stories/14/07/29/first-responders-at-fault-for-some-problems-at-paulsboro-toxic-spill-ntsb-says/.

254   Matthau, "Fighting to Prevent NJ Chemical Disaster."

255   Jane Kay and Cheryl Katz, "Pollution, Poverty, and People of Color: Living with Industry," *Scientific American*, June 4, 2012, https://www.scientificamerican.com/article/pollution-poverty-people-color-living-industry/.

256   "Train Derailment Causes Chemical Spill of Vinyl Chloride in Paulsboro," *South Jersey Times*, updated November 30, 2012, http://www.nj.com/gloucester-county/index.ssf/2012/11/train_derailment_prompts_evacu.html.

257   Sharon Lerner, "The Teflon Toxin, Part 6," *Intercept*, December 16, 2015, https://theintercept.com/2015/12/16/toxic-firefighting-foam-has-contaminated-u-s-drinking-water-with-pfcs/.

258   Kyle Bagenstose and Kristina Scala, "Chemical Taint from Firefighting Foam Being Investigated at Military Bases Across US," *Burlington County Times*,

May 1, 2016, http://www.burlingtoncountytimes.com/news/horsham-pfos/
chemical-taint-from-firefighting-foam-being-investigated-at-military-bases/
article_1c6092ca-0c87-11e6-b42a-cf24e0df95b3.html.

259   For this section on the military and foam exercises, I rely on Tracy Carluccio
(deputy director of the Delaware Riverkeeper Network), interview with author,
January 17, 2017.

260   For this section, I rely on Tom Roeder and Jakob Rodgers, "Toxic Legacy: Air
Force Studies Dating Back Decades Show Danger of Foam That Contaminated
Colorado Springs–Area Water," *Gazette*, updated October 25, 2016, http://
gazette.com/toxic-legacy-air-force-studies-dating-back-decades-show-danger-
of-foam-that-contaminated-local-water/article/1588446.

261   Roeder and Rodgers, ibid

262   Roeder and Rodgers, ibid

263   Kyle Bagenstose, "Dangers of Firefighting Foam Discussed in 2001, Document
Shows," *Intelligencer*, June 9, 2017, http://www.theintell.com/news/horsham-
pfos/dangers-of-firefighting-foam-discussed-in-document-shows/article_
d4a5bbbc-4a25-11e7-ae80-4314c84eab0c.html.

264   Kyle Bagenstose, "Unwell Water History," *Intelligencer*, May 18, 2017, http://
www.theintell.com/news/horsham-pfos/unwell-water-history/article_1aeaed76-
8bf5-11e6-b1f7-4fb2cc450c6d.html.

265   Kyle Bagenstose, "Ivyland Woman Sues Navy after Finding High PFOA
Blood Level," *Intelligencer*, January 12, 2017, http://www.theintell.com/news/
horsham-pfos/ivyland-woman-sues-navy-after-finding-high-pfoa-blood-level/
article_83b1fada-d8e8-11e6-b2c4-7f62537e561a.html.

266   Sharon Lerner, "The Teflon Toxin, Part 6," *Intercept*, December 16, 2015, https://
theintercept.com/2015/12/16/toxic-firefighting-foam-has-contaminated-u-s-
drinking-water-with-pfcs/.

267   Bruce Finley, "Peterson Air Force Base Dumped 150,000 Gallons of PFC-laced
Water into Colorado Springs' Sewer System," *Denver Post*, updated October 19,
2016, http://www.denverpost.com/2016/10/18/peterson-air-force-base-laced-
water-spill/; ---, "Drinking Water in Three Colorado Cities Contaminated with
Toxic Chemicals above EPA limits," *Denver Post*, updated September 23, 2016,
http://www.denverpost.com/2016/06/15/colorado-widefield-fountain-security-
water-chemicals-toxic-epa/.

268   Roeder and Rodgers, "Toxic Legacy."

269   Specifically, this firefighting foam either contains or breaks down into PFOA
or PFOS. Some military bases continued to use these hazardous materials as
of 2015, when Lerner published this piece. Hopefully, the military will join the
companies and nations that have banned its use. For more, see Lerner, "The
Teflon Toxin, Part 6."

270   Rich, "The Lawyer Who Became DuPont's Worst Nightmare."

271   Captain Paul Eidman (professional fisherman/angler and marine
conservationist), interview with author, May 15, 2017.

272   Rich, "The Lawyer Who Became DuPont's Worst Nightmare."

273   Sharon Lerner, "The Teflon Toxin, Part 3," *Intercept*, August 20, 2015, https://
theintercept.com/2015/08/20/teflon-toxin-DuPont-slipped-past-epa/; the
regulatory/corporate revolving door is also explored in Callie Lyons, *Stain-
Resistant, Nonstick, Waterproof, and Lethal* (Connecticut: Praeger, 2007).

274   Rich, "The Lawyer Who Became DuPont's Worst Nightmare."

275   Rich, ibid

276   Information about drinking water regulation in this paragraph provided by
Brady Dennis, "In U.S. Drinking Water, Many Chemicals Are Regulated—But
Many Aren't," *Washington Post*, June 10, 2016, https://www.washingtonpost.com/
national/health-science/in-us-drinking-water-many-chemicals-are-regulated--
but-many-arent/2016/06/09/e48683bc-21b9-11e6-aa84-42391ba52c91_story.
html?utm_term=.f028880ffe64.

277   Lerner, "The Teflon Toxin, Part 3."

Chapter 6: The Paving of America

278   George Draffan, "Taking Back Our Land: A History of Railroad Land Grant
Reform," Railroads and Clearcuts Campaign, November 1998, http://www.
landgrant.org/takingback.pdf.

279   Julie Morse, "Checkerboard: Putting Western Forest Pieces Back Together,"
nature.org, December 3, 2014, http://blog.nature.org/science/2014/12/03/
checkerboard-western-forest-pieces-washington-montana-conservation-land-
connectivity/.

280   George Wuerthner, "Why Is Logging Dying? Blame the Market," *High Country
News*, June 15, 2016, http://www.hcn.org/articles/why-is-logging-dying-blame-
the-market.

281   Morse, "Checkerboard."

282   Morse, ibid

283   "Incident Information," State of California, modified September 23, 2016,
http://cdfdata.fire.ca.gov/incidents/incidents_stats?year=2016.

284   Morse, "Checkerboard."

285   For this section on Truckee and the Sierra Nevadas, I am indebted to Perry
Norris (executive director of the Truckee Donner Land Trust), interview with
author, April 28, 2017.

286   S. M. Stein et al., "Wildfire, Wildlands, and People: Understanding and
Preparing for Wildfire in the Wildland-Urban Interface—a Forests on the
Edge Report," United States Department of Agriculture, Forest Service, Rocky
Mountain Research Station, January 2013, https://www.fs.fed.us/openspace/
fote/reports/GTR-299.pdf; Devin Fehely, "Over 100 Million Dead Trees Pose
Wildfire Threat in California," *CBS San Francisco Bay Area*, June 2, 2017, http://
sanfrancisco.cbslocal.com/2017/06/02/100-million-dead-trees-wildfire/; Keith
Ridler, "Scientists Try Bacteria to Halt Invasive Cheatgrass Overwhelming the

West," *Los Angeles Times*, November 13, 2016, http://www.latimes.com/nation/nationnow/la-na-invasive-cheatgrass-20161110-story.html.

287 David Bunker, "Forest Land Is Being Turned into Housing," *Tahoe Daily Tribune*, October 12, 2005, http://www.tahoedailytribune.com/news/forest-land-is-being-turned-into-housing/.

288 Bunker, ibid

289 Bunker, ibid

290 T. W. Crowther et al., "Mapping Tree Density at a Global Scale," *Nature* 525 (September 2015): 201, http://www.nature.com/doifinder/10.1038/nature14967.

291 Ashley Kirk, "Deforestation: Where Is the World Losing the Most Trees?" *Telegraph*, March 23, 2016, http://www.telegraph.co.uk/news/2016/03/23/deforestation-where-is-the-world-losing-the-most-trees/; Nell Greenfieldboyce, "Tree Counter Is Astonished by How Many Trees There Are," National Public Radio (*All Things Considered*) September 2, 2015, http://www.npr.org/sections/goatsandsoda/2015/09/02/436919052/tree-counter-is-astonished-by-how-many-trees-there-are.

292 Charles Q. Choi, "The Lost Forests of America," *Live Science*, April 23, 2009, http://www.livescience.com/7725-lost-forests-america.html.

293 "Wetlands: A Global Disappearing Act," http://www.ramsar.org/sites/default/files/documents/library/factsheet3_global_disappearing_act_0.pdf.

294 T. E. Dahl, "Wetlands: Losses in the United States 1780's to 1980's," United States Department of the Interior, Fish, and Wildlife Service, Washington D.C., 1990, https://www.fws.gov/wetlands/Documents/Wetlands-Losses-in-the-United-States-1780s-to-1980s.pdf.

295 "Wetlands: A Global Disappearing Act."

296 All data on the Mississippi in this paragraph are from Adam Wernick, "Louisiana's Coastline Is Disappearing at the Rate of a Football Field an Hour," Public Radio International, September 23, 2014, https://www.pri.org/stories/2014-09-23/louisianas-coastline-disappearing-rate-football-field-hour.

297 All data on wilderness destruction from David Maxwell Braun, "Catastrophic Declines in Earth's Wilderness Areas Over the Last 20 Years, Study Finds," *National Geographic*, September 8, 2016, http://voices.nationalgeographic.com/2016/09/08/catastrophic-declines-in-earths-remaining-wilderness-over-the-last-20-years-study-finds/.

298 James E. M. Watson et al., "Catastrophic Declines in Wilderness Areas Undermine Global Environment Targets," *Current Biology* 26 (2016), https://voices.nationalgeographic.com/files/2016/09/watson_wilderness_2016.pdf.

299 You can learn more about Apple Pond Farm and schedule a visit to this special place at http://www.applepondfarm.com/about-us.

300 Dick Riseling, (owner, Apple Pond Farm), conversation with author, May 13, 2017.

301 Derek Thompson, "What in the World Is Causing the Retail Meltdown of 2017?" *Atlantic*, April 10, 2017, https://www.theatlantic.com/business/archive/2017/04/retail-meltdown-of-2017/522384/.

302 Thompson, ibid

303 Ethan Rothstein, "Even Developers Agree the U.S. Has Way Too Much Retail Space," *Forbes*, April 5, 2017, https://www.forbes.com/sites/bisnow/2017/04/05/even-developers-agree-the-u-s-has-way-too-much-retail-space/3/#36f7d11136f7.

304 For this background on Hamilton Township, I am indebted to George van Amelsfort, interview with author, March 28, 2017. See also, Delaware Rivkerkeeper Network, "New Jersey Stormwater management implementation: a case study of Hamilton Township, Mercer County," May 2010, http://www.delawareriverkeeper.org/sites/default/files/resources/Reports/Hamilton_Twp_NJ_SWM_Implementation_Report.pdf.

305 Anne Pickering, "Bishop Tube Facility Started in 1951, Now Abandoned," *Daily Local News*, updated June 2, 2007, http://www.dailylocal.com/article/DL/20070602/TMP01/306029998.

306 Ralph Vartabedian, "How Environmentalists Lost the Battle Over TCE," *Los Angeles Times*, March 29, 2006, http://articles.latimes.com/2006/mar/29/nation/na-toxic29. See alternative URL: https://greeneconomics.blogspot.com/2006/03/.

307 Vartabedian, ibid

308 Vartabedian, ibid

309 Vartabedian, ibid

310 Pickering, "Bishop Tube"; Philip L. Comella and Craig B. Simonsen, "EPA Classifies Trichloroethylene (TCE) as Human Carcinogen," *Workplace Safety and Environmental Law Alert Blog*, September 29, 2011, http://www.environmentalsafetyupdate.com/environmental-compliance/epa-classifies-trichloroethylene-tce-as-human-carcinogen/.

311 Pickering, ibid

312 For this story, I rely on Paula Warren's presentation at a public meeting in East Whiteland Township, Pennsylvania, June 7, 2017, and on personal conversations throughout the spring of 2017.

313 "ToxFAQs for Trichloroethylene (TCE)," Agency for Toxic Substances and Disease Registry, accessed July 14, 2017, https://www.atsdr.cdc.gov/toxfaqs/tf.asp?id=172&tid=30; "Trichloroethylene Toxicity: What Are the Physiological Effects of Trichloroethylene?," Agency for Toxic Substances and Disease Registry, accessed July 14, 2017, https://www.atsdr.cdc.gov/csem/csem.asp?csem=15&po=10.

314 For this section, I am indebted to Liz, Kate, and Larry Stauffer, interview with author, April 10, 2017.

315 For the prospective purchase agreement between Pennsylvania's Department of Environmental Protection and Constitution Drive Partners (a unit of

O'Neill Properties), see Jon Hurdle, "Chesco Residents Urge Officials to Reject Development Plan for Contaminated Site," National Public Radio (State Impact), April 25, 2017, https://stateimpact.npr.org/pennsylvania/2017/04/25/chesco-residents-urge-officials-to-reject-development-plan-for-contaminated-site/; Michaelle Bond, "On toxic site abandoned for decades, developer sees townhouses sprouting in Chesco," philly.com, April 10, 2017, http://www.philly.com/philly/news/pennsylvania/toxic-brownfield-development-East-Whiteland-ONeill-DEP-Bishop-Tube-Malvern.html.

316   Amanda Mahnke, "Planning Commission Discusses Sports Fields at Bishop Tube, Uptown Worthington Rentals," *Malvern Patch*, May 27, 2011, https://patch.com/pennsylvania/malvern/planning-commission-discusses-sports-fields-at-bishop6ec8bd9e8d.

317   Tom Myers, "Technical Memorandum: Review of Bishop Tube Superfund Site and an Assessment of the Site's Proposed Residential Development," prepared for the Delaware Riverkeeper Network, March 23, 2017, http://www.delawareriverkeeper.org/sites/default/files/DRN%20to%20PADEP%203.27.17_1.pdf.

318   Michaelle Bond, "On Toxic Site Abandoned for Decades, Developer Sees Townhouses Sprouting in Chesco," *Philly.com*, updated April 10, 2017, http://www.philly.com/philly/news/pennsylvania/toxic-brownfield-development-East-Whiteland-ONeill-DEP-Bishop-Tube-Malvern.html.

319   "Overview of the Brownfields Program," United States Environmental Protection Agency, accessed July 14, 2017, https://www.epa.gov/brownfields/overview-brownfields-program.

320   Ledyard King, "President Trump's Budget Would Cut Superfund Toxic Cleanup Program by 30%," *USA Today*, updated April 7, 2017, https://www.usatoday.com/story/news/politics/2017/04/07/president-trumps-budget-would-cut-superfund-toxic-cleanup-program-30/100168436/.

321   King, ibid

322   All data on Love Canal taken from Associated Press, "'Love Canal' Still Oozing Poison 35 Years Later," *New York Post*, November 2, 2013, http://nypost.com/2013/11/02/love-canal-still-oozing-poison-35-years-later/.

323   Deidra Ashley, "Cancer 'Hot Spots' in Florida May Be Associated with Hazardous Waste Sites," University of Missouri School of Medicine, accessed July 14, 2017, https://medicine.missouri.edu/2017/03/cancer-hot-spots-in-florida-may-be-associated-with-hazardous-waste-sites/.

324   Ashley, ibid

325   Fred Stine (citizen action coordinator at the Delaware Riverkeeper Network), conversation with author, May 6, 10, 2017.

Chapter 7: Can We Afford a Green Amendment?

326   For this discussion, I am indebted to David Warne (assistant commissioner, Watershed Protection Program, New York City Department of Environmental

Protection) and Adam Bosch (director of public affairs, New York City DEP Bureau of Water Supply), interview with author, April 18, 2017.

327 Some theorize this is because the water's pH level, at 7.2, is nearly neutral (with purity being 7.0). See Rachel Nuwer, "Why Is New York Tap Water So Good?," *Edible Manhattan*, March 7, 2013, http://www.ediblemanhattan.com/departments/liquid-assets/theres-something-in-the-water/.

328 Tim Sprinkle, "The Secret of New York City's Mythic Bagel-Making Water," *Quartz*, October 7, 2014, https://qz.com/263351/the-secret-of-new-york-citys-mythic-bagel-baking-water/.

329 Albert Appleton and Daniel Moss, "How New York City Kept Its Drinking Water Pure—In Spite of Hurricane Sandy," *Huffington Post*, updated January 23, 2014, http://www.huffingtonpost.com/daniel-moss/new-york-drinking-water_b_2064588.html.

330 Appleton and Moss, ibid Specifically, the authors state that "there was a 75 percent to 80 percent reduction in farm pollution loading."

331 Correspondence with Adam Bosch, director of public affairs, Bureau of Water Supply, NYC DEP, June 28, 2017.

332 The program itself is premised on partnership with local organizations. For example, the Catskill Watershed Corporation and the Watershed Agricultural Council, along with other development corporations, make possible the septic repairs and agricultural accommodations discussed in this profile. As Adam Bosch notes, "The partnership model is part of what makes our watershed protection program unique, successful, and a model for others."

333 Megan Cartwright, "Don't Go in the Water," *Slate*, July, 2015, http://www.slate.com/articles/health_and_science/medical_examiner/2015/07/crypto_in_swimming_pools_swimmers_diarrhea_caused_by_a_parasite_that_chlorine.html.

334 The water does undergo limited treatment to ensure quality. For a succinct overview of New York's water sourcing and treatment, please see Emily S. Rueb, "How New York Gets Its Water," *New York Times*, March 24, 2016, https://www.nytimes.com/interactive/2016/03/24/nyregion/how-nyc-gets-its-water-new-york-101.html?_r=0.

335 Motoko Rich and John Broder, "A Debate Arises on Job Creation and Environment," *New York Times*, September 4, 2011, accessed May 10, 2017, http://www.nytimes.com/2011/09/05/business/economy/a-debate-arises-on-job-creation-vs-environmental-regulation.html.

336 Steven Overly, "Donald Trump Tells Detroit Auto CEOs That Environmental Regulations Are 'Out Of Control,'" *Washington Post*, January 24, 2017, https://www.washingtonpost.com/news/innovations/wp/2017/01/24/donald-trump-tells-detroit-auto-ceos-environmental-regulations-are-out-of-control/?utm_term=.cfb0ba3ad90a.

337 All figures on regulatory compliance and benefits in 2012 taken from Jim Tankersley, "Report: New Regulations Cost $216B and 87 Million Hours

of Paperwork. What Do They Reap?" *Washington Post*, January 14, 2013, https://www.washingtonpost.com/news/wonk/wp/2013/01/14/report-new-regulations-cost-216-billion-and-87-million-hours-of-paperwork/?utm_term=.87de12e35564.

338   Lindsey Cook, "Seriously, Go to College," *US News & World Report*, August 17, 2015, https://www.usnews.com/news/blogs/data-mine/2015/08/17/study-benefits-of-a-college-degree-are-historically-high.

339   For this discussion on the Clean Air Act, and all monetary figures, I borrow from Alan H. Lockwood, "How the Clean Air Act Has Saved $22 Trillion in Health-Care Costs," *Atlantic*, September 7, 2012, https://www.theatlantic.com/health/archive/2012/09/how-the-clean-air-act-has-saved-22-trillion-in-health-care-costs/262071/. This article was an excerpt from his book *The Silent Epidemic: Coal and the Hidden Threat to Health* (Boston: MIT Press, September 2012).

340   "Government Regulation: Costs Lower, Benefits Greater Than Industry Estimates," Pew Charitable Trusts, May 26, 2015, http://www.pewtrusts.org/en/research-and-analysis/fact-sheets/2015/05/government-regulation-costs-lower-benefits-greater-than-industry-estimates.

341   David Brodwin, "The High Cost of Dirty Water," *US News & World Report*, June 8, 2015, https://www.usnews.com/opinion/economic-intelligence/2015/06/08/epa-clean-water-rules-benefits-outweigh-its-costs.

342   American Sustainable Business Council, "Small Business Owners Favor Regulations to Protect Clean Water," July 2014, http://asbcouncil.org/sites/default/files/asbc_clean_water_poll_report_july2014_sv_final_140721v2sm.pdf.

343   Avery Fellow, "Environmental Cost of Business Estimated at $4.7T Annually," *Bloomberg*, April 17, 2013, https://www.bloomberg.com/news/2013-04-17/environmental-cost-of-business-estimated-at-4-7t-annually.html.

344   TEEB for Business Coalition, "Natural Capital at Risk: The Top 100 Externalities of Business," April 2013, http://naturalcapitalcoalition.org/wp-content/uploads/2016/07/Trucost-Nat-Cap-at-Risk-Final-Report-web.pdf.

345   Fellow, "Environmental Cost of Business."

346   TEEB for Business Coalition, "Natural Capital at Risk"

347   Chari Towne, *A River Again: The Story of the Schuylkill River Project* (Pennsylvania: Delaware Riverkeeper Network, 2012), p. 11.

348   Towne, ibid, p. 12.

349   Towne, ibid, p. 14.

350   Towne, ibid, p. 33.

351   Unless otherwise stated, all information on the Delaware River in this section is from the Delaware Riverkeeper Network's "River Values: The Value of a Clean and Healthy Delaware River," April 2010, http://planphilly.com/uploads/media_items/http-planphilly-com-sites-planphilly-com-files-rivers_valus_report_final-pdf.original.pdf.

352   Andrew Balmford et al., "Walk on the Wild Side: Estimating the Global Magnitude of Visits to Protected Areas," *PLOS Biology*, February 2015: 13, https://doi.org/10.1371/journal.pbio.1002074.

353   Chris Mooney, "Natural Protected Areas Get 8 Billion Visits per Year. That's Higher than World's Population," *Washington Post*, February 24, 2015, https://www.washingtonpost.com/news/energy-environment/wp/2015/02/24/new-study-proves-that-human-beings-love-nature/?utm_term=.94d7b0d3ff78.

354   Catherine Rayburn-Trobaug, "Ecotourism in the U.S.," *USA Today*, accessed July 17, 2017. http://traveltips.usatoday.com/ecotourism-us-10980.html.

355   Catherine Cullinane Thomas and Lynne Koontz, "2016 National Park Visitor Spending Effects," Fort Collins, Colorado: National Park Service, April 2017: 13, https://www.nps.gov/subjects/socialscience/vse.htm.

356   James R. Houston, "The Economic Value of Beaches—A 2013 Update," *Shore & Beach* 81 (2013): pp. 3, 5.

357   Gerald J. Kauffman et al., "Economic Value of the Delaware Estuary Watershed," University of Delaware, June 2011, http://www.ipa.udel.edu/publications/DelEstuaryValueReport.pdf.

358   Alexis C. Madrigal, "The Blood Harvest," *Atlantic*, February 26, 2014, https://www.theatlantic.com/technology/archive/2014/02/the-blood-harvest/284078/.

359   Kieron Monks, "Why This Crab's Blood Could Save Your Life," CNN, updated January 5, 2015, http://www.cnn.com/2014/09/04/health/this-crabs-blood-could-save-your-life/.

360   Ted Lee Eubanks Jr., John R. Stoll, PhD, and Paul Kerlinger, PhD, "Wildlife-Associated Recreation on the New Jersey Delaware Bayshore," New Jersey Division of Fish and Wildlife, February 16, 2000, p. 49.

361   C. C. Sutton, J. C. O'Herron and R. T. Zappalorti, "The Scientific Characterization of the Delaware Estuary," Delaware Estuary Program, 1996.

362   Kauffman et al., "Economic Value of the Delaware Estuary."

363   D. Munro, et al, "Oyster Mortality in Delaware Bay: Impacts and Recovery from Hurricane Irene and Tropical Storm Lee," *Estuarine, Coastal and Shelf Science* 135 (2013), http://hsrl.rutgers.edu/abstracts.articles/Munroe_2013_ECSS.pdf. Significant storms have taken their toll on the oysters, reducing harvests because of the freshwater flow dynamics that had harmful impacts on the Delaware Bay oysters.

364   David R. Boyd, *The Environmental Rights Revolution* (Vancouver: University of British Columbia Press, 2012), 5.

365   Boyd, ibid, 5.

366   Zachary Davies Boren, "Major Study Finds the US Is an Oligarchy," *Business Insider*, April 16, 2014, http://www.businessinsider.com/major-study-finds-that-the-us-is-an-oligarchy-2014-4.

367   Nathan Rott, "How the EPA Became a Victim of Its Own Success," National Public Radio *(Morning Edition)*, February 17, 2017, http://www.npr.org/2017/02/17/515748401/how-the-epa-became-a-victim-of-its-own-success.

Chapter 8: Fighting for a Green Amendment

368 Jerry Williams (toxic tort attorney), interview with author, March 10, 2017; Michele Baker (New York Water Project founder and tireless advocate), interview with author, April 27, 2017.

369 Jesse McKinley, "After Months of Anger in Hoosick Falls, Hearings on Tainted Water Begin," *New York Times*, August 30, 2016, https://www.nytimes.com/2016/08/31/nyregion/hoosick-falls-tainted-water-hearings.html?_r=0.

370 McKinley, ibid

371 "Filtering Water Fears in Hoosick Falls Demands an Independent Probe," *New York Daily News*, July 5, 2016, http://www.nydailynews.com/opinion/filtering-water-fears-hoosick-falls-independent-probe-article-1.2696368.

372 "Slide Show of Hoosick Falls Water Crisis," *Albany Times Union*, updated May 2, 2016, http://www.timesunion.com/local/article/Timeline-of-Hoosick-Falls-water-danger-6768897.php#photo-9102470 (see image 16 of 46).

373 "EPA Statement on Hoosick Falls Water Contamination," December 17, 2015, http://www.villageofhoosickfalls.com/Media/PDF/EPAStatementHoosickFallsWaterContamination.pdf.

374 Dan Turkel, "Officials Took Months to Warn Residents of a Tiny New York Village of an Impending Disaster in Their Water Supply," *Business Insider*, March 5, 2016, http://www.businessinsider.com/delay-in-warning-hoosick-falls-residents-not-to-drink-water-2016-3; Brendan J. Lyons, "Concerned Citizens Pack Hoosick Falls Water Hearing," *Albany Times Union*, updated January 15, 2016, http://www.timesunion.com/local/article/Concerned-citizens-pack-Hoosick-Falls-water-6760001.php; "Slide Show of Hoosick Falls" (image 26 of 46).

375 Scott Waldman, "Hoosick Falls Confronts Poisoned Wells and an Uncertain Future," *Politico*, March 23, 2016, http://www.politico.com/states/new-york/albany/story/2016/03/hoosick-falls-confronts-poisoned-wells-and-an-uncertain-future-032864.

376 Matthew Hamilton, "Erin Brockovich: Attend Village, Town Meetings," *Albany Times Union*, January 31, 2016, http://www.timesunion.com/local/article/Erin-Brockovich-to-address-Hoosick-Falls-water-6795132.php.

377 Kenneth C. Crowe II, "Gov. Cuomo: $10 Million Heading to Hoosick Falls," *Albany Times Union*, February 12, 2016, http://www.timesunion.com/local/article/Hoosick-Falls-students-worried-by-PFOA-6827170.php.

378 Matthew Hamilton, "Hoosick Falls–Inspired Law Extends Statute of Limitations," *Albany Times Union*, updated July 21, 2016, http://www.timesunion.com/local/article/Hoosick-Falls-inspired-law-extends-statute-of-8401980.php.

379 Hamilton, ibid

380 Media Release, "Hoosick Falls Kids Call for Constitutional Right to Clean Water," EffectiveNY, January 1, 2017, http://effectively.org/2017/01/01/hoosick-falls-kids-call-for-constitutional-right-to-clean-water/.

381 For the following discussion on constitutional amendments, I am indebted to Jordan Yeager (environmental attorney), interview with author, April 20, 2017.

382 For an overview of the process please explore "Amending state constitutions," *Ballotpedia: The Encyclopedia of American Politics*, https://ballotpedia.org/Amending_state_constitutions. There you will find in-depth and technical discussions for how to alter state constitutions.

383 Florida changed its constitution in 2006, requiring this supermajority. See Howard Troxler, "Florida's 60 Percent Rule May Doom Amendments on Ballot," *Tampa Bay Times*, October 25, 2010, http://www.tampabay.com/news/politics/stateroundup/floridas-60-percent-rule-may-doom-amendments-on-ballot/1130300.

384 With the exception of Delaware, the only state in which the legislature can amend the constitution without consulting the people ("Amending State Constitutions," *Ballotpedia*).

385 New York State Bar Association, "Report and Recommendations Concerning the Conservation Article in the State Constitution (Article XIV)," August 3, 2016, p. 12, https://www.nysba.org/ArticleXIVreport/.

386 Bar Association, ibid p. 13.

387 "The Right to a Clean and Healthful Environment," New York People's Convention, http://nypeoplesconvention.org/685-2/the-right-to-a-clean-and-healthful-environment/.

388 "*Gasland*: HBO documentary key driver of opposition to fracking, study finds," *Guardian*, September 2, 2015, https://www.theguardian.com/environment/2015/sep/02/gasland-hbo-documentary-fracking-opposition.

389 For more information on *Sacred Cod*, see Alexander C. Kaufman, "New England Cod Fishermen Share Coal Miners' Plight in This New Documentary," *Huffington Post*, April 11, 2017, http://www.huffingtonpost.com/entry/sacred-cod-documentary_us_58ed1547e4b0ca64d919d595.

390 Thomas L. Friedman, "Smart Approaches, Not Strong-Arm Tactics, to Jobs," *New York Times*, January 25, 2017, https://www.nytimes.com/2017/01/25/opinion/smart-approaches-not-strong-arm-tactics-to-jobs.html?_r=0.

391 Franklin L. Kury, Statement to the House of Delegates of the Pennsylvania Bar Association, 1970, reprinted in *Clean Politics, Clean Streams: A Legislative Autobiography and Reflections* (Maryland: Lehigh University Press, 2011).

392 Klein, *This Changes Everything* (New York: Simon & Schuster, 2014), pp. 294–295. For a more extensive examination of Blockadia, see pp. 293–336.

393 Explore the Sane Energy Project's work at saneenergyproject.org.

394 Michelle Nijhuis, "The Teen-Agers Suing over Climate Change," *New Yorker*, December 6, 2016, http://www.newyorker.com/tech/elements/the-teen-agers-suing-over-climate-change.

INDEX

Canada, Alberta tar fields, 105–6

Canalos, Asha, 97–103, 105, 125, 242

cancer

and air quality, 25, 138

from benzene exposure, 21

from chemicals in drinking water, 24

in children, 27

from fracking proximity, 77, 93–94

from heavy metal accumulation in human bodies, 26

from PCB exposure, 141–42

from PFOA exposure, 132, 227

prevalence of, 27

from TCE exposure, 175, 176, 177–78

from vinyl chloride exposure, 146, 148, 152

Cannonsville Reservoir, New York, 196

Canyon Resources, 46

Cape France Enterprises v. Estate of Peed, 55–56

carbon dioxide gas, 37, 78, 87–90

carbon monoxide and Clean Air Act, 138

Carluccio, Tracy, 3, 72, 94, 133–37

Carpenter, David, 77

Carrillo, Sandra, 141

Carson, Rachel, 50

Carter, Jimmy, 182

Castile La Mancha, fracking moratorium in, 83

Castille, Ronald D., 10, 234

Catskill Fund for the Future, 199

Catskill mountain range, 195–201, 198

cattle ranching

DuPont toxic dump sickens rancher, 132–33

fracking vs., 67–71

as natural capital cost, 205–7

caviar industry, 28, 255n51

Ceballos, Gerardo, 31–32

cellular damage from PFOS firefighting foam, 154

Central Valley, California, 80

César E. Chavez High School, Manchester, Texas, 20

CFCs (ozone-depleting chlorofluorocarbons), 203–4

Chambers Works facility on the Delaware River, DuPont's, 133–37

checkerboard land ownership in the American West, 163–67

chemicals. *See* fracking chemicals; industrial contaminants; *individual chemicals*

chemical testing facilities, 134

Chesapeake Bay sturgeon, 30

children

and air pollution, 24–25, 26–27, 254n38

cancer prevalence increase, 1990–2009, 27

chemically-sensitive children and nearby vinyl chloride spill, 146–48

and current funding for fossil fuel infrastructure, 38

excluding from joys of nature, 39–40

Hoosick Falls's children speak up about PFOA contamination, 225–26, 227–28

incidence of leukemia in Manchester, Texas, 20

and injustice of polluting our environment, 246–47

maladies from air pollution, 24, 26–27

Our Children's Trust, 245

playing in PFOS firefighting foam, 154

politicians on development of "natural